Art Directing

FOR VISUAL COMMUNICATION AND SELLING

AD

Art Directing

FOR VISUAL COMMUNICATION AND SELLING

The Art Directors Club of New York

Visual Communication Books

Hastings House, Publishers, New York

Acknowledgements

To all who have so generously contributed their experience and their time in perfecting the plans for this book, and who have helped to bring it to completion, our sincere appreciation is extended.

Special acknowledgement should be made to the presidents of the Art Directors Club of New York during whose administrations this publishing program was developed and carried on: Roy W. Tillotson; John Jamison; Julian M. Archer; Frank Baker; William H. Buckley.

We owe a debt of gratitude, as always, to the efficient work on this project by the permanent staff of the Club under the direction of Winifred G. Karn, executive secretary, and Janet K. Brewster, assistant secretary.

Library of Congress Catalog Card Number: 57-8644.

Published simultaneously in Canada by S. J. Reginald Saunders, Publishers, Toronto 2B.

Printed in the United States of America.

To Louis Pedlar, who in 1920 conceived the idea of starting an Art Directors Club;

To Earnest Elmo Calkins, who for many years has been a leader in advertising and the graphic arts;

To our first three presidents—Richard Walsh, 1920; Heyworth Campbell, 1921; Joseph Chapin, 1922—who succeeded in making the Club a vital organization during a difficult period,

To Roy Tillotson, for the vision of recognizing the possibilities in the idea for this book when it was first presented to him;

To all the succeeding presidents of the Club who have given so generously of their time and talents in carrying out significant programs over the years;

This book is gratefully dedicated.

Book Committee

EDITOR-IN-CHIEF	*Nathaniel Pousette-Dart*
HONORARY MEMBERS	Richard Bach Earnest Elmo Calkins Richard Walsh
SUPERVISOR OF COPY	Henry M. Havemeyer
SUPERVISOR OF DESIGN	Alberto P. Gavasci
TRAFFIC MANAGER	C. Edward Cerullo
ASSOCIATE EDITORS	Gordon Aymar Robert H. Blattner Mahlon A. Cline Wallace Elton Suren Ermoyan Arthur Hawkins Peirce Johnson* Lester Rondell Arnold Roston Karsten Stapelfeldt Roy W. Tillotson
COMMITTEE MEMBERS	James C. Boudreau Stuart Campbell Charles Coiner J. Walter Flynn Juke Goodman Wallace Hainline Paul Lang John Peter Robert West

* Deceased

TREASURER
Mahlon A. Cline

PUBLICITY DIRECTOR
Edward R. Wade

EXECUTIVE SECRETARY
Winifred G. Karn

ASSISTANT SECRETARY
Janet K. Brewster

SPECIAL RESEARCH COMMITTEE
Rufus A. Bastian, *Chairman*
George W. Booth
Marc Brody
Louis N. Donato
Bob Jones
William Knudsen
Edmund Marein
Jack Skolnik
Rollin C. Smith
Al Stenzel

6

Contents

FOREWORD

rt directing has long since earned the right to be classed as other than an occupation for the artist or designer *per se*. It is a *profession* concerned primarily with visual problems . . . the visual communication of ideas . . . visual selling.

Today the two dominant factors are idealism and practicality, equally important in the world as a whole, and in the fields of industry, advertising and publishing. The one gives inspiration and creation, the other gives discrimination, balance and accomplishment. The one creates the dynamic motivating ideas; the other directs the practical work of the world.

This book, therefore, is based on actual concepts of practicality and idealism . . . practicality, because the art director realizes that in order to meet his own obligations, he must give the service that the business world demands; idealism, because he does not believe it necessary to sacrifice personal or professional standards in the fulfillment of his prescribed tasks. He knows that only by maintaining high ideals will he have a dynamic influence on all the visual means of communication.

These facts take on added significance when we realize that the public at large is becoming more and more visual-minded; and doubly so when we consider our tremendous population growth. In 1900 there were some 76 million people in the United States of America; at present, we have around 168 million and, by 1975, it is predicted that we shall have at least 200 million.

To satisfy the ever-increasing needs of this growing population, science and industry are well equipped to furnish all the services and goods necessary. But to help in the problems of distributing these goods and services, all forms of promotional media must become more effective. It is here that the art director exercises a key function.

More than six years ago, when plans were first made for the publication of this book, there was only a vague idea of how art directors functioned in different kinds of organizations in the fields of advertising and publishing—and in industry. It was only after numerous talks and forum discussions that we arrived at a realization that the art director's job in wooing public acceptance, and breaking the bottleneck of sales resistance, required many different methods of approach.

So the book was not completed "over night." Rather, it was hammered out of the exciting experience, the work and hard thinking of some sixty creative people who have participated vitally and enthusiastically in their professional capacities. Each contributor was chosen because of his special ability and long experience in his own field.

The major purpose of ths book, then, is to study and analyze the functions of the art director, his emergence from the past, his responsibilities—present and future—in our ever "dynamic expanding economy."

11

Nathaniel Pousette-Dart

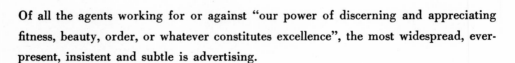

The Art Director and the National Taste

By Walter O'Meara

*Quoted from his article in the 31st Annual
of National Advertising and Editorial Art
of the Art Directors Club of New York*

Of all the agents working for or against "our power of discerning and appreciating fitness, beauty, order, or whatever constitutes excellence", the most widespread, ever-present, insistent and subtle is advertising.

Employing as it does practically every medium of expression—including a few new ones of its own invention—advertising reaches people in more ways, in more places, and at more times than any other form of communication except speech. More money is spent on it, perhaps, than on all the rest of the so-called arts combined. It certainly reaches and influences the desires, decisions—and tastes—of more people than any other kind of persuasion.

I have known few art directors who did not have a keen awareness of beauty, order and fitness, and who did not possess a firm belief in their practical value. These men have certainly exercised a strong and constructive influence on the character of advertising, and indirectly on the taste and discrimination of all the people whom advertising reaches.

The art director has been among the first to recognize the role that the fine arts can play in industry and commerce; and he has provided a new and lucrative market for established talent.

He has worked patiently, diligently—and with an understandable amount of profanity—to improve the quality of mechanical reproduction, printing, typography, and the various other technical processes involved in his work.

Also, I must add, he has managed to impart to those with whom he labors a certain sharing of his own enthusiasm, so that even the dullest and most unesthetic copywriter or account executive finally comes to grasp a little of his appreciation for beauty, order and fitness—and begins to understand how these can be translated into practical (and profitable) advertising terms.

There can be no doubt that the art director has helped greatly to direct one of the most powerful influences of our time into positive and constructive channels. I think it is about time for somebody to say the things about him that he cannot—and would not want to—say about himself. I am happy to have had the privilege of doing that pleasant job.

Emergence of the Visual Concept

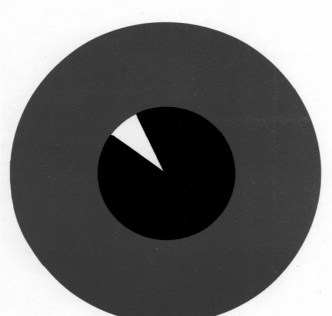

Part 1 *Designed by* Alberto P. Gavasci

The Man With the Visual Message

by Stanley Resor

Chairman, J. Walter Thompson Company

THE art director in the modern advertising agency has a long heritage. In order to make clear his position today it may be well to sketch the background of the advertising agency business.

The Early Agencies Were Space Buyers

Advertising as a separate activity engaging the full time of certain people goes back at least two hundred years to the eighteenth century. The "advertisement solicitor" was a recognized—though humble—figure in the London of Dr. Johnson. But the advertising agency, as distinct from the advertising staff of publications, seems to be an American innovation and made its appearance in the early years of the Republic. The modern agencies trace their roots back to the period following the Civil War, when the rapid westward expansion of the population and the railroads created many new markets. This movement brought with it the establishment of many new newspapers and stimulated the growth of national magazines. In this situation a central agency that could buy space in a variety of publications became a necessity to any manufacturer attempting to conduct a regional or national business in consumer products.

The early agencies were thus primarily buyers of space for manufacturers' copy. One of the early agents reported in later years that he was aghast when an advertiser first asked him to write and "fix up" an advertisement. He resented being asked to do the advertiser's work for him. Another agent, who got his start as a space buyer, contracted in advance for national magazine space at wholesale and then sold it at retail to advertisers. After the value of magazine space had been established in this way, the publishers began to set their own prices to advertisers, including a sales commission to cover the cost of agency service. To sell the space the agencies began to suggest copy and illustrations.

The Art Manager Appears

One of the large early agencies employed about 50 people, but had only one copywriter, the proprietor himself. Illustrations were handled by the "art manager". This is the first instance I can find of the position of art director in an agency. The date is about 1880. This art manager purchased illustrations from various artists as occasion required. He then had wood engravings or zinc etchings made and turned these cuts over to the agency's typesetting department. Final plates were made by an electrotyper. "There was

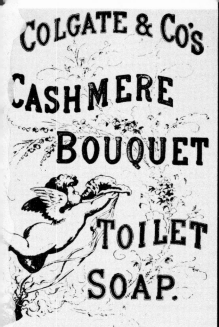

LORD & TAYLOR,

Importers and Wholesale and Retail Dealers in

DRY GOODS.

Nos. 255, 257, 259 & 261 Grand Street, cor. Chrystie, N. Y.

little attempt at that time to make advertisements beautiful," writes the historian of this agency. "The intent of the picture was to convey a definite idea of the article to be sold."

Somewhat later the pictorial "character" made its appearance in advertising and took its place beside the illustration of the product. The famous cook, "Rastus", who recommended Cream of Wheat, was drawn from a photograph of a real chef in Kohlsaat's Restaurant in Chicago. Aunt Jemima was originally a cotton doll included in pancake flour packages as a premium and designed to be stuffed and sewn up by children in the homes where the flour was used. Later, Alonzo Kimball was commissioned to execute an oil painting portraying Aunt Jemima. Sunny Jim, Phoebe Snow and many of the others were creatures of the imagination. But for a time artwork was simply an added element in advertising, bought "as occasion required" and changed but little from year to year.

The Modern Agency Provides Many Services

In the first years of the twentieth century drawings and photographs of products in use became more frequent and more attention was given to display type and to layout. Copy, layout and illustrations were changed more often than had been the practice hitherto. To produce this kind of advertising the art director was a necessity. He was soon a fixture in all the service agencies, acting not only as a middleman between copywriters, artists and typographers, but also one of the group shaping the advertising message.

The modern agency, offering a full range of services in media analysis, merchandising plans, copywriting and art was developed in approximately its present day pattern at the time of World War I. Since then individual agencies have grown in size and many new agencies have been formed. Special services of many kinds have been added; including groups of services in radio and television. In the planning of television the art director plays an important part, and his role throughout as a member of the creative group in the agency has remained as it was when his function was first generally established some fifty years or more ago.

The Art Director's Place on the Team

The reader of this book will find ample materials to help him in forming a picture of the modern art director's role in advertising. My own observations here should be taken simply as a few added touches to the picture this book develops.

Some art directors once conceived it as their duty to elevate with taste and beauty an otherwise somewhat drab and workaday form of communication. They were missionaries to the heathen, and the artists they summoned to help them often in the past adopted an attitude of condescension to the demands of commerce. Nonetheless, whether they came reluctantly or gladly, many fine artists have added to the effectiveness of advertising. Sir John Millais' painting of his grandson blowing bubbles, purchased and used widely by Pear's Soap, was perhaps the first joint venture between the fine arts and modern advertising. From that day to the publication of Edward Steichen's photographs in the advertisements of Pond's, and since then, many fine artists have made advertising both more agreeable and more effective.

But the modern art director is something more than a new kind of patron for the artist. The art director, like the copywriter with whom he is so closely allied, is a man with a message. He has a story to tell. He must gain attention for that story, and he must lend the story force and persuasiveness. Some have said that the task of the art director is to deliver the reader to the copywriter in a favorable frame of mind. This statement suggests that the art director is a sort of bird dog. To my way of thinking, the relationship between the art director and the copywriter is at once more equal and more intimate than that between hunter and hound, and less predatory in character. Both art director and copywriter are together trying to tell a story that the advertiser wants to get across and that the reader, if his attention can be caught and held, wants to hear. Their job is to make that story, despite all the distractions the reader may be subject to, as clear and as cogent as possible. In short, art directors and copywriters are advertising men.

Advertising as a Social Force

Advertising today is a profession in which the art director may well be proud to claim a part. The hopes of the world have been stirred by the miracles of the American economy. America has demonstrated that want and the fear of want can be banished, that every man's family can have some of the good things of life. Increasingly it is becoming clear that at the base of this seeming miracle is the daily American practice of expanding markets by studying human needs, fitting production to them and calling the attention of people to their own needs and the products that meet them.

Advertising is central to this process and so is central to the great movements in the world today. In times past the major efforts of mankind were directed to the building of temples or of palaces for the use of the few and the astonishment of the many; and the artists of the day were proud to design and decorate them. At the present time the major efforts of mankind are directed toward making every man's home a fit dwelling for free and responsible citizens. In that effort, resting squarely on effective communication concerning needs and products, advertising men and artists who work with them play a vital part. They are, as they should be, in the main stream of our times.

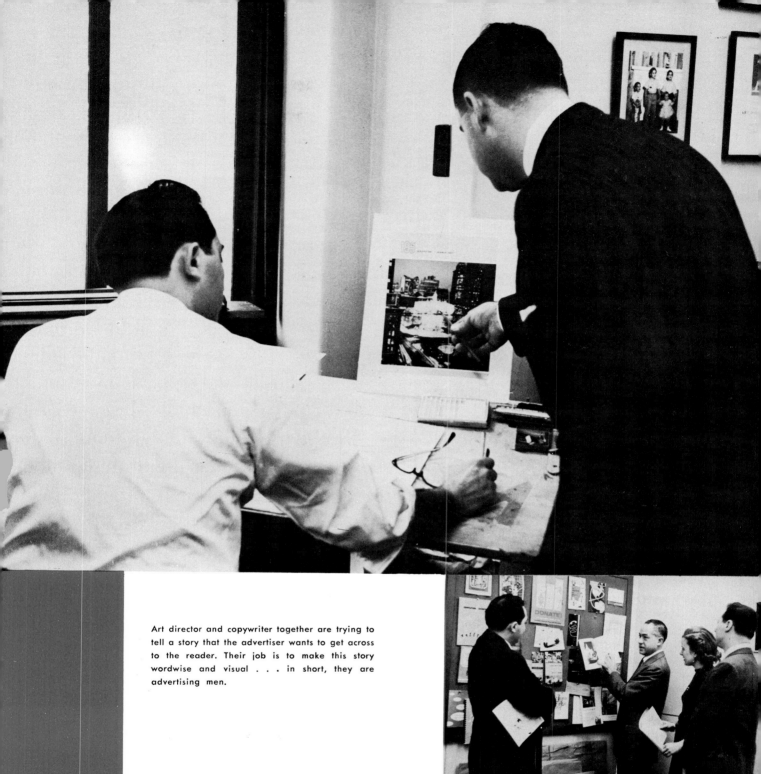

Art director and copywriter together are trying to tell a story that the advertiser wants to get across to the reader. Their job is to make this story wordwise and visual . . . in short, they are advertising men.

19

Blackstone Studios

Visual Excitement
in Modern Publishing

by Gardner Cowles

President and Editor of Look Magazine,

President of the Des Moines Register and Tribune

BECAUSE the publishing business is such an old one, people have a tendency to think of it as being rather static and unexciting in comparison with some of its younger contemporaries. Actually, it's about as static as a cruising taxi cab and about as unexciting as a hurricane.

In fact, during the past 20 years there has been a virtual revolution in the publishing business, and the art directors of the nation have played a huge part in it. I personally am convinced that they will play an even larger part in the future.

Background for Revolution in Publishing

The reasons are basic, and can perhaps best be highlighted by the events of the past few decades. In the 1930's, the Cassandras sounded the death knell for magazines and newspapers. Radio, they said, would make printed media as out of date as Sanskrit. Then came television—and more dire predictions about the future of publishing. Yet look what's happened.

In 1935—during radio's heyday—the magazines whose circulations are measured by the Audit Bureau of Circulations, had a total circulation of roughly 76,000,000. And in 1948, when, for all practical purposes, the era of television actually started, total circulation of these magazines was just under 141,000,000. Today it's well over 160,000,000.

At the same time, newspaper circulation has also been increasing. Since 1935, total circulation of daily newspapers has grown from approximately 38,000,000 to over 55,000,000.

These gains by printed media did not come automatically. They came for a number of reasons—and one of the most important reasons is that competition actually *is* the life of trade. Radio in its prime was a rough, tough competitor. It had newness. It had glamor. It had aggressiveness. By contrast, magazines and newspapers were the old guard in the media field.

The Influence of Radio

With the advent of radio, astute publishers quickly realized that they had to make their publications better than they ever had been before—and they started making constructive moves to hold their place in the communications sun.

They actively sought better ways of gaining the attention and interest of readers—and one of the most obvious ways was, of course, to increase the visual appeal of their publications.

Magazines started using more color, and newspapers started using color, too. They adopted new printing techniques. They gave increased emphasis to illustrations of various kinds. They improved their layouts. They chose more appealing type faces. And finally

they started broadening their editorial bases to appeal to more and more people, and they started using an abundance of photographs.

Both the broadening of editorial bases and the wide-scale use of photographs were amazingly slow in coming. Publishers, for some reason, seemed to feel that people's interests were limited by such things as income levels, education, sex, etc.—and magazines particularly planned their editorial fare to appeal only to specific groups of people.

I personally feel that radio, with its great variety of programs, helped dramatize to publishers the wide interests people actually have and the great unanimity of those interests. I also think that some research which was conducted by the Des Moines *Register* back in the late 1920's helped considerably in this respect —as well as in focusing attention on the great appeal of photographs.

The Pictorial Era Emerges

Although none of us on the *Register* had any idea at the time what we were getting into, the research turned out to have some mighty far-reaching results— and eventually led to what was generally considered the most radical advance in modern journalism.

George Gallup, who was then a graduate student of psychology and a graduate instructor in the Journalism School at the University of Iowa, had just developed a new method for the scientific measurement of reader interest, and we decided to test this measuring technique on readers of the *Sunday Register*. The research showed conclusively that pictures ranked very high in reader interest; that pictures which were related to each other ranked even higher; and that solid, unrelieved blocks of text invariably got below-average readership. With this evidence before us, we started experimenting with picture stories, and with stories combining pictures and text. The result was a 50% increase in the *Sunday Register*'s circulation.

Photographs had, of course, been in use in publishing since the turn of the century, and even before the Gallup research a number of publishers had been making extensive use of them. But the Gallup research offered such convincing evidence of their comparative effectiveness in relationship to text—and of their increased effectiveness when they were used as an integral part of a story—that publishers of both newspapers and magazines were bound to be impressed.

As a matter of fact, my brother John and I were so impressed ourselves that we started thinking about the possibilities of a national magazine employing the picture story technique—plus a new editorial concept which involved a departure from the standard publishing practice of directing editorial appeal only to a specific group of people.

The Gallup research had shown us not only that well-selected pictures increased the interest-value of virtually all subject matter but also that pictures spoke a universal language, appealing to people of all kinds and of all ages. For that reason, we felt that a magazine employing a "picture language" could successfully reach and inform millions of people — regardless of age, sex, income, employment, or education.

In the meantime, Henry Luce had also become intrigued with the huge potential for a national magazine employing pictorial journalism. His version—*Life*—appeared on the nation's newsstands in November, 1936, and our version—*Look*—appeared in January, 1937.

Visual Communication of Ideas

The over-night success of both these magazines brought into sharp focus—on a national basis—the tremendous effectiveness of visual material for faster communication of ideas, and gradually practically all magazines began putting more and more emphasis on pictorial treatments. Today you can even find magazines containing more pictures in a single issue than are contained in an average issue of *Life* or *Look*.

In recent years, there has also been a great upsurge in the use of other visual material in magazines and newspapers, and I believe this trend will continue to accelerate. Publishers have actively sought ways and means of communicating to their readers faster—and in more understandable form—and this has led to the increased use of design in graphic presentation.

In addition to an increased emphasis on quality in fiction illustration, publications have moved into the area of the fine arts. Paintings by old and modern masters are being used not only as great works of art but as illustrations as well. The emphasis on art quality has tended to raise the standards of all art work in magazines and has influenced the efforts of many advertisers in the publication field.

In increasing their attention to visual presentation, magazines and newspapers have found that maximum effect is achieved if photos, graphs, maps, cartoons, illustrations and paintings are used in place of words, as well as with words—and this is one of the reasons why the art director has come to play an increasingly important role in the editorial concept of modern magazines. He is no longer just a planner of illustrations and a liaison between the editor and the artist. Today's magazine art director plays a major part in the publication structure, from formulation of editorial ideas to the production methods by which the magazine is printed.

And, as I said before, I'm convinced that in the years ahead the art director will play an even more important role than he does right now. In my judgment, the great success of television has only served to emphasize the great love of the public for visual treatment—and the result is almost bound to be even greater emphasis than there is now on visual techniques in printed media.

Creative Imagination

by Nathaniel Pousette-Dart

Art Consultant

Both the man of science and the man of art live always at the edge of mystery, surrounded by it; both always, as the measure of their creation, have had to do with the harmonization of what is new and what is familiar . . . with the struggle to make partial order in total chaos.—Margaret Halsey.

23

IT IS unquestionably true that all the creative arts have some fundamentals in common, since basically they function through the same laws. These fundamental laws do not change; they only seem to change because new aspects have been discovered at different times in the history of art. Just as Einstein's discovery of new aspects of old laws has changed our concepts of time and space, so Cezanne's experiments with form and color, in painting, led to the discovery of an abstractionism which had existed in music for centuries. Each art is formed and given character through the ends it serves.

Since both advertising and illustrative art serve ends other than those of pure art, both, as art, must be compromised. A recognition of this fact would clear up much confused thinking on the subject.

Methods for Stimulating Ideas

Mr. James Webb Young in his book, *A Technique for Producing Ideas*, (Advertising Publications, Inc., Chicago) worked out the following method for creating ideas for utilitarian purposes:

"First, the gathering of raw materials, both the materials of your immediate problem and the materials which come from a constant enrichment of your store of general knowledge.

"Second, the working over of these materials in your mind.

"Third, the incubating stage, where you let something besides the conscious mind do the work of synthesis.

"Fourth, the actual birth of the Idea — the 'Eureka! I have it!' stage.

"And fifth, the final shaping and development of the idea to practice usefulness."

On pages 44-45 of our book, Mitchell Havemeyer shows a comprehensive and suggestive chart which illustrates the first steps in Mr. Young's method of stimulating the creative imagination.

"When Karl Pearson compared man's brain to a telephone exchange handling incoming and outgoing calls, he took in only a small part of its activity: it is a power station, a storage warehouse, a library, a theatre, a museum, a hall of archives, a court of justice, a seat of government," wrote Lewis Mumford in *The Transformations of Man*.

It is true that, in the field of advertising, style, freshness, fashion and effectiveness dominate — so we cannot expect this work to have the profundity, timelessness, basic sincerity and conviction which are demanded of creative works in the field of the fine arts. However, if we accept the idea that there are various levels of creativity — then we may derive pleasure from all art manifestations. We may enjoy a jazz composition — but if we were to equate it with a Bach fugue, it would mean that we have no conception of the difference between a powerfully organized work of art and an amusing and clever bit of syncopation. The one lives forever, the other is exciting but ephemeral. No matter on what level a work of art may be, however, creative imagination is of vital importance.

What is a Creative Act?

The philosophers, aestheticians and critics over the years have tried to give a lucid definition of an inspiration and a creative act without a great deal of success, because here we deal with a problem which is just as difficult to explain as the question, "What is Life?" Life is a mystery — so are inspiration and creative acts.

We may say that a creative act is based on an inspiration — but then we must define inspiration. We may say that an inspiration is a quick realization of a unified whole, but we still have not pinned it down because we may achieve an all-over unity which has no inner validity or life. Inner life in a work of art is just as vital to creation as to the existence of man.

"The factor in which a true genius excels often is not judgment or memory or even intelligence, but creative imagination, the highest achievement of man's new brain. The remarkable human capacity to see, in what we call the mind's eye, images of things that our eyes have never seen makes it possible, in addition to bringing together new mental patterns of things unseen, to bring from the unconscious mind striking new combinations of thought patterns. This we call inspiration."[*]

An inspiration is usually preceded by a great deal of study, research and thought, but it is not directly dominated by the intellect. Once an artist has created a work of art, it may be examined by the intellect, which acts as an analytical instrument and helps him to correct its shortcomings.

In creative painting Picasso and Matisse have shown that one idea, through new inspirations and conceptions, may lead to many new works. So an artist, while working on a canvas, may have several new inspirations; but with each one the whole work must be changed to conform to it. El Greco made many copies of some of his paintings but each one was an original creative work in itself.

Influences: Past and Present

The techniques used today in the commercial fields are based on the work of the modern creative painters of twenty-five or thirty-five years ago in Europe — on Cubism, Fauvism, Dadaism, Futurism and other schools and on the sincere creative work of such artists as Cezanne, Van Gogh, Picasso, Matisse, Rousseau, Seurat, Gris, Klee, Chirico and Kandinsky.

[*]Quoted from an article in the *Atlantic Monthly* called "How the Brain Works" by George R. Harrison, Dean of the School of Science at M.I.T.

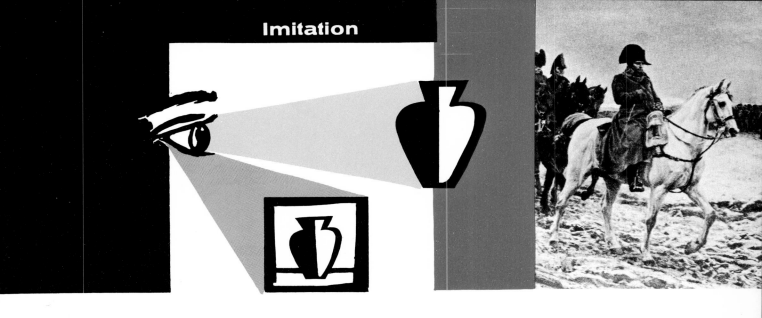

Imitation

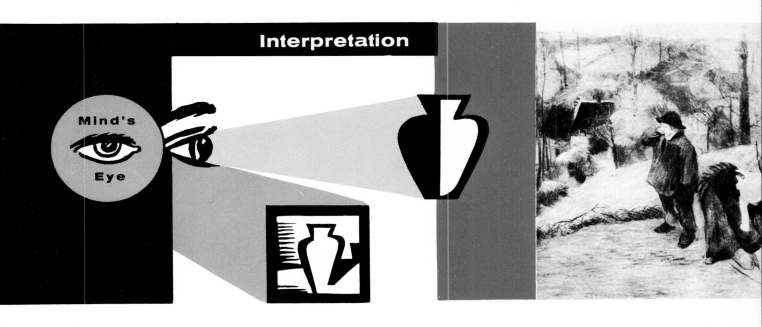

Interpretation

Mind's Eye

Creation

CREATIVE
IMAGINATION

Mind's Eye

PAST
EXPERIENCE

Picasso

Klee

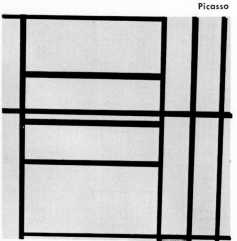

Mondrian

Miro

That the best art directors and designers of today seem to concur in this opinion, is evidenced by an A.I.G.A. exhibition being held, as I write this, at the Library of Congress, "Modern Art Influences and Printing Design." The following quotations are taken from their catalogue, one under the heading "Art Influences" and the other from the summary:

"A tremendous change has taken place in visual communication during our time. The designer of printing today has a wide range of possibilities at his command inspired by the artists who initiated new visual forms. These forms have been referred to as the new language of vision. The exhibit features certain of the abstract art movements that are considered to be the most influential in changing graphic design. Basically the main current of inspiration was abstract art. One stream evolved in geometric forms based on the art theories of Cezanne that widened into Cubism. Another was non-geometric or free in form which emerged as Abstract Expressionism and grew into Surrealism.

"The contemporary graphic designer who has been well grounded in the theories and forms of art of the past, both traditional and modern, is the most successful and often the most daring. Though his work reveals his understanding of earlier examples, it is distinctive, new and fresh."

Today the advertiser has a wonderful audience: one that is sensitive, alert and intelligent. He need no longer worry about going over the heads of people.

In this book the art directors show their greater awareness of the possibilities of the Creative Imagination — not only in solving problems, but in continually creating "greater new things under the sun."

26

Art Directing...
Advertising Agencies

Part 2 *Designed by* Oscar Krauss

World Change...
The
Art Director's
Challenge

by Elwood Whitney

Senior Vice President and Director, Foote, Cone & Belding

NOT too many years ago an art director could accurately be described as the "ugly duckling" of business life. Most executives took rather a dim view of anyone or anything remotely associated with this strange creative world when it came in contact with the world of commerce, and if a company found itself in the "unfortunate" position of requiring an art director's services, such a job was, more often than not, barely tolerated. "Art Director" was an ignominious title at best, and the poor wretch who held it was treated accordingly.

He (at that time it could never have been a she) was generally thought to be a disappointed artist: a long-haired, grubby-fingernailed, *atelier* type with absolutely no practical business acumen. Art directors, any businessman would tell you quickly, operated on a cloud high above the more practical folk concerned with the everyday chore of running a business for profit.

Happily, over a long and painful period of time, both art directors and the attitude of business toward them have changed substantially. I do not believe that there are many occupations today, either in business or professional life, which offer as much challenge and opportunity as can be found in the art director's field.

There are few occupations where the contribution factor is generally acknowledged to be so vast, and even fewer where the ceiling on what a man may earn is so unlimited. For the most part, an art director's earnings are in direct ratio to what he can contribute, and since this is an age of expansion—where everybody is in everyone else's business—the scope of his contribution is bounded only by his own ability.

How the AD's Status Has Changed

What brought about this great change in the art director's status? What raised him from the paint-stained nonentity of 20 years ago to a point where business holds him in esteem and clamors for his services?

The only answer, I think, lies in the profound changes that have taken place in our American economy. Our industrial revolution is over; no longer must the emphasis be on ever-increasing production, for we have demonstrated beyond doubt that we can produce at fair prices more than enough goods for our own needs and still have a surplus for export to other parts of the world. Much of our industry is not operating at the full capacity of which it is capable.

Our problem today is learning how to utilize fully the fruits of our production and this problem will take on added importance as time goes on because the technology of production is far ahead of the technology of sales. Continued prosperity depends on the skill with which we are able to channel a growing torrent of products from machines to consumers. This has resulted in a marketing revolution.

And today, among the most important facets of the marketing operation are those fields in which the art director's talents are particularly applicable and necessary: in product design, in packaging, in advertising, merchandising and sales promotion.

There are today more than 500,000 trade-marked items in this country, of which about 10,000 are actively vying for consumer attention and dollars. To operate successfully in this intensely competitive market, a businessman must make the public both want his product and prefer his brand. He must, in other words, establish personality for his brand. And despite the continuing power of the written word, the fact remains that the most memorable brand personalities have been established through unique packaging, attention-getting illustrations in printed advertising, and unusual sales promotion and merchandising devices. All these are the special province of the art director in industry.

Product and Package Design

In the field of product design the art director, working hand in hand with the engineer, the draftsman, the designer and the sales manager, has helped change the face, form and personality of countless products in recent years. Scarcely an item comes to mind that hasn't undergone an evolution in design, structure, engineering, decoration, packaging or, at the very least, a color metamorphosis.*

Because we must sell in competition with other quality products that perform satisfactorily—in a market where automobiles all run, fountain pens all write and detergents all get clothes clean—it is no longer sufficient for a product to "work." It must also, to borrow a phrase, "look sharp, feel sharp and be sharp." And keeping that fine edge on a product is one of the art director's primary responsibilities.

The accent on sharpness quite naturally led the art director into the field of package design. Consider the food field, for example. Almost every product to be found in the supermarket today, whether it be in a plastic bag or wrap, a can, bottle, package or box, has been radically changed within the past few years. The degree depends only on the particular product category and the intensity of competition. Changing a product's appearance, and hence its personality, is no longer something to be frowned upon or feared; it is frequently a marketing necessity. Products must be improved to keep pace with increased competition and the art director, through his package design, must reflect these changes and improvements.

Products today must also speak for themselves, for this is an era of self-service when a thousand products shout from the shelf for consumer attention. Only the art director's good, clear thinking—embodied in skillful design—enables the personality of one product to be heard above the clamor of competition.

Visual Selling

And one of his most important functions, of course, is the counsel and assistance the art director is able to offer in the preparation of the advertisement that is his

* See Donald Deskey's views about this, page 158—Ed.

company's most powerful means for building consumer recognition and brand acceptance.

It is the function of the illustration in printed advertising to attract attention through the size, shape, content and color of the picture; to stimulate desire; to arouse interest through dramatization or psychological appeal; to convince by adding realism; to create atmosphere or mood; to induce action to aid product identification; or tell a complete picture-continuity story.

All these things the art director, by his background, training and instinct, can help bring to fruition in the finished advertisement. Upon how well he does his job and upon how well he supervises its execution, where that is his responsibility, the success of a campaign and success of the product in the marketplace may depend.

Point of Sale—Dealer Helps

His job doesn't end with the product, its package and an advertising program, of course. The ingenuity with which the art director can quickly demonstrate his product's superiority to the consumer via dealer displays, banners, bins, floor stands and other promotional and merchandising devices all add to or subtract from the product's ultimate sales. Even more important, his creative ability and imagination affect the resale of a product. It is on this repetitive habit of buying the same brand that "brand preference"—the most precious ingredient in product leadership—is based.*

The art director has still another opportunity to put business eternally in his debt. This is the "no man's land" in our changing market picture—dealer education and dealer helps, a sadly neglected yet fertile field. It

is an area where no manufacturer, wholesaler, distributor or any of their salesmen has real knowledge. The art director who prospects here is most certain to strike pure gold.**

Television—Challenge to Art Directing

On the debit side of the ledger it is necessary to note that not always have art directors made the most of their opportunities. To cite just one example, many have been left at the post in an important field on which they should already have left an indelible mark—television. In my opinion, there are too few art directors in business today who have bothered to interest themselves in this dynamic medium. I have never understood why. Perhaps it's pernicious inertia.

Whatever the reason, the result has been that the creators, writers, directors and producers in television too often dominate the medium, each in his own specialized way. This came about simply because the opportunity was big and somebody had to get the job started. At the beginning, no one knew more than anyone else. No one was a specialist. Today, the nonspecialist in television is a rarity. Perhaps we could more easily evaluate the position of the art director in television if we reduced the whole equation of the medium to primary terms. I refer to the commercial.

The better commercials are—the more interesting, palatable and digestible they are—the more acceptable the medium. And television, after all, is a medium just as the publishing business with its newspapers and magazines is a medium. Publishers can't stay in business without advertising and neither can television. So

Design/Norman Schoelles, vice president in charge of package planning, Lippincott & Margulies, Inc.

Kent Cigarette package designed by Sam Marsh AD/Fred Sergenian, Young & Rubicam.

30

when we talk about TV commercials, we're really talking about personality-building ads. And since this is a visual medium, by all odds it should be the greatest challenge in the world for the art director.***

That, unfortunately, hasn't always been the case. Art directors have all too frequently fumbled an opportunity to get in on television's ground floor. Perhaps it is not too late to make amends—the boom in color television, where the art director's talents can be used most profitably, is only now getting under way—but with every passing day it becomes more difficult to "join the club."

Creative Visual Thinking

I have only one other observation, but it is an important one. It applies to all visual-minded, creative people who have a large part of their facility in their hands.

I urge that you first use your head, that you use your brain, before you put pencil to paper. Try to understand what the problem is, what the facts are that make it a problem. Analyze what you know, sorting out facts in a logical rather than an emotional manner. Then, once the problem and the procedure are clear, you can pull out all the stops with every attention-getting device of which you are creatively capable.

This discretion will be appreciated by people in business. It demonstrates that you are trying to help them solve their problems in a logical, businesslike way. It also puts you in an enviable position for you have, in addition to your ability to think, a tremendously important extra talent: you can picture your thoughts.

The importance of the thinking man increases. In a period of great change such as we are now undergoing, everything is transient and temporary. If we are going to do business during this period of emergence, we must try to understand the reasons for these things being as they are. This part is relatively easy. The business pages of our country are filled with information about every contributing factor to our changing economy: our growing population, our added income, our growing list of new products, and the changes in the living and shopping habits, the changes in the political, social and economic beliefs of our customers. All we have to do is dig, read and absorb.

But you won't understand how these enormous changes are outmoding all our accepted selling appeals and methods unless you mix with people where they live and work and shop. You cannot get understanding sitting at your drawing board.

That, as I see it, is the challenge of the future. How well the art director does his job—designing, improving and selling products—will have a great deal to do with the success and, indeed, the whole future of business. Nothing can remain static and exist for long, for this is a world of change.

And a world of change is an art director's world: a world of golden opportunity.

* Techniques of point-of-sale advertising are discussed by Stuart Leech, page 150, and Paul Lang, page 152—Ed.

** A graphic case history on dealer helps, by Alberto P. Gavasci; is presented on page 104—Ed.

*** See, in this connection, the views of William Duffy, Harry McMahan, Paul Smith, Georg Olden, page 112 ff.—Ed.

Still from "The Cat", a TV series for Simmons Beautyrest. This is the prototype of a new development in the graphic use of animals in advertising. AD/Stephen Frankfurt.

Point-of-purchase display designed by Robert Gage for Max Factor

The
Art
Director . . .
Plus
Value
for
Management

by Wallace W. Elton

Vice President and Director,
J. Walter Thompson Company

ONCE upon a time, within the memory of men now engaged in "management" of the advertising business, there were no "art directors." To refresh your memory on that score turn back and reread Mr. Stanley Resor's introduction to this volume. What we term the "art director" was a creation of business necessity. Note that he was first called the art "manager."

Business terminology is often a matter of expediency. Today both "manager" and "director" seem inadequate terms for the men about whom this book is written. In fact, the term "art director" probably will change within a few decades. Even now, the "art director" of television fulfills a role quite different from that of the "art director" of printed media.

Management and the Art Director

There are different interpretations of the term "management." Webster defines it with the help of such words as judicious, executive, and control; which also could be used to define the work of many art directors.

Let's assume that in American business the term "management" frequently is applied to the group of men who are paid to run an enterprise or interest. The trap in this assumption lies in thinking that, as in baseball and in the theatre, management generally is composed of non-performers. That's not the case in our business.

Many of the great advertising agencies are captained

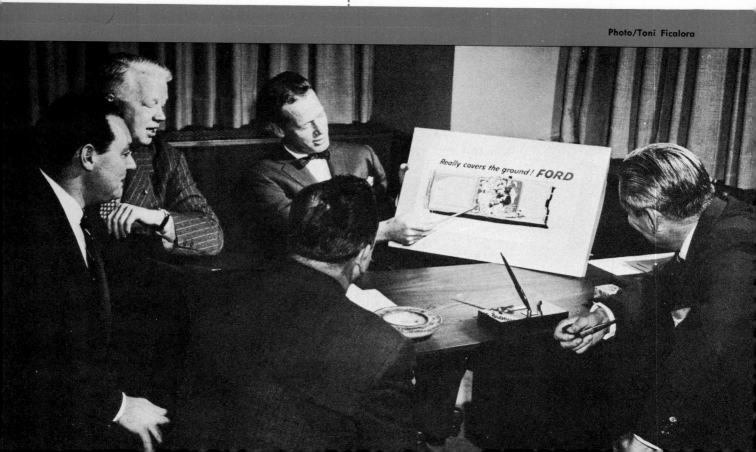

by men who are performers. They are creators. They deal in ideas. They have a compulsion to influence, to change, and to improve. The *produce* ideas.

The ideas they produce have much to do with the organization and staffing of their own businesses as well as with the selling of goods and services. For instance, management has had a considerable influence on the development of the art director as a factor in the whole field of commercial communication.

Agency Management—a Case History

Here's a typical example . . . set forth as a case history which could have happened anytime in the last 30 years.

Back in the days when no advertising agency billed more than $50,000,000 and commercial copywriting was a training ground for movie script writers and novelists, a Young Man approached graduation from a liberal arts university.

The Young man had some talent for drawing. As much out of curiosity as anything, he had taken courses in art and photography in addition to the prescribed curriculum at his college. He earned pocket money doing cartoons for local shops and advertising agencies.

And he wrote, too, because he was The Editor of a college publication.

The month before he graduated there was an advertisement in his college publication that was headlined, "Have you ever thought of Art Directing as a profession?" The advertisement was by a Big Advertising Agency. The Young Man thought this was worth a call.

Two weeks after graduation, he was working for the Big Advertising Agency as a layout man in the art department. A notably articulate and persuasive Art Director-Vice President had told him the Management of the Agency was looking for talented trainees with liberal arts educations.

The Vice President said the Management felt they could train a man in lettering, typography, layout, and art buying, but they did not have the time to teach him English, public speaking, history and all the things that helped toward an understanding of people.

The Management, he said, felt that the agency would better serve its clients if its art directors had more to offer than a graphic talent alone. He said further that men entering the agency under this program would be encouraged to become acquainted with all phases of the business. They would be given an opportunity to become advertising men, not just layout specialists.

This enlightened program represented a major agency recognition of the Art Director as something more than a frustrated artist, an illustrator doing double duty or a production man who also does the art buying. It recognized the art director as an advertising man.

The Young Man was one of several beginners who benefited from that program. Most of them remained in the advertising business, although circumstances and advancement took them to other agencies. They performed in a manner that justified the faith an enlightened management showed in hiring them.

One of them became head art buyer and then executive art director of another large agency. Later he became a vice president and senior account executive.

Another advanced through a vice presidency and senior art directorship to a position as creative chief of his agency.

A third became a vice president and supervisor in copy, art, and television. Still another became vice president and head art director of his agency.

So the judgment that one agency management showed in taking a new look at the training of art directors eventually strengthened the management of several agencies.

"Don't Cry . . . Act"

The moral of the foregoing story, if it has one, is that management hopes the art director will be much more than a graphic specialist. Many art directors hope the same thing, but it is difficult to turn the hoping into doing.

Recently, the National Society of Art Directors' official magazine, *Art Direction,* published an editorial under the title, "Don't cry . . . act." It read as follows:

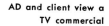

Photos/Ed Jacoby

AD and client view a
TV commercial

Reviewing preliminary layouts

3

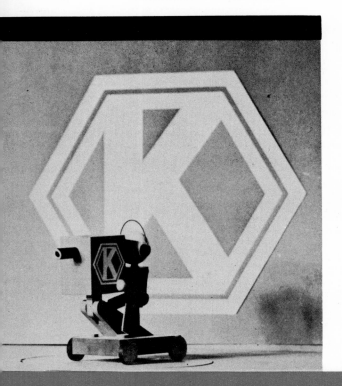

TV "logotype" for Kraft Foods Company.

Photo/Charles Kelloway—Christy Studios

"ADs have done a lot of crying about their bottom of the totem pole lot and some blame it all on the word art. Art isn't any nastier a word than copy. The word, the title, is what the profession makes of it. . . . The AD won't be held back by his title, only by his own individual ability to think and speak and act on the broader levels of sales management."

None of this means that the art director can throw away his drawing board or that he can divorce himself completely from the daily problems of typography, reproduction and design. He is expected to be a specialist and the guardian of good taste in everything concerned with graphic communication. It is taken for granted that technical skill, professional knowledge and a certain amount of talent are possessed by a good art director. He has a plus value for management when he goes further than that.

The AD's Basic Requirements

Most art directors realize their need for a complete education and a broader understanding of business and social forces. Not long ago, the member clubs of the National Society of Art Directors were polled on their opinions of art schools. They were asked what the graduates of those schools most needed to be better equipped for landing a job.*

The number one requirement, as you might expect, was thorough training in the mechanics and in the graphic processes and skills of the business. Any member of a management team would be in agreement on that requirement.

The second requirement, with which management would agree also, was a more complete schooling in the humanities or what the universities call a liberal arts education. Some people would say this can be acquired through a great and continuing curiosity about the people of the world in which we live.

Certainly inquisitiveness can be a rewarding trait.

* See also the section on "Education and Training", beginning on page 188, for details about current programs.—Ed.

The research experts are the most inquisitive people in business and they are a potent force in advertising today. But inquisitiveness, like inventiveness, is of no use without direction or without the desire to influence. One job of management is to supply the direction in any effort. What management can not always supply is the desire and knowledge to influence people.

One of management's best sources of that desire and knowledge should be among art directors. The tools and the knowledge to influence people are part of the art director's stock in trade. The desire to exert an influence with that stock is not always evident. Although it should not be too common among creative people, perhaps there is the same difference in this respect among art directors as among people of all vocations.

Are You a "Speculator" or a "Rentier"?

The distinguished dean of advertising men, Jim Young, composed a particularly pertinent passage on this basic difference between people. Jim quoted the Italian sociologist, Pareto, and spoke as follows to advertising men.

"Pareto thought that all the world could be divided into two main types of people. These types he called, in the French in which he wrote, the *speculator* and the *rentier*.

"In this classification *speculator* is a term used somewhat in the sense of our word 'speculative.' The *speculator* is the speculative type of person. And the distinguishing characteristic of this type, according to Pareto, is that he is constantly pre-occupied with the possibilities of new combinations.**

"Note particularly that word *pre-occupied*, with its brooding quality.

"Pareto includes among the persons of this speculative type not only the business enterprisers—those who deal with financial and business schemes—but those engaged with inventions of every sort, and with what he calls 'political and diplomatic reconstructions'....

"The term used by Pareto to describe the other type,

** Art directors please note.

the *rentier*, is translated into English as the stockholder —though he sound more like the bag holder to me. Such people, he says, are the routine, steady-going unimaginative, conserving people, whom speculators manipulate.

"Whatever we may think of the adequacy of this theory of Pareto's as an entire explanation of social groups, I think we all recognize that these two types of human beings do exist. Whether they were born that way, or whether their environment and training made them that way, is beside the point. They *are* ...

"But it seems to me that the important point for our purpose is that the *speculators*, or reconstructors of this world, are a very large group. Theirs at least is the inherent capacity to produce ideas, and it is by no means such a rare capacity. And so, while perhaps not all God's chillun got wings, enough have for each of us to hope that we may be among those who have.

"At any rate, I propose to assume that if a man (or woman) is at all fascinated by advertising it is probably because he is among the reconstructors of this world. Therefore, he has some creative powers; and these powers, like others, may be increased by making a deliberate effort to do so, and by mastering a technique for their better use."

Mastering Creative Powers

Most art directors would rather be classed as "speculators" than as "rentiers." Particularly, if they have aspirations to take part in management. One way to succeed in that direction is to heed Jim Young's observation that creative powers may be increased "by mastering a technique for their better use."

The art director who realizes that the solution to creative problems may include but does not end with the selection of a type face or an artist; the art director who knows his business so thoroughly that he can relate it to all the other tools of advertising; the art director who can be articulate and influential in the development of commercial communication ... that's the one who is on his way to "management" recognition.

Photographer/Sol Mednick

The Art Director in the Larger Agency

by Charles T. Coiner

Vice President in Charge of Art, N. W. Ayer & Son, Inc., Philadelphia

THIS summary of the functions of the art director, and his relationship with the other people and other departments in the advertising agency where he is employed, applies for the most part to the larger agency, in which a highly developed organization and well defined responsibilities are essential.

An advertising agency is composed of talented writers and artists, experts in planning, media, TV, radio and public relations, client representatives or account executives, and expediters of various kinds. The physical equipment of an agency is relatively unimportant.

In order to use fully the abilities of these different specialists, and to avoid wasting talent through misdirection or overlapping areas of authority, the assigning of definite responsibilities is vital. Each department of the agency (Plans, Merchandising, Representation, Copy, Art, Radio-TV and others) must be given definite responsibilities which belong to it alone.

The Art Director's Responsibilities

At one time art responsibilities were not firmly and clearly assigned. When agencies first began building up art staffs, their primary source of talent was painters, etchers and others who were mainly interested in and trained in the fine arts. The reason for this, of course, was that years ago there were no schools for teaching art or design other than fine art schools. In time, many of these artists developed a great interest in advertising design and made it their profession, becoming topnotch art directors.*

The art director's duties originally covered the mechanical production of the advertising as well as crea-

* Refer back to Stanley Resor's statement about this. See also the section on "Education and Training" for comparison with present methods, page 185—Ed.

tive work. This involved art buying, type specification, the correcting and approving of engravings, and so on. The head of the engraving staff was, in those days, often merely a runner between the art department and the engraver's shop. In addition, the art director in many cases spent a good part of his time helping to represent the agency in dealing with clients. We now recognize that these duties can be handled better if assigned to specialists trained in those fields, rather than by assigning them to the art director.

The job of the art director should be to visualize effective ways of presenting the message to the reader or viewer, and to execute the format. No one else in an advertising agency is properly equipped to do this job. It also provides the specialist in art with a wide field of operation and adequate responsibility, if the agency is of fair size.

By confining his responsibilities to this area the art director can use his creative talents all through his working hours. To be sure, he must consult with the art buyer, the engraver and the typographer, but he does not assume the responsibility or direct the work in these fields. Most sizeable agencies support the art director with the help of lettering men, sketch artists and research people.

The Organization Viewpoint

The present-day art director has to be a good organization man. He is a link in a chain, all links of which must be equally strong in order to provide the best possible service to a client. It is vital, therefore, that the art director understand the importance and function of each link in the chain. His work cannot be done in an ivory tower. Sound layout design depends on good coordination with other departments of the agency.

Other departments can provide valuable foundation material for the art director's work.

No artist who does not understand organization operation, or who resists the idea of working as a part of an organization, can become a good agency art director. Such artists can best serve themselves and advertising by working on a free-lance basis or in some other capacity outside the advertising agency. This is not meant to disparage the talented artist who cannot conform to organizational procedures. But there are many artist-designers who are so individualistic that it is difficult for them to work as part of an agency organization. It is probably a good thing for advertising that there are such people; they help make up the great pool of free-lance talent available to agency and advertiser. Some of our best art directors, too, operate on a free-lance basis and do excellent work. The agency art director, however, must be the type of person who can thrive in an organization.

How the AD Works

The art director's work usually starts when the basic strategy for a campaign is being planned. In the planning stage, information is collected from all possible sources to answer various questions. What are the basic objectives of the advertiser? What kind of people do we want to reach? What are the best ways to reach them? What should be the main theme of the message to be conveyed?

Then, if publications are to be used, there are tactical questions to be answered. Which publications will best reach our audience? What frequency will be used? How can the space units be divided in the most effective way? Color, or black and white? The answers to all these questions map out a route along which copy and art will travel. The art director will pick up his pencil only when he has this information before him. Any uninformed thinking on his part can only produce results which should, and most likely will, end in the waste basket.

After the planning stage, the next step involves meetings between the copy writer and art director, during which various layout approaches are discussed by both parties. Sometimes an early agreement can be reached. More often, however, the art director will withdraw to his drawing board and begin to experiment with "roughs" or pencil versions of possible layouts. When he hits on an idea which seems to fill requirements, the writer is consulted. If an agreement is reached, work may begin on a more comprehensive layout.

Layouts and Finished Art

The "rough" layout is usually too sketchily done to submit to the advertiser. Generally it is necessary to do a more comprehensive pencil or chalk version on tissue which will be mounted on board. If the client is inexperienced in advertising, or if the material is to be presented to an advertising committee in the client's organization, it is often necessary to show with some exactness how the advertisement will look when published. In this case a layout will be rendered, using a very finished sketch illustration, headlines, which have actually been lettered, and type set in position. This type of comprehensive layout was frequently used in the past. However, it is expensive to produce, and takes time. The more modern trend is to submit to the client rougher layouts in which the illustrations are suggested rather than rendered in detail.

After approval by the client, the layout goes to the art buyer. At this time, also, the typographer consults with the art director as to type faces and overall typographic effect.

The art buyer consults with the art director on all important commissions, so that finished artists who are satisfactory to both parties can be selected. Very often art buyers and art directors will consult while the layout is being created, because the director may have the style of a finished artist in mind while he is working on the layout. A preliminary "sketch"—photography or art—may be undertaken at this point.

Finished art must meet the art director's expectations and be approved by him. The engraving expert, however, takes full responsibility for the quality of the completed engravings, once he has accepted the finished art as practicable for engraving. The art director does not tell the engraving expert how to make engravings. He does, however, expect the reproduction to match the art work within the limitations of printing inks, printing paper and printing processes.

Television Coordination

Problems of television art are usually handled by an art director specializing in TV, who is familiar with all the different techniques and developments in the field of TV commercials (See page 112.) Part of his job is to coordinate the commercials on television with printed advertising. In this way, the art themes and treatment in all types of media will have a "family resemblance," multiplying their effectiveness with readers and viewers and getting the greatest possible impact from the entire program of advertising.

It will be seen, therefore, that the art director in the larger agency has a well-organized job in which he must function in close cooperation with all of the creative departments for maximum effectiveness. The basic aim is to create a visual selling message.

An
Art
Director
Must Be
More
Than An
Artist

by Lester Rondell

Group Supervisor, Grey Advertising Agency

THE fundamental problems of the art director are the same, regardless of the billing of the agency. Art direction is one of America's newest professions. Not too many years ago the art departments of advertising agencies and magazines were staffed only with "layout men" and "paste-up" boys. When a paste-up boy grew up, he became a layout man. Now, due to technological advancement and the introduction of rubber cement, the "paste-up" boy has been replaced by a "mechanical" man. And as advertising and publishing developed into the major industries they are today, the layout man became an art director.

Dr. Agha, one of our most distinguished leaders, has always objected to the title "art director," on the ground that it suggests a traffic cop standing at an intersection directing some art north and some art south. He has maintained that we do more than merely *direct* art— we create some of it, guide, encourage and inspire much of it—and then supervise all of it towards its ultimate reproduction. Agha thought then, that perhaps we should be called "art supervisors." But that too is inadequate. At any rate, I think the title is less important than the actual role art direction is performing today in the business of advertising.

39

The AD Must be an Artist—and More

One frequently hears remarks about the responsibility of art direction in elevating the taste of the public. I used to argue that way myself. But in recent years I have come to believe that the elevation of taste is not a function of art direction. I do feel, however, that inasmuch as art direction is primarily and obviously concerned with art, an art director who is also an artist is better equipped to realize the full potential of his position. And if he is a conscientious, talented artist, his work will necessarily tend to elevate the taste of those exposed to the results of his efforts.

But in order to cope with all the demands of his job, an art director must be more than an artist. He must be a businessman too, which means he must be an artist—not for art's sake—but for business' sake. But this does not mean he cannot serve business and industry best by the use of originality and good taste, and by employing the finest technical and creative assistance available. The more ways art direction demonstrates that good art means good business, the more freedom art

directors will be given to develop their ideas. And this is a goal worth attaining, both for the artist and the businessman.

Varied Responsibilities

The responsibilities of an advertising agency art director can be quite varied. They include the scheduling of time for the preparation of layouts, lettering, finished art, photography and retouching, and for engravings to be made. This can frequently become a complicated and detailed operation requiring considerable art and mechanical reproduction knowledge.

A familiarity with the various methods of reproduction is of great importance. For unlike a fine art painting, drawing or etching, the printed page is the only exhibit the public ever sees. It is true that the technical advancement of engraving and printing has accomplished wonders, but there are still many limitations that must be considered in the handling of artwork so that the maximum effectiveness can be retained on the printed page.

In addition to space advertising the art director also handles all creative problems connected with posters, packaging, printing and, now, television.

In most advertising agencies the art director is responsible for the buying of all the finished art, photography and lettering that appears on the printed page. In this capacity he should be thoroughly familiar with the work of the art studios, photographers, illustrators, and fine art artists. Advertising is using fine art more and more, and when properly applied it can be extremely effective. Because art buying can be so time consuming, some agencies employ "art buyers" who do all the interviewing and purchasing.*

The art director works closely with the production department on type and special instructions on engraving. He supervises the preparation of rescales for different sizes of the same advertisement. He will check and approve all finished engravings prior to submission to the client and the publication. Any or all of these activities may require conferences with the client, account executive, copywriter, traffic manager or production man.

Layout and Design

Layout is the outstanding single function of art direction, and depends on a number of factors for its successful execution. A good advertising layout has to be much more than just a slick rendering and arrangement of the various elements. It must be the plan for an advertisement that will arrest the eye of the reader; project the point and purpose of the message simply and succinctly; create in the mind of the reader the desire to *buy* something, from a cake of soap to a trip to South America.

The design and appearance of the final ad can also arouse an emotional response that will affect the reader in different ways. People will react to certain shapes and tones and colors unconsciously. The advertisement should make the reader feel and remember what is most advantageous for the advertiser. Therefore, the visual impression of the advertisement should reflect the quality of the product, and enhance the believability of the message.

Let me hasten to add in deference to copywriters that I think the words in the advertisement are very important, even if there are only a few of them—the fewer the better. But for the purpose of our discussion we will confine our remarks to visual presentation.

The different techniques for rendering a layout include pencil, pen, pastel or water color. The purpose of the layout is to simulate the visual effect of the printed page and therefore the technique should be

*Refer also to Nathaniel Pousette-Dart's views on "the creative imagination", page 23—Ed.

One of a series of trade paper ads for Wesson Oil that ran in 2-color full-page units. Advertising in trade publications must be designed to appeal to the particular needs and interests of the industry the product is used in.

The object of the Relska Vodka campaign was to convey a distinctive brand identification to a product that suddenly became a commodity. Aimed at a "class" audience in a competitive market, the ads appeared in 4-color full-page newspaper space and in magazines.

chosen accordingly. A well developed technique, or method of rendering can enhance the expressiveness of the layout. To achieve this the art director should have a good working knowledge of illustration, lettering, type, photography and design in order to graphically indicate what the final advertisement will look like.

The basic elements in practically all advertisements are a picture, caption, copy and signature. The arrangement of these elements must be carefully planned. Sound judgment should be exercised in determining the "kind" of art to be used; illustration, photograph, painting, or drawing. There should be a good reason for the style of caption used—if set in type, what type? If hand lettered, what style? The arrangement of the copy must be given careful attention as to placement, character, and size of type.

A successful advertisement is usually the result of the combined thinking of many minds. The basic purposes of the campaign or advertisement are discussed and outlined in a meeting of the plans board consisting of contact, research, copy, art and media. Following this meeting, copy and art will meet again to develop specific themes, based wherever possible on the findings of research and marketing. The art director will execute or supervise the rendering of the layout.

Advantages of Smaller Agencies

I do not think there is any real difference in the function of an art director of a small, medium-sized or large agency. In terms of research or merchandising the large agency may have greater facilities to offer a client. But in the actual creation of an advertisement— the copy, art and engraving—a large agency is just a group of little agencies under one management.

The smaller agency affords the art director a greater opportunity to participate more directly in the many elements that contribute toward building the best ad. He can take an active part in the planning, research, media, merchandising and marketing problems, because of a less complicated departmental set-up.

Another advantage of the smaller agency is the opportunity to work on a variety of accounts. This serves as excellent training for the beginner and is most stimulating and challenging for the art director. It requires solving problems in all forms of media from 40-line newspaper ads to 4-color, full-page magazine advertisements and outdoor posters. Television has also become a vital part of the job from general planning to storyboards.

The accompanying illustrations indicate the diversification I am talking about. They are examples of some of the jobs produced in our agency, and each represents but one of many in individual campaigns.

"Cover girl" theme which has proven effective in attracting women to Sweetheart Soap in a campaign that ran in women's magazines in black-and-white and planned for frequency.

Small space 2-color units in Sunday supplements used for Tabasco campaign designed to combine maximum of "class" brand identification with frequency of insertions.

42

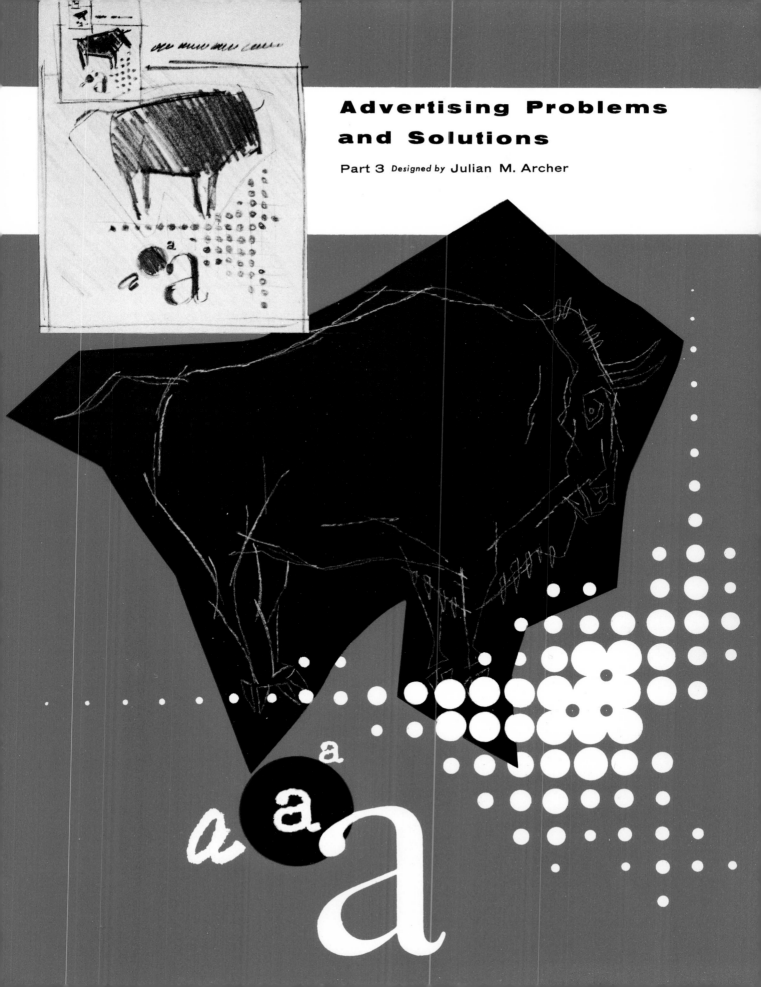

Advertising Problems and Solutions

Part 3 *Designed by* Julian M. Archer

Springboards to Help Stimulate Advertising Ideas

by Henry M. Havemeyer

President, Hoyt Howard, Inc.

PRODUCT

INSTITUTIONAL

SERVICE

SALES OBJECTIVES

A LOOK AT COMPETITION

MEDIA
reaching the consumer

RESEARCH
market
. .
reader behaviour

BENEFITS SHOWN BY PRODUCT OR SERVICE:

in use
not in use
variety of uses
end uses
technical details
product being ma
. .
quality
pride of ownershi
snob appeal
information offer
price

CHECKLIST FOR IDEAS

contests
sample offers
symbols — all typ
similes
analogies
. .
testimonials
continuities

POWER HEADLINES
question and
startling-
statement
techniques
. .
unexplored

THIS diagram will not create ideas. It does not pretend to offer a reading-from-left-to-right time-table. The approaches are grouped rather loosely with no attempt at formula.

It does, however, do two things: (a) serves as a checklist to keep us out of creative ruts, and (b) suggests that, in planning fresh advertising, all concerned would do well to consider the possibilities listed to the left before, for example, plunging at once into premature thinking about illustration techniques.

A point to remember — a good advertising idea can originate anywhere; but its recognition and development can be facilitated by mature analysis.

CONVENTIONAL

picture, headline,
copy, logo

all type

EDITORIAL

NEWS
TESTIMONIAL
celebrities
models
plain people
contests
case histories

CARTOON
(single)

CONTINUITY
cartoon strips
picture-caption
series
"before & after"

PICTURE-CAPTION
(without continuity)
. .

unexplored

FORMAT

MODERN

SHOCK CONTRASTS
texture
rhythm
form, color
line, tone
content

TYPE DEVICES

"WHITE SPACE"

SYMBOLS

NON-OBJECTIVE
(decorative
devices)
. .

unexplored

ILLUSTRATION

HUMOROUS

DECORATIVE

HISTORICAL

ROMANTIC

DRAMATIC

REALISTIC

TECHNICAL

ART TECHNIQUES

An Exciting
Visual Problem

by Charles Faldi
*Vice President and Director of Art,
Benton & Bowles, Inc.*

ADS are composed of two kinds of copy. Word copy and picture copy. It's not important which comes first in the preparation of the ad, so long as there is a good marriage of the two.

Perhaps because of the product itself, the answer to this problem was a relatively simple one. Its elegant design and jewel-like character were woven into a series of provocative situations where the major visual interest was focused on the product.

This campaign provides an excellent example of the kind of effective contribution an art director can make. But in order to do this he must understand the problem fully and exercise good judgment and practical imagination toward its successful solution.

I have chosen this series because it depicts the art director's creative ingenuity. There were ever so many sketches made before this unusual concept went into production. For his theme the art director made a high fashion, decorative, and unique use of the product. I'm sure this series will be memorable both in the trade and by the consumer.

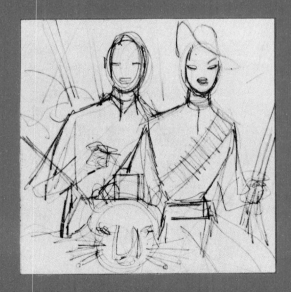

47

BROTHERS TO THE ONE'S AT HOME

BROTHER TO THE ONE'S AT HOME

Brother to the ones at Home

Brother to the ones at Home

Four Steps
to a Solution

by Gordon M. Wilbur

Art Director, N W. Ayer & Son, Inc., Philadelphia

THE copywriter furnished the manuscript for this advertisement before any layout work was commenced. The art director prepared rough tissues showing four different situations. These roughs were taken to the client who chose the composition which was felt most suitable to show the advantages of the Airlight telephone booth. This was rather unusual because we usually submit a finished comprehensive to A. T. & T.

After receiving client approval to proceed to photography, estimates were obtained from several photographers. The client had requested that the photograph be taken in Hamilton, Ohio. Because of the distance and the possibility of many difficulties that might be encountered, the art buyer felt that we had to arrive at a definite estimate and remain with it. We wanted to avoid the "cost plus" method of working in order to keep the photographer conscious of expenses, which otherwise could get out of control.

Enter the Art Buyer

The art buyer chose photographer Arnold Newma because of his ability to handle location work well. His work for *Life* indicated this. His work also has a dramatic mood quality about it, and above all, we wanted a dramatic shot.

Mr. Newman's estimate for the job was well worked out. His price came between the high and the low estimates that had been submitted by other photographers. The names of the various photographers were actually given to the client and we had highly recommended Newman above the others. The art buyer handled all of this groundwork in order to remove this detail from the art director.

The art buyer made all the basic arrangements with the photographer and with the Cincinnati & Suburban Telephone Company located in Cincinnati. Arnold Newman, his assistant, and the art buyer went to Cincinnati. The art buyer again worked with the men at the Cincinnati & Suburban Telephone Company to arrange a location, police protection, the obtaining of an Airlight phone booth and other details.

When the prints for the job were delivered they were reviewed by the copywriter and the art director, as well as the art buyer, and the necessary retouching was done before submission to the client for his approval.

The unusual problems which arose during the actual photography were handled smoothly. These were production problems—procedural problems within a large but closely knit corporation, but not really unusual where work of this type is concentrated in the hands of an art buyer.

Art Buyer: Edward W. Warwick.

49

A LIGHT IN THE DARK—More and more outdoor telephone booths are being placed at convenient locations. They are available for service 24 hours a day. They supplement the hundreds of thousands of telephone booths in buildings, stores, hotels, gas stations, airports, railroad stations and bus terminals.

Brother to the Phones at Home

No matter where you go, you are never far from a public telephone. North, south, east and west, they are conveniently located to serve you.

They are all brothers to the telephones in your home or office and connected in a nationwide family. From them you can call any one of fifty million other telephones nearby or across the country . . . and thirty-five million in other countries.

So the next time something comes up when you are away from your home or business—or you're thinking of someone who would like to hear your voice—just step in a convenient telephone booth and call.

You can travel far in a few minutes—save steps, time and money—and get things settled while they're fresh on your mind.

BELL TELEPHONE SYSTEM
"It means so much to keep in touch"

Sometimes You Start With a Picture

by Gordon Wilbur

A RECENT newspaper campaign for Plymouth was started a month or two previous to this advertisement. We had convinced our client that it was wise to show a photograph of the car rather than a drawing in the announcement advertising, because car drawings had over the years reached such extremes of stretching that the public discounted these drawings.

The first photographs used for newspapers had been changeovers from color transparencies made for the magazine advertising. These changeovers were retouched to preserve all the photo qualities, but with values accentuated to increase contrast. They were satisfactory, but the art director and art buyer on the account felt that newspaper art would be much improved if the car were photographed especially for newspaper reproduction. Irving Penn, the photographer we selected, was enthusiastic about the possibilities.

The other people on the account were convinced of the opportunity for improvement in the newspaper art, and the experimental photograph which we proposed was authorized. The general view of the car was discussed within the creative group and with the photographer before work was started. The exact angle and the lighting were developed by the photographer, with the cooperation of the art director and the art buyer.

An Unusual Procedure

This procedure was unusual in that no layout had been prepared for the advertisement, and because of the layout problems which were so closely tied up with the angle of the car, the art director was present at the shooting, together with the art buyer. The art director watched the general conception of the picture, and the way its shape affected the layout possibilities and the desire for drama. The art buyer watched for the atti-

5

SUDDENLY, IT'S 1960...

In one flaming moment, Plymouth leaps 3 full years ahead! Plymouth's traditionally great engineering brings you the fabulous new Fury "301" V-8 ... revolutionary new Torsion-Aire ride ... exciting sports-car handling ... new super-safe Total Contact Brakes ... dramatic Flight-Sweep Styling. The car you might have expected in 1960 is at your Plymouth dealer's *now!* See it! Drive it! Own it!

➤ PLYMOUTH!

tude of the car, roundness, separation of forms, contrast of values, surface qualities and reflections. Where one person's interest conflicted with another's it was settled by a satisfactory adjustment or the detail of lesser importance was given up.

The result of the experiment was a dramatic photograph with strong, simple contrast and natural high surface reflections in the car; no retouching to explain shapes or bring out non-existent separations was required. Retouching was limited to increasing contrasts which existed in the photograph and correcting details of reflection produced by the mechanical limitations of our reflecting surfaces.

Reproduction proved excellent in both large papers and small—even those with the most undependable reproduction looked well.

Art Buyer: Gordon M. Wilbur, Associate Art Director.

51

Graphic Simplicity . . .
Dramatic Impact

by William Bernbach

President, Doyle, Dane, Bernbach, Inc.

and Robert Gage

Art Director, Doyle, Dane, Bernbach, Inc.

Rough Comp.

Thumb-nail Sketch

AS professional skill advances, it becomes increasingly difficult to distinguish technique from substance. The technical excellence with which a good idea is executed will often make or break that idea. On the other hand, even a technical genius will not make a *bad* idea come off.

We therefore always concern ourselves first with the quality of the idea. We are ad builders and not copywriter and art director. An ad is just pictures and words util some great idea brings them to life.

The first assignment we give ourselves is to define the purpose of the ad as simply and succinctly as possible. We measure the success of our efforts in terms of how dramatically and imaginatively it achieves the purpose of the ad, and not by the isolated graphic beauty of the page or the cleverness of the words.

In the case of Ohrbach's, the purpose of the ad is to tell the reader that here she can get high fashion at a low price. Aware of the tremendous competition for the readers' attention, we searched for a way to express this thought in the most provocative, yet the most simple terms. If we could find a single symbol that would express more than one thought, we knew we could achieve a graphic simplicity that would add to the dramatic impact of the ad and at the same time make the thought easier to grasp. We found it in the price tag which was a symbol of price and the price tag string which could serve the purpose of binding someone. By simply using the string to tie up a fashionable looking woman and the price tags as a background for the words "tied up by high prices?", we said everything that needed to be said with a minimum of words and pictures. Yet the incongruity of using the price tag in such a manner made for a startling and therefore attention-getting visual.

52

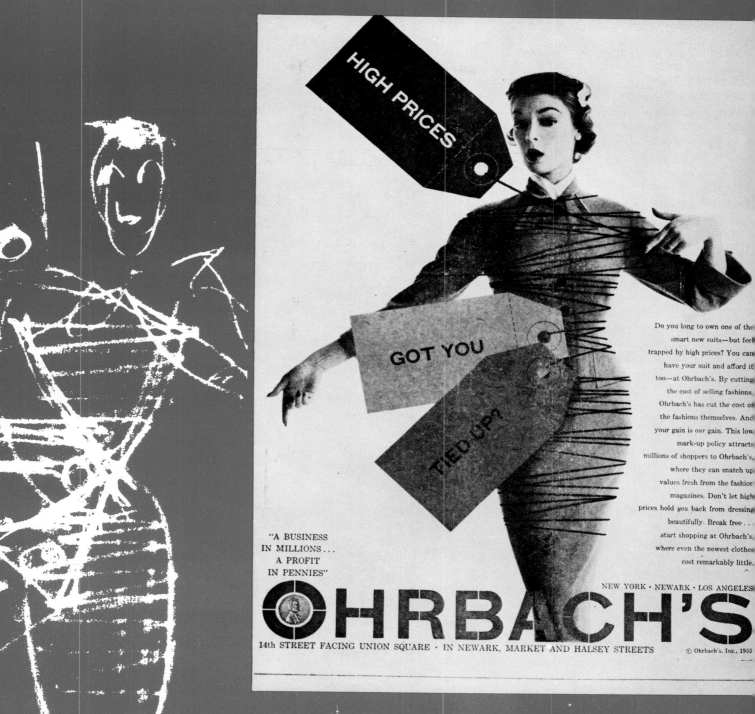

HIGH PRICES

GOT YOU

TIED UP?

Do you long to own one of these
smart new suits—but feel
trapped by high prices? You can
have your suit and afford it
too—at Ohrbach's. By cutting
the cost of selling fashions,
Ohrbach's has cut the cost of
the fashions themselves. And
your gain is *our* gain. This low
mark-up policy attracts
millions of shoppers to Ohrbach's,
where they can snatch up
values fresh from the fashion
magazines. Don't let high
prices hold *you* back from dressing
beautifully. Break free . . .
start shopping at Ohrbach's,
where even the newest clothes
cost remarkably little.

"A BUSINESS
IN MILLIONS . . .
A PROFIT
IN PENNIES"

NEW YORK · NEWARK · LOS ANGELES

OHRBACH'S

14th STREET FACING UNION SQUARE · IN NEWARK, MARKET AND HALSEY STREETS

© Ohrbach's, Inc., 1953

Finished Ad

53

The International Art Director
...His Problems Overseas

by Francis Von Dumreicher

Art Director, International Division, McCann-Erickson, Inc.

GENERALLY speaking, at first glance there is not too much difference between a domestic and an international art director. Both must be perceptive, flexible, and *au courant* with the trends and tastes of the day. Both are engaged in communication; are concerned with problems of creation and productivity.

The major difference is in the area covered which, in the international field, is literally the whole world. It is hard enough to convey an idea when one works in the same cultural environment with the group to which the idea is directed. Imagine how much more difficult it is when one must consider the widely varying sensibilities of many such groups, thousands of miles apart. Yet these are the dimensions of the job.

Attributes of the International AD

The international art director must strive to be an all-around man. His ideal is da Vinci, the epitome of the Renaissance—interested in everything and able to do anything. His sympathies and understanding should literally be as wide as the world. His professional attainments should be of a comparably high character. He must know that a type of art which will be accepted in one country will be rejected, or will prove meaningless in another; and that while testimonials, for example, work well in the United States and Latin America they are often received skeptically in Europe.

Yet his attainments cannot be limited to art forms. He must know buying habits too— as demonstrated in half a hundred widely dissimilar marketing areas. He

5

must know how goods are displayed and sold in Brussels, Buenos Aires or Bombay. He keeps his eyes open in market-place and bazaar, drug store and supermarket. He is aware of how the newer types of research can be used to direct and certify creative recommendations, and how the real and underlying reasons for human motivation can be ascertained and turned to the advantage of his clients. He is, above all things, a sincere and sensitive *adapter* of good ideas and methods from everywhere.

If he operates in this way, the international art director will proceed soundly and without undue reliance on mood or caprice. In many overseas markets this is still a revolutionary attitude. Hence, part of his job is to convey such ideas to his other offices in an appeal-ing or convincing way. He must be salesman, diplomat and psychologist; for he is, after all, an American. Other peoples are proud and sensitive—especially if they are creative; they do not respond to a "bulldozer" approach, and must be given an opportunity to find their own way to the correct conclusions. So regarded and helped, they will often react favorably and with startling speed to the suggestions made; which is only basic common sense in dealing with human nature, wherever found. It is trite but true that people are really much the same everywhere; yet each time it is discovered anew, the simple fact comes as a heart-warming revelation.

Indeed, this is one of the more inspiring and hopeful sides of this work. When we find the human motif that

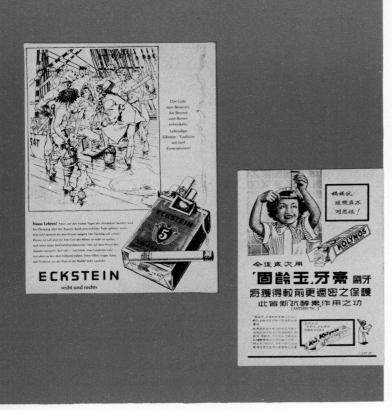

for its posters and exhibits; Germany for its designers and typography; France (and increasingly Italy) for fashions; England for fine handling of national newspaper advertising; Scandinavia for functional displays; Latin America has some outstanding painters.

It is desirable that all offices (of an international agency) be kept informed of these availabilities. Several years ago I installed a Central Creative Committee whose purpose is to review our entire overseas production, and since our agency has twenty-two offices in this category, the volume is considerable. All forms of visual advertising are evaluated. Sometimes new layouts are prepared to implement the suggestions made. Each month I try to choose one subject for discussion and criticism.

This operation is augmented by the dispatch to interested offices of new product data, as well as information on new techniques in any medium; we also send them our own domestic campaigns, plus any other unusual handlings of problems with which we know they are concerned. Add to these activities a two-way training program for personnel, the study of international media and frequent trips to other countries for on-the-spot liaison, and it is clear that the life of the international art director is far from dull. It is full of challenge and crisis. No two days are ever alike. And therein lies its fascination.

Qualifications of an Overseas AD

A word to those who seek positions as creative art directors in foreign branches of U. S. advertising agencies. Obviously, knowledge of the language is needed for such everyday routines as marking copy and art for typographers, printers and engravers. But more important still—the art director should cultivate an intimate understanding of the idioms, customs and psychology of the overseas customer, who often differs sharply from his American counterpart. He must master those visual techniques and understand those copy appeals which will be most effective with the people he is trying to reach. One way of doing this is to study the native newspapers, magazines, radio programs, movies, posters and other media. It is also desirable to learn the language of the man in the street.

The overseas art director must sometimes be more resourceful than if he were in the States, where first-rate photographers and artists of all kinds are at his beck and call. He will often be required to "import" art from a neighboring country, substitute photographs for drawings (or paintings for photographs) and generally exercise ingenuity in making the most effective *local* advertising with the means at his disposal.

makes us all kin, no traditions of narrow nationalism can stand against it.

Methods and Techniques

One of the prime functions of the international art director is to serve as a clearing house of information and experience—both to and from his overseas offices. This includes the readability as well as the design aspects of typography. It extends to the use of the Polaroid camera for layout purposes, for example. It even comprehends such small and obvious short cuts as the substitution of the charcoal pencil for graphite pencil plus India ink.

Nearly every country has a contribution to make to the techniques of art direction. Switzerland stands out

5

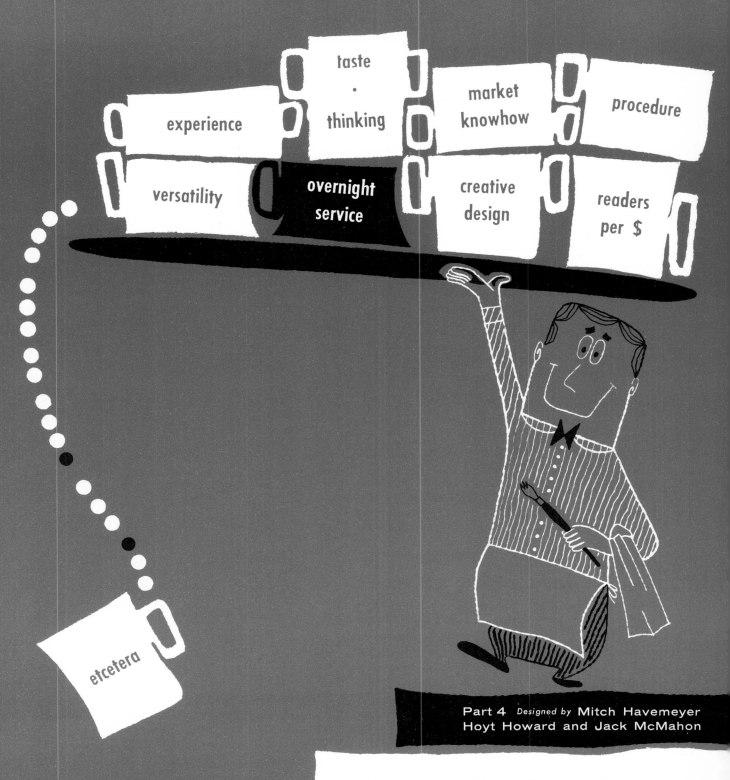

Part 4 *Designed by* Mitch Havemeyer
Hoyt Howard and Jack McMahon

The Studio Art Director

The Consulting Art Director

The Consulting Art Director

by Arthur Hawkins

Consulting Art Director and Designer

WHILE the atomic age has not yet produced a noticeable effect on the publishing and adtising businesses, the second half of the twentieth century has, nonetheless, seen a phenomenal development in the processes, skills and materials serving these— and other—industries.

Never have such a wide variety of art expressions been put to work to sell goods. And never has there been available such a bountiful supply of capable artists —designers, cartoonists, illustrators—to produce this. Even easel painters today are showing a willingness— and ability—to undergo the discipline required by the industrial field. And art schools across the country are ever grinding out a fresh contingent of hopefuls eagerly straining to "get into the act."

New Tools and Skills

The recent rapid development in photography has almost overnight provided advertisers and publishers with an exciting and practical tool with which to sell soft goods, foods, liquors and every conceivable type of merchandise. Color photography has come into *common* use with the perfection of color film, development processes and photographic skill. And a choice is offered of color transparencies, carbro prints or synthetics expertly rendered from black-and-white prints.

In support of these art forms there is offered a wide assortment of type faces—machine and foundry—with new up-to-the-minute styles being introduced almost monthly; an assortment of film lettering, the variety of which almost defies the imagination; and hand lettering of every conceivable nature.

To put all these services and skills to work, to select the most suitable art forms or technique for the job at hand, to coordinate and prepare the work for the engraver, the offset printer, the lithographer or silk screen printer, the experienced hand of one or more trained art directors has become indispensible—as evidenced by the present practice of every advertising agency in the country worthy of the name, and by many publications, department stores and manufacturers.

Why a "Part-Time" Art Director?

But what about industries having an insufficient volume of business—or an insufficient demand for creative work—to warrant the employment of an art director? For them the answer is an art director working part time—a consulting art director.

This man—the free-lance art director, as he may sometimes be called—has the same duties, performs the same functions, as any other art director except that he may work for several businesses, or publishers or agencies at the same time, receiving an agreed fee for a stipulated, scheduled work program—one day a week, two days a week, four mornings a week, etc.—but he may work irregularly as business pressure requires.

The consulting art director may work directly with management, planning, visualizing or laying out advertisements; he may design packages, posters or displays, booklets, annual reports or direct mail pieces; he may design TV commercials or layout the pages of a magazine or company publication.

Or he might work in collaboration with the regular company art director, providing a fresh creative viewpoint, a new approach, a different technique or medium of illustration to an old and tiresome problem.

To perform his job efficiently the consulting art director must be prepared to specify type, direct photography, supervise production and printing. He has to know color, paper, printing, engraving. In short, he must be prepared to fill-in in any creative or executive capacity required up to and including client contact.

New Help for the Agency Art Director

by Hoyt Howard
Secretary-Treasurer, Hoyt Howard, Inc.

IN this have-an-account-today-lose-it-tomorrow era, more and more advertising agencies (whether medium, small or large) are finding that it is good business sometimes to call on the services offered by a consulting art director. As advertising grows more visual and the importance of the attention-getting idea becomes more widely understood, the need for consulting AD's (as well as those on salary) will increase.

Today's consulting art director is helping advertising agencies in four general areas. They are:

1.—Developing *fresh ideas*
    on a specific account problem.
2.—Handling the *overflow* from an art director.
3.—Advising and/or visualizing
    for *specific markets*.
4.—Handling the *non-space material*
    that must support an advertising campaign.

Fresh Ideas

These will flow more readily if the consultant is called in at the earliest possible stage. The agency need only to acquaint him with the client's sales objectives, the current agency plans for the specific account problem, the file of competitors' advertising (perhaps a word about "sacred cows.") and let him go to work. Grant him the permission also to suggest his own campaign. Even some new thinking on a logotype or trade mark has been known to open up a format and increase the readership. In this way the consultant often gets approval to do things that the agency art director has been restricted from doing.

Overflow

This is the result of the art director temporarily having more work than he can handle. Here the consultant augments the art director in the same way that an art studio augments the agency "bullpen." The art studio renders comprehensive layouts from roughs that are completely thought-out by an art director; the consulting AD does the same thinking and rendering that the art director would do if he had the time. It is obvious, however, that proper thinking takes longer than proper rendering.

Specific Markets

Here a specialist among consulting ADs may be called for. The agency may be temporarily inexperienced to handle visually a new field that has suddenly opened up due to acquiring a new account or having an important account enter the new field. With the part-time services of the consulting specialist in that field, the agency can face expansion of account responsibility without hasty major reorganization.

Non-space Material

Made up of those things that are often unprofitable to the agency and/or nuisances to the art director—dealer aids, statement enclosures, folders, charts, posters, trade ads, booklets, tags, postcards, labels, point-of-sale material, annual reports, and even catalogs—but which are *very* important to the client. In this area the agency may find it wise to have the consulant work with the client and report to the agency.

What Motivates the Consultant?

Although the consulting art director is the newest phase of this new art directing profession his batting average is very high. His interest in the client's objective is the same as the agency's: success means more business. This, plus the very fact that he is making a good living on his own, is proof of the consulting AD's ability to be of real tangible help. Furthermore, his continuing success with an agency hinges on his enthusiasm for, and interest in, even the least exciting problems. For even the smallest job *can be done better*. Clearly the consulting AD, by the very nature of his work, cannot afford to get stale. The main reason he accomplishes this is the mental procedures and creative techniques that he has learned from years of thinking, studying, rendering and succeeding.

A Reliable Teammate

Because the consulting AD has had years of inside-the-agency experience, on many accounts, his understanding of the art director and his job makes him a reliable teammate. It would seem, then, that the more agencies in which he has held a job, before opening his own business, the more aware he is of variations in agency and account philosophies.

What the consulting AD wants to hear most, of course, are statements like these:

"Our new account is confident that the proposed campaign will do the job."

"We have just received the Starch figures on the first ad and the noted rating is way up."

"That catalog sold all the plant can produce for the next season."

"Our client added two more publications to the schedule when he saw those layouts you did for us."

How does the consulting art director charge for all this? He may work in several ways: by-the-hour (like a plumber), by-the-day (like a bricklayer) or by-the-job (like a shoemaker). However, when the consultant has earned the confidence of the agency, he is allowed to do his work, then send in his bill (like a lawyer).

Art Direction in the Studio

... Versatility Plus

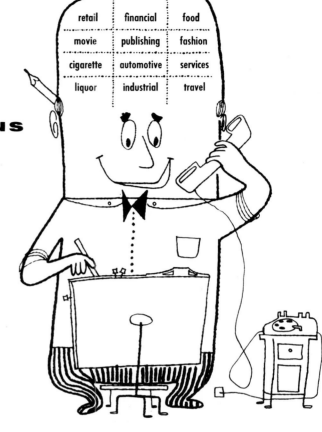

retail	financial	food
movie	publishing	fashion
cigarette	automotive	services
liquor	industrial	travel

by Bert W. Littmann

Vice President, Pahmer & Littmann, Inc.

THE art director in a studio is necessarily a very special kind of breed. He must possess the resourcefulness of a fox, the tenacity of a leech, the toughness of a bulldog, and the strength of a lion . . . to say nothing of talent.

Rare as this specimen may be, he is a basic necessity that every studio must have if it is to survive, and grow. A studio creates its reputation on the abilities and personalities of its owners or managers, and builds a foundation for its future on the quality of its staff. But it is the "inside man" who is the cornerstone that holds the whole framework together.

What Makes the Studio AD Tick?

In order more efficiently to explore the personality and talent demands of the studio art director we can group them into three main requirements. They are:

1. *Versatility* — In agencies, publications and individual companies the art director produces consumer ads, trade ads, booklets, and so on. He utilizes the same logos and type styles, follows approved formats, and in general promotes the policies created by his company. This in no way infers that he is any less capable or original than the studio art director. It's simply a matter of quantity. While the "regular" AD may have three accounts the studio AD may have 15 or 20 accounts. He must know the styling and production of every type of advertising market from lingerie to locomotives. He must be able to quickly gather about him all the necessary art talent, staff or freelance, to produce a job. He might be called upon to find a certain fabric, a new line technique, an unusual type of display construction, or a better way of matching color. His mind must be a department store of services. In most studios he is also his own production chief — familiar with all phases of reproduction, printing, and mailing.

Television demands all this knowledge, and more. The latest TV techniques and money-saving short cuts must constantly be sought by the studio AD. He must be aware of the technical requirements of the networks and scenic designers — and in many cases must co-ordinate his TV output with various trade unions.

In short, he must be a veritable Answer Man, with the know-how to tastefully create and produce anything asked for by a client, from a lowly 14-line mechanical to the loftiest full-page illustration.

2. *Durability* — The studio art director must be built to "take it" — mentally, as well as physically. He will be constantly harrassed by client and employer to produce faster, better, and cheaper. He will be perpetually besieged by suppliers for more time and by free-lance artists for more money. From morning to night he will be allocating work and arranging more schedules than the train dispatcher on a railroad.

Through it all he must maintain an outer calm that commands respect from his staff. He must know the strengths and weaknesses of his bull-pen and be able to listen to and solve their individual problems, to coerce stubborn temperaments, and to wet-nurse promising beginners into mature artists. He can't afford to have an ulcer.

3. *Salesmanship* — "Who's minding the store while the boss is away?" Every studio owner must be 100% sure of the answer to this question, for while he and his salesmen are outside contacting clients the only responsible art-wise person at the studio is the AD.

If a client should phone in, it becomes the art director's job to reassure him of the progress of his particular job and to determine the time of delivery. The intelligent studio AD soon learns the "power" of positive thinking" in the studio-client relationship, and goes on to develop the tact of a diplomat.

Sometimes he will be required to pick up jobs when other salesmen are occupied elsewhere, and in this case "represents" the studio in every sense of the word. The studio AD is the extra "salesman" whose client-contacting efforts go a long way in determining the difference between profit and loss for his studio.

These are the basic requirements of the studio art director. You might logically ask — "Does such a studio superman really exist?" Seeking the perfect studio art director is like seeking the perfect wife . . . you must compromise on a person who is fairly well-rounded, knows most of the techniques, is good in tight spots, and possesses to some degree the qualities of versatility, durability and salesmanship.

In the final analysis the qualified studio AD can look forward to a job that offers the opportunity to build his own staff as he wants it, a chance in most cases to share in the profits, and the knowledge of greater security because in the studio operation an account lost does not necessarily mean a job lost.

The Studio Art Director

YES indeed, the art director — a form of humanity with as many sides as an octagon, with the arms of an octopus — has, in the average studio, the job of layout man, visualizer, art manager, price figurer, and chief worry wart. This is especially so when all is going smoothly and serenely, the work for the morrow all laid out and assigned, then, *boom* — at a quarter to five Joe Jenks, agency art director (and good client), tinkles the telephone and announces that he has a rush job that must be done by nine the next morn. Then all Cain breaks loose, and the well-organized organization goes to pot. So let's just chat a bit about Paradise, where the AD is an *art director*.

Types of Studios

In order more readily to clarify the work, let us list the various types of studios:

The studio with artists working on salary throughout. Here the art director has two functions. One is to direct and traffic the work through the studio, designating the man to do the particular job, and generally co-ordinating the work from start to finsh. Actually, in this case, he is an art manager; the responsibility for the execution of the job is his. His second duty may be to create and design layouts which in turn are given to the artists in the studio to put into comprehensive form or to finish. In this type of studio

by A. Halpert

Halpert — Dane Studio

the artist's time is a factor and time slips must be kept, for final pricing. This is also up to the AD.

The studio with part of the staff on salary and part on a free-lance or percentage basis is another. The art director may be part of the free-lance group, in which case his function is to create and render ideas and layouts only, on a percentage arrangement. Or he may be an idea man solely, with the rendering of visuals and comprehensives done by the artists in the studio. Or again, as in the first studio discussed, he may have the double duty, especially if he is salaried, of creating layouts and seeing them through the studio, using both the free-lance and salaried men.

The studio that represents top illustrators, has still another type of art director. Here the creative work has been done by the agency or magazine art director, and the illustrator follows the layout in general, with whatever of his own originality and composition and design he can put into the illustration. Obviously this art director's job is not one of creating or visualizing. Here again he sees the job through, assigning the job to the artist who has been designated by the magazine or agency, and follows the job to completion and delivery. He does not necessarily have to be an artist, but good taste and art judgment are prime requisites. This type of studio generally has salesmen who bring in the jobs. From then on the responsibility is the art director's. Not a creative art director to be sure, in this case, but a very important cog in art direction. This studio is referred to as "artists' representative".

Some art directors are owners of or partners in a studio. An art director in this situation may be a creative man, working at a drawing board and also a contact man, seeing clients and picking up jobs. There are no set rules in the studio business. If an art director is highly creative and is more valuable to the studio at the drawing board, that's where he should be. If he has contacts and personality, plus creative ability, then part of his time should be spent seeing clients and part as an inside man.

As in the agency business, the larger art studios employ a number of art directors who are specialists, such as in the fashion field, or on the bold, punchy type of layouts, or booklet and brochure designers. The studio that specializes in television commercials has a different problem than the general studio; therefore, its art directors are trained and equipped for that phase of visualization and art.

But, we've been talking about Paradise, where each man has a particular job to do, serenely, without fuss or fury. Ah, how nice, what a sweet life — then — tinkle, tinkle — boom, the 9 A.M. deadline — and Paradise goes down the drainpipe. But, with all this, the job of studio art director has a great many facets, covers a wide field, and can be most interesting and profitable for those with creative ability.

New Help for Magazines and House Publications

by Tobias Moss

*Advertising Manager/Director,
A. I. Friedman, Inc., Consulting Designer*

GENERAL magazines (the big boys) with healthy national circulations are constantly being revamped; undergo frequent cover changes and inside revisions. Sparkling, contemporary typographic treatments, clever layouts, better illustrations and a more interesting use of photographs are all indicative of the trained art director—plying his visual trade. These talented creative ADs are well-paid, *full time* employees.

What About the "Lesser" Magazines?

What about them? And the many, many trade magazines, house organs and business papers? Issue after issue of most show a dull sameness; old-hat typography, standardized handling of art and photos, unimaginative layouts—all evidence of amateurish art direction, if any. In most instances the publisher is trying to save money (commendable). Just-out-of-school art graduates are tagged with the title "art director" and then do everything but direct art. The editor usually doubles in brass, and gets fouled up in the problems of trying to conceive layouts as well as plan and edit the contents of a publication. He usually has to gather material, write, and handle innumerable production details. Editing and art directing are seldom, if ever, two functions which any one person can perform successfully in the preparation of a magazine. Many house and trade magazines published today are painful graphic evidence of this obvious truth.*

Happily, more and more publishers are aware of the necessity for good design, interesting make-up and readable typography. But do they know that wielders of good taste can be hired? Men of business appear to regard art and design warily. They are loathe to seek out a consulting art man, fearful of the cost of an imponderable luxury—art direction. Perhaps design and good taste do not readily lend themselves to a

* See Lester Beall's views on this also, page 96—Ed.

dollar yardstick, yet few will deny its value. The cost of other production factors—printing, typography, illustrations, photographs and engravings—is accepted, seldom question. But the man—*a free-lance consulting art director*—who can bind these elements together and package the jig-saw into a well-integrated organ of information is almost ignored in budget appropriations.

Good Design to Fit the Budget

This man can be had . . . and his professional fee is not exorbitant. He can give the magazine a more commanding and authoritative "feel"—without making it look foreign to its own field. He'll bring contemporary style and good looks to an old-fashioned page, window dress material, think out problems and contribute editorially, too. For the sake of continuity it is best that this "magazine doctor" be called back frequently. A layout designed for a specific problem cannot be "picked up" again and again. No amount of formulae, in themselves, can produce good design. He knows his business and any editor or publisher can "get together" with this professional art director on a free-lance basis. His fees are dependent on the complexity or frequency of publication, and time needed to do a creditable job.

Fundamentally, editors and publishers want their publications to have a professional appearance. A professional appearance is just as important in an industrial publication as it is in any other publication. Above all else, the industrial editor—the same as the editor of a newsstand magazine—must turn out a publication that will interest readers—the appearance factor is of vital importance.

Sure, there's a price tag for a qualified consultant's knowledge, taste, ability, experience—his is a specialized skill. But it's value received. The result is justified by a better magazine!

The Bitter Pills and Sugar Coating of Pharmaceutical Advertising

by Herbert Lubalin

Executive Art Director, Sudler & Hennessey, Inc.

PHARMACEUTICAL advertising has its unusual aspects. The same peculiarities of the industry that enhance the creative opportunities of the pharmaceutical art director are also his deterrents.

Contrary to popular belief, he does not enjoy fabulous budgets, but must produce art and design comparable to the finest employed in nationally advertised consumer campaigns for little more than "trade" advertising appropriations.

A Concentrated Market

The pharmaceutical industry is, in many respects, the most competitive segment of the industrial advertising world. Seldom have so much money and talent been expended by so many companies to reach so few prospects. Virtually all our advertising is directed to some 160,000 M.D.'s. The doctor, representing a professional group with ethical standards, regards pharmaceutical products as a serious part of his medical practice. It has become an important function to supply him with educational as well as promotional information. Therefore, the pharmaceutical industry has found it necessary to rely on personal contact as an adjunct to the usual methods of advertising. This contact is established through a vast detail force of highly-trained, educated men who can gain the attention, respect and confidence of the physician. Coupled with detailing, the pharmaceutical manufacturer makes available a generous amount of professional product sampling. This is a costly effort, but necessary to provide the doctor with a knowledge and a means of evaluating a product.

5

Therefore, before the art director enters the picture, a large part of the total advertising budget has already been allocated. The remainder is spent, in varying proportions, on medical journal ads and direct mail.

The pharmaceutical industry carries on what amounts to a multi-million dollar trade campaign. Low space rates keep design and art costs at a minimum. The amounts usually allotted in the pharmaceutical budget fall far short of the 10% allotment customary in consumer product advertising.

Direct mail presents a similar picture. The pharmaceutical industry is the largest direct mail advertiser in the world. The demands of its audience for educational and informative literature can be satisfied only by a consistent flow of material, ranging from postcards to elaborate house organs. Here again, only a small part of the promotional advertising dollar reaches the art budget. Printing, typography, paper, engravings and mailing cost consume the rest.

Budgets Cannot Limit Creativeness

These budgetary limitations would ordinarily curtail creativeness. But the stimulation provided by an intelligent audience helps to offset this handicap. The pharmaceutical art director is forced to seek new visual techniques and is kept alert by the constant demand for fresh ideas. He recognizes the importance of the doctor's confidence, and therefore, must confine his creativity to an unexaggerated presentation of pharmaceutical facts. The M.D. is a busy man and must be reached with simplicity. He is hypercritical and must be reached with restraint. The glamorous product photograph and beautiful-woman testimonial of consumer advertising, certain humorous applications, the eye patch and the tattoo, have little place in pharmaceutical advertising. Instead, the art director must transform seemingly dull elements, such as case histories, literature abstracts and highly technical language, into visually attractive, effective selling tools. The special meaning behind professional symbols and the very language of medicine itself must therefore be fully understood.

In spite of these problems imposed on the art director, by maintaining the highest standards of advertising art and design, he has helped to bring a measure of prestige not only to himself, but to the pharmaceutical industry as well. Both top advertising talent and the unrecognized artist and designer, have been drawn to this industry because of the creative challenge it represents, and the opportunity it offers to enhance a reputation, or to develop one. To a large extent the success of pharmaceutical advertising has resulted from the combined efforts of these artists and the pharmaceutical art director.

Pictured here are examples of pharmaceutical media and promotion advertising. The spontaneous appeal of this material, all produced on limited art budgets, is hard to surpass — at any price. The doctor receives dozens of these mailings every week; he receives scores of medical journals containing hundreds of ads; he is confronted in this maze of literature, with an abundance of formulae, charts, graphs, product claims and prescriptions. We are convinced of our success as art directors when this busy, harried man reads our message and prescribes products we help to promote.

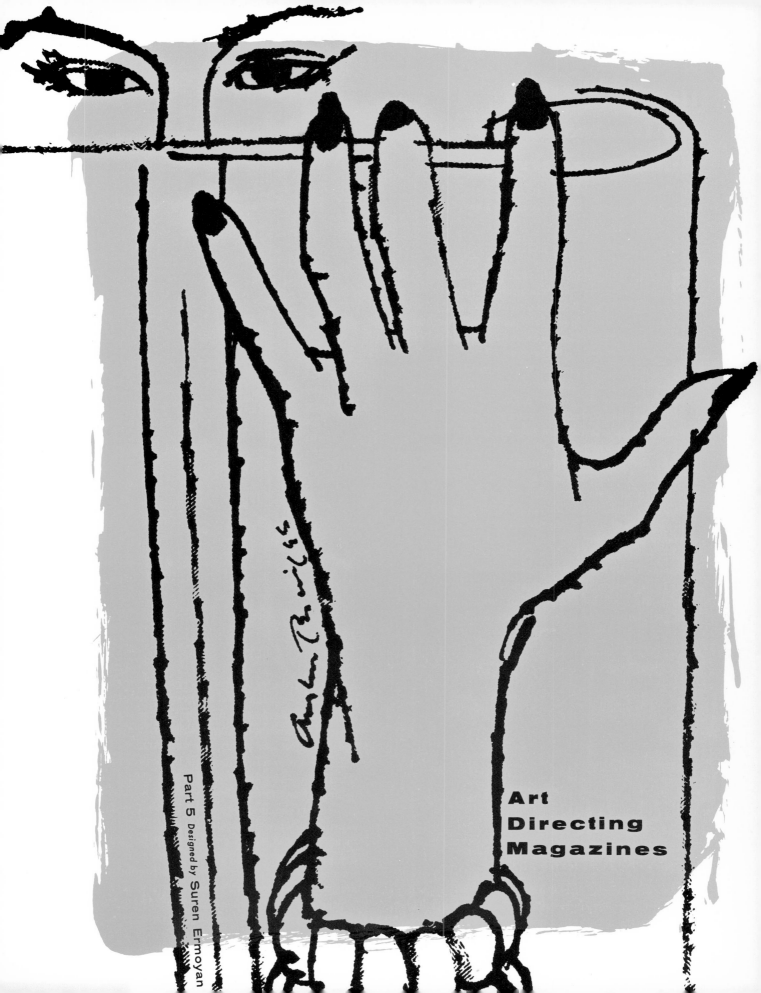

Part 5 Designed by Suren Ermoyan

Art
Directing
Magazines

How Magazine Art Directors Build Readership

by Suren Ermoyan

Senior Vice President, Visual Director, Lennen & Newell, Inc.

BECAUSE magazines are vital instruments of communication, and an outstanding characteristic of American life, it has become almost fascinating to observe how vastly the need for specialized information has increased. Magazines face constant competition for public attention and have become laboratories of experimentation in the graphic arts, particularly in illustration, typography and the studied arrangements of diverse matter on the printed page.

Women's magazines, for example, are distinguished by certain characteristics in function, information and graphic form, which they all have in common. Functionally they are designed for the woman. Their information is characterized by the nature of their editorial matter. In graphic form these magazines are distinguished by their visual interest, simplicity and flexibility. The aim of each magazine, however, is almost invariably unique and the standards of taste, style, and quality it has set must surely be reflected in its physical make-up. In all the departments of these magazines the goal is perfection, for American women turn to them confidently for definitive advice or guidance in all matters pertaining to fashion and home making.

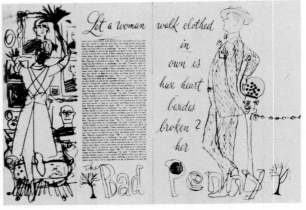

Complex Problems for the AD

Art directing a major magazine today is one of the most complex undertakings in publishing. Therefore, here the art director must be a business executive with an understanding of editorial "angles", an awareness of reading trends, all of which condition him to be a vital contributor to the success and progress of his particular magazine. He applies the necessary visual common denominator that the average woman can grasp with ease and speed, while maintaining a taste and style that everybody can understand.

Under the guiding hand of the editor-in-chief, the art director translates the editorial matter into compelling visual terms. Here is where his rigorous discipline, his shaping of precise values and technique for expediting work is capitalized on. The editorial elements are hand-picked and hand-adjusted with an alert eye to comprehensive fitness, resulting in a successful integration of all the components in producing a magazine that effectively achieves its purpose.

Magazines are planned and developed (often several months) in advance; and issues are kept in constant play until deadlines. Several different printing processes may often be used in the make-up of various

magazines, so constant thought must be given to the physical limitations of each page. Some pages bleed; others don't. This calls for accurate production knowledge on the part of the art director.

We are indebted to research for establishing the importance of formats, pictures, layouts and the position of headings. Typography in a magazine is nothing more than a set of pictorial symbols and a dynamic vehicle for the transmission of words and meanings; hence, it is a great mistake to consider it merely as a technical element. Used ill-advisedly, typography can severely handicap the layout, illustrations and text.

Design Expresses the Idea

In working with artists and photographers, the best results are achieved when the *idea* is the primary consideration. After making a rough layout, the art director should give specific briefing on the nature of the problem, and serve notice that he expects the artist or photographer to rely on his own resources and come through with an improvement over the rough layout. Every opportunity should be given the artist or photographer to exercise imagination, to respond with fresh layers of his talent. This is the only way to keep working relationships *alive*.

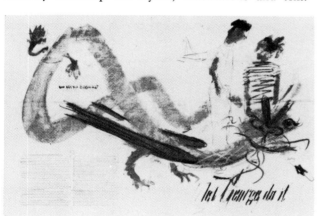

Why all the stress these days on good design? Many magazines seem to be *getting along* without it. But since design plays a vital role in the expression of ideas, does it not seem logical that *good* design must in turn enhance any magazine? Unfortunately, some people still cherish the notion that design is something to be *added on* instead of being an inherent quality which can result only from a process of trial and error. But remember also that the art director is at a disadvantage for it is usually difficult for him to defend his aesthetic judgment and matters of taste. There are times when a degree of compromise is necessary, but above all the art director must maintain creative integrity because the ultimate responsibility for the magazine's appearance is his.

Design and Visual Flow

Let us observe how consciously the visual flow and character of a magazine are handled. A study of magazine *design* describes the development of graphic patterns based on analytically determined standards: (1) *Analysis* of the editorial problem, (2) *Development* of the visual elements, (3) *Integration* of these elements into design patterns. *Format design* develops through the integration of the design factors (illustration and typography) into visual flow patterns that provide the necessary continuity. This continuity guides the reader through a sequence of pages. Since each visual unit is generally two facing pages, these units must integrate with other units to provide uninterrupted flow. The art director gives each series of units their unique appearance through the application of a variety of spatial sensations on the pages. This variety of sensations provide the stimulation necessary for seizing and holding the reader's attention. Only when the art director understands the total relationship of all these factors, can he truly influence visibility and legibility on the pages of a magazine. This visibility and legibility become then his personality, his visual signature.

Because a magazine art director deals with ideas and concepts, a liberal arts background is a prime requisite. Combine with this, specialized graphic arts training, experience in layout, lettering, type faces, printing techniques, art and photography. Then move into field work and gain experience and practice in design of magazines if possible. A job in the art department of a magazine, no matter how limited it may seem at first, will provide an opportunity to develop an understanding, through experience, of the various stages of graphic communication. Here you can learn a point of view, a method of approach, techniques of thinking and working. Beware of imitation, get ahead on your own talent and ingenuity, and measure problems by your own scale. And above all, be yourself.

Examples of pages from
Good Housekeeping and
Town and Country magazines

Salty sheers

It now goes: We shall see *sheers* by the seashore. A low-hugging, long-sleeved lumberjacket of Fisba dotted Swiss, $7.95. The short bird's-eye piqué shorts, $5.95, and bra, $4.95. All, Harrold. At Bloomingdale's; Woodward & Lothrop, Washington; Rich's, Atlanta

The tough-tender look we find the most fun: a sweatshirt of dotted organdy, edged in ribbing, $5, with taut cotton gabardine shorts and matching bra, $4. All by Jane Irwill. Saks Fifth; Lazarus, Columbus; Frost Bros., San Antonio; H. Liebes, San Francisco

Art Directing
the Fashion Magazine

by Bradbury Thompson
Art Director, Mademoiselle

THERE are numerous editorial departments with which the art director must be concerned on a magazine such as *Mademoiselle*. But, because the cover and some 80% of the pages are devoted to fashion, his principal job is with that department.

In the art direction of fashion pages the first step is usually a meeting attended by the editor-in-chief, the managing editor, the fashion editor and her entire staff, as well as the beauty editor when her problems are related to fashion. Here, for the issue concerned, its unifying theme (which might be "College", or "Career", or "Suburbia") is reviewed, and each section and page is discussed in relation to the theme. After the fashion department has outlined the clothes to be shown on each page, appropriate backgrounds are considered and the photographers are selected.

At other meetings the assignments of the various pages are presented to each photographer. Although suggestions are offered to him, he is free to produce a photograph that is creatively his own idea and composition, with the understanding only that the clothes be clearly shown. A fashion stylist is present at the actual posing to assist in matters of clothing.

The first results of a black-and-white photographic shooting are the contact sheets, which the art director examines with the editors and the photographers. A number of enlargements are ordered, from which a final selection is agreed on.

7

Mademoiselle ®

Twentieth Anniversary issue

The Heart of Fashion

The Heart of Fashion

for spring

for trousseaux

for romance

February 1955...35 cents

The Layout

At this point comes the layout with photographs; this must include the necessary information regarding the amount of copy and headings. A pencil layout is made which is subsequently produced by the art director's assistants in the form of a comprehensive layout with photostats of the photographs. The use of dummy type in this comprehensive makes it easier for the editors to write for a given area and size of type, as ultimately is to be used on the pages. When this layout is completed photostatic copies are made for approval by the departmental editor and the editor-in-chief.

The assistant art directors then follow through in assigning the photo retouching and mechanical drawings. They are also responsible, with the art director, in the checking of engravings. The final page proofs are initialed by the art director, assistant art directors and by all the editors concerned.

The AD's work with departments other than fashion is on a more personal basis, as the departments are smaller and are fewer pages to cope with. In the case of fiction, the story is first discussed with the fiction editor and decision is made on an artist whom it is felt can produce a sympathetic illustration. When he has read the manuscript, the artist is encouraged to create his own interpretation. In fact, the layout is made upon completion of the artist's work to avoid restricting his creativeness with a preconceived layout.

Solutions to the particular problems of other departments—such as health and beauty, college, career —are, in the main, arrived at through the art director's collaboration with their editors.

The foregoing is a summary, in rather sketchy terms, of a creative process which is ever challenging to the art director, constantly stimulating his efforts to present in sparkling visual form the editorial content of the magazine and its appeal to women's interests.

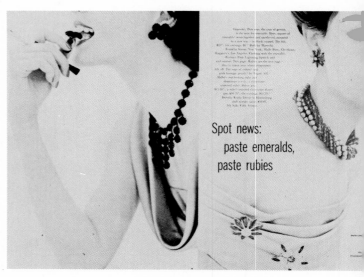

Spot news:
paste emeralds,
paste rubies

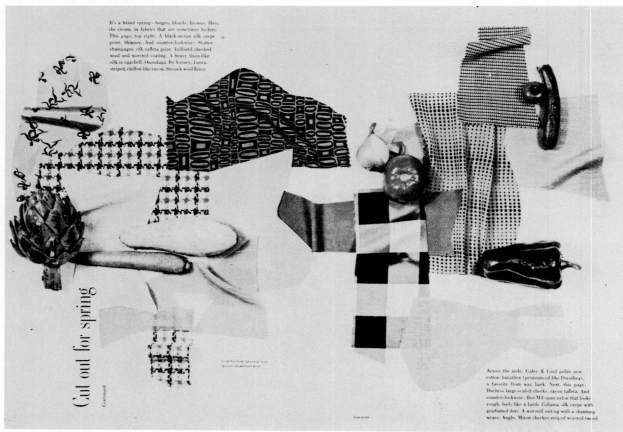

Cut out for spring

VEGETABLES FOR GOURMETS

If you are really as fussy as a gourmet about the taste of what you eat, you will have to grow your own vegetables. The best-tasting kinds are little-known varieties that you can't find in any market because they don't look big enough to sell at a profit. Plant the kinds described here

The only reason for growing your own vegetables is to get better flavor than you can buy. Stores carry vegetables that look well and sell well but don't taste worth a darn—at least by gourmet standards. That's all because the farmer is concerned with size not flavor. He's out for whopping bigness, so he lets his crop fully mature. It's not only more salable, but is tough enough to withstand rough handling en route to market. Trouble is once vegetables reach this stage of maturity their real flavor is gone. So if you have a discriminating palate, grow your own.

Flavor in vegetables is an inherited quality. It is at its best in some obscure half-forgotten varieties that farmers find unprofitable to grow. So you must discover these kinds for your garden.

Inheritance isn't the whole story, of course. You'll need a sunny place, for sunshine fills your vegetables with sweetness. You'll have to harvest correctly, usually daily, to catch your crop vegetables at the peak of their flavor. (Farmers grow kinds that ripen evenly because they want to cut the whole field in one swoop.)

You'll probably want to pick most things when they are still in the baby size, an extravagance farmers cannot indulge in because this cuts the size of the crop drasti-cally—a limitation of little importance to you because you can just plant a few more rows of each vegetable than specified on the yield charts. The best chefs, incidentally, wouldn't think of using the big, over-grown vegetables featured by most markets.

Farmers know that what they sell is rather tasteless. They don't eat this stuff themselves; they grow an entirely different set of varieties for their own table. Here they ignore looks and size of vegetables and pick them when they're young and tasty.

You have to look in the seed catalogs of the specialists to find many of these most flavorsome vegetables. So send now for new catalogs, look for the following:

Beans: Virginia Stanton says, "Make them stringless, if you please—and good for freezing so I can cook an extra amount." (She does two frying pans full each time and freezes those left over for winter dinners.) She grows Burpee's Stringless for tenderness and taste and Kidney Wax (the latter for color variations).

Dr. Carleton conducted extensive trials on beans last summer from France, Sweden, Germany, and England. "I'm full of beans," he says. His pets remain the two oldtimers, both pole beans—Blue Coco and Lazy Wife. Blue Coco is a brilliant purple-podded variety that (Continued on page 111)

Collaborating Editors:
Virginia Stanton
Dr. R. Milton Carleton
William E. Swain
Harry B. Logan

The above article tells the reader that the best-tasting vegetables are the little-known varieties that can't be found in the markets, but must be grown at home. We felt that a literal photographic illustration should not be used, since the vegetables to be depicted were no different in appearance than ordinary ones. The decorative approach gave opportunity to display the unusual subjects in an unusual way. The artist, Dudley Huppler, used a striking pen-and-ink stipple technique. The rough incorporated only the overall basic design.

Art Directing
the Service Magazine

by Wallace F. Hainline

Art Director, House Beautiful

THE art director of a service magazine has the most complicated, encompassing and in a sense, the most commonplace of all subject matter—the way people live. His job is to help interpret all the facets of living—graphically, attractively, and with authority, for an audience of human beings who themselves are pretty well acquainted with the problems of keeping a roof over their heads. The scope involved would seem to call for a real expert—one who knows as much about beating eggs and planting tulips and arranging furniture as he knows about studs and lally columns and mixing concrete. Well, he need be no miracle man but he must certainly know something about all of these things and a few hundred other items like them. Otherwise he will have no legitimate basis of judgment for ordering and evaluating the artwork and photographs which are destined to persuade or inform several million readers who count on his magazine for ideas and information.

And, apart from all this, he should have insight into the emotional reactions, the likes and the dislikes of human nature, for he is dealing with such concepts as home, family life and personal tastes.

Acquiring the Right Background

How does the art director of a service magazine acquire this kind of background? The chief requirement is that he keep alert to everything he sees and experiences. Everybody has an acquaintance with most of the matters that affect living. The art director, however, must do more than casually eat his meals or mow the lawn or order the carpenter to repair the door sill. He must so sharpen his perception, so observe the details of daily living, that he can relate these experiences and the mechanics and principles behind them to the demands of his job.

Specifically, on a magazine like *House Beautiful,* which is devoted to showing the highest standards of American living, the art director faces the problem of presenting practical solutions to living problems in a way that lifts them above the commonplace. The goals are to present the factual, stylishly—yet with clarity—and to create a mood or aura of desirability. For in this day and age the editorial pages of a service magazine face some pretty sharp competition from several sources.

The most obvious competition is in the advertising pages of the same magazine. Indirectly, editorial material in a magazine like *House Beautiful* is a type of merchandising of both ideas and products. The layout of editorial pages therefore requires the same attention to visual "sales pull" as the layouts turned out by an advertising agency art department, which generally use a direct selling approach. Editorial pages should stimulate the reader to accept an idea, and to want to buy the merchandise involved with the idea. At the same time, they must preserve the line of distinction between the commerical and the inspirational, which is what establishes the editorial personality of a magazine.

Rough Layouts

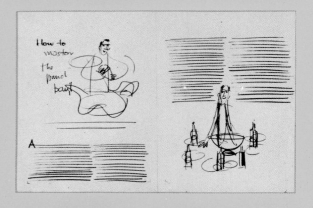

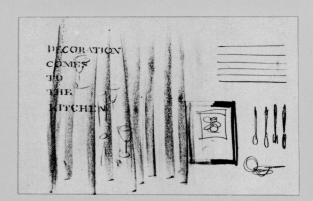

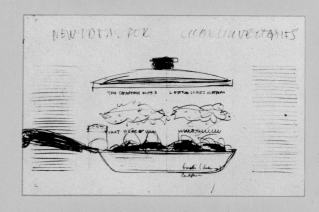

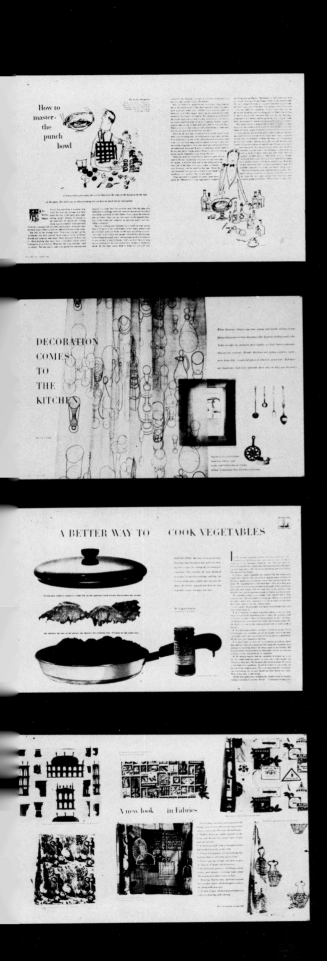

But competition doesn't stop here. The competition of other magazines has grown tremendously in the past twenty years. While the interests of home were once pretty well confined to the so-called "Shelter" magazines, there is now scarcely a magazine on the market which does not have at least a section devoted to home-making. The time when a general magazine or a woman's magazine was 75 percent fiction has passed, so that most art directors these days are faced with the presentation of home-making ideas. This transition has made the field more competitive, but has in consequence improved the visual presentation considerably.

Today's service magazines are covering a far wider range of subject than their obvious material, like home decoration, architecture and gardening. They are branching out into such fields as art, science, music, travel, psychology, even philosophy. This has widened the scope of art work.

Creating Distinctive Editorial Pages

The result of all this is the need for an art director to familiarize himself constantly with all sorts of techniques in artwork. Again everything he sees is grist for his mill, not to copy verbatim, but to use as inspiration. He should keep an eye on the art in fields unrelated to his immediate matter. He can pick up clues to fresh approaches from magazines, books, exhibits, fine art, the stage, window displays, in fact from everything about him. Any one of these can be the spark that will lead to a solution when he most needs it, a month or a year from now. To create distinctive editorial pages, then, the art director must know well, and feel so strongly the overall policy and message of his magazine that its character comes through like a signature, on every page he designs.

At *House Beautiful* the art staff, in addition to the art director, consists of three associates who handle layout, paste-up and production. The magazine is printed in Philadelphia, so for accurate page make-up the composing room is given a paste-up of illustrative material, type in position. Since we see only one proof for corrections it is very necessary that the key layout be accurate.

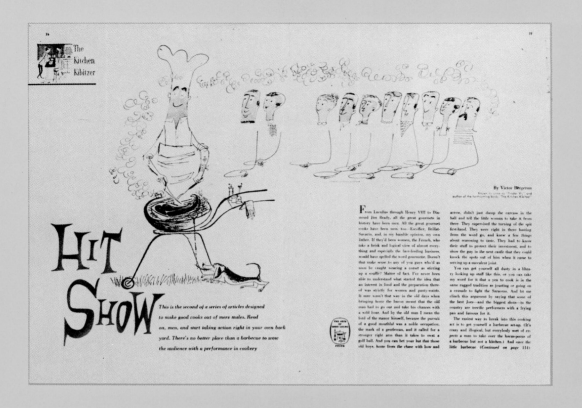

This piece about outdoor barbecuing was written by Victor Bergeron, famous restauranteur, author and world-renowned gourmet—otherwise known as Trader Vic. The choice of Marilyn Hafner as illustrator was a happy one. Her lively, humorous drawings enriched the salty style. Trader Vic's very rough ideas were given to Mrs. Hafner with the copy, and the salient ideas requiring illustration were discussed. Her interpretive talent is such that she was given freedom to do what she liked. These pages were designed from a drawing she submitted, rather than from a pre-planned layout.

This article in *House Beautiful* describes the good family life and the need to record a family's journey through the years — requiring an illustration with realism and charm. Photographer William Helburn was successful in handling this difficult assignment. The models were well cast; the action natural. One has the feeling that he is an unseen visitor watching a little family pageant. A number of roughs were given to the photographer with a copy of the story and a general description of the type of illustration wanted. It was then up to him to produce models, props and action.

Art Directing
the Family Magazine

by Otto Storch

Art Director, McCall's

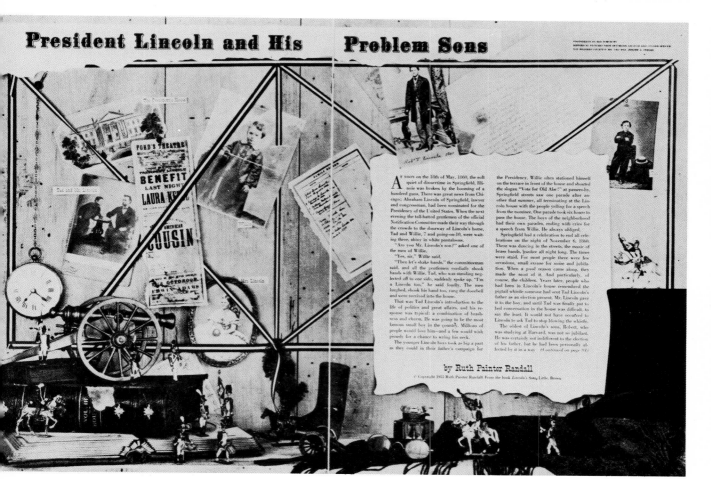

A well-directed, well-coordinated layout, and illustrations that illuminate ideas can keep the reader's eye just where it should be—riveted on the page until the entire content has been absorbed. We are a picture-minded people in this country and, as we become more and more so, dozens of bright and colorful publications compete for readers' attention; within each of these there are dozens of subjects and departments, and many dozens of handsome, compelling ads. The magazine art director must take all this into consideration and try to make his magazine different from the others—give it a personality and authority of its very own, while still avoiding the freakish or tasteless. The art director must at all times view the magazine as a whole and try to supply a logical, pleasant sequence of visual effects—a sequence that will keep the reader turning the pages right to the end.

To do this successfully, it goes without saying that an art director must know his trade and must have a staff that can carry through ideas. At *McCalls,* for example, the art staff consists of ten people with various duties that cover layout, styling and production.

hair goes bright   for the holidays

It takes on sparkle and excitement
to match the season and make a
woman feel, appropriately, her prettiest.
The magic? Color. The top swatch
of each beribboned pair at left
is hair—unadorned. The second shows
how a rinse or tint makes it come alive
to give new life to eyes and skin. A beautiful
way to shine at the Christmas parties—or all year round

The girl pictured above has brown hair—as do most American women. It's pretty, but neither as flattering nor as glamorous as it might be—and so is the photograph at left. For this picture the model used hair coloring, as thousands of women—blonde, brunette and red-haired—are doing to give more glow to a lighter color to their hair. How is it done? Very often at home with either temporary or permanent colorings. Temporary rinses dramatize color by adding highlights. They often come in a shampoo, usually can be washed out. Permanent colorings are longer-lasting and they should be applied the first time in a salon. A successful hair-coloring job not only brightens the hair but gives a corresponding glow to skin tones. To make it successful, remember: Don't have a permanent less than two weeks before or after any type of hair coloring. Make a skin-sensitivity test every time before using a permanent coloring, unless it's made of vegetable dye. Follow directions exactly and be proud of a prettier you.

by MIRIAM GIBSON FRENCH

Two Moments of Importance

To my mind, there are two moments in the preparation of material for a magazine that are of supreme importance to the art director, and indeed determine the ultimate success or failure of his work. The first is the preliminary editorial conference that outlines the material to be presented and the thinking behind it. It is of utmost importance for me to be a participating member of this meeting. I can learn exactly what is behind the editorial decision to run the piece, exactly what it is intended to accomplish and the general tone and "color," if you will, that the piece demands. The second decisive moment is concerned with my instructions to the photographer, illustrator and layout men. I must be able to convey accurately to them what I expect to have, and they in turn must be clear about their own procedure.

McCall's goes to visit Monticello, home of Thomas Jefferson—brings the great kitchen and beautiful dining once back to life with foods and flavors Jefferson once cherished

FEAST DAYS AT
MONTICELLO

by WADE ASHBEE

At *McCalls*, I have the opportunity of dealing with almost every kind of magazine department from fiction to feature, to health to household, in color and black-and-white, in photograph, drawing and painting. I deal with a number of editors, all specialists in their own fields, all distinctly different in temperament and editorial outlook. But I find my job is made easier by the fact that all are agreed on one point of utmost interest to the art director. And that is that *planning* is vital. They want, just as I want, to have a clear visualization of what they are going to accomplish *before* they start. This avoids wasted time and effort by everybody, art and editorial departments alike. They know, just as I do, that compromises must be made from time to time. A deathless bit of prose may have to be sacrificed to make the page come alive visually. A magnificent photo may have to be reduced to snapshot size, or a layout squeezed more than I'd like, to make the meaning come through. But because our preliminary planning is thorough, I think we are often able to come through with a minimum of sacrifice to either art or editorial ideas.

So the magazine art director's job is basically one of communication, both with the readers and with the writers and editors who supply the non-visual material. Given a clear line of communication between the AD and his colleagues, form and meaning can be given to their ideas—bring life and emphasis to printed words.

by Doris Hume

LITTLE MISS INNOCENT

Guaranteed to snuff out an old flame:

A bit of wisdom—and a piece of chalk—

in the hands of a child like Deedee

OF ALL the girls in Linsdale, Jenny Barth was the last one you would have expected Holt Mercer to marry. Holt has much better than average good looks: being old J. D. Mercer's nephew he went right from college into the law firm of Mercer and Talbot; and he had been engaged to Iris Weldon.

As for Jenny—well, she was named Jennifer, but somehow you wouldn't be able to call her that with a straight face if you had to. She's Jenny. Medium brown hair and medium brown eyes, a slightly tilted nose and a mouth about a quarter-size above medium. She has what is called a "feminine" figure, meaning she wasn't designed by Nature to wear slacks—and has the rare good sense not to. Cute little feet and straight legs, though not long enough. That's a physical description of Jenny. You can't get the rest of her into words as easily. Depends on the angle from which you're viewing. Now, take Miss Simms, remaining relative of Linsdale's founder, who reads psychology in-stead of romances, who knows all and tells more. "That Jenny Barth," Miss Simms said once, "can act as cattle-headed as a *maiden*." It could be that, after a Cuban vacation, Miss Simms sought an occasion to use the word, but with all the good intentions in the world you'd never call Jenny the intellectual type. On the other hand, take the people down at Ricknell Realty where she worked: from Mr. Ricknell, Sr., down to Sim, the office boy, they always said, "Heya, Jenny. How's the gal?"

Iris Weldon, an orphan, was living that year with her grandparents and creating a male stampede in Linsdale, but when she and Holt met it seemed to be combustion at first sight. One look and she marked him for her own. Her grandmother's friends made approving sounds and said this was what Iris needed to steady her and bring out her best; for Miss Simms had insisted that it was frustra-tion at not having met the man who was her match that made her high-tempered and *(continued on page 96)*

ARMORED for flight, the pilot of a modern jet surveys the varied instruments on the scratched bubble which is his office. In his Martian rig, he seems all goggles above, oxygen mask below, scarcely man at all.

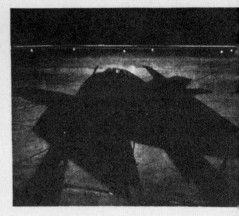

FULL THROTTLE, flying a tight and fixed V at formation, three F-86s go howling into the sunset. Their afterburners, gulping fuel at hundreds of pounds a minute and fretting it to the radiant white heat, blaze with their own inner.

EARTHBOUND, a runway's dazzle, seen by a low-angle camera, halts a truck silhouetted against the bright mountain of the Colorado below the set.

These spreads from *Life* and *Look* indicate the wide range of material the picture magazine art director must cope with.

LIFE

NOVEMBER 23, 1936 10 CENTS

LIFE

AS MIDDLE EAST CRISIS WORRIES THE WORLD
NEW EGYPT DISPLAYS ITS POWER

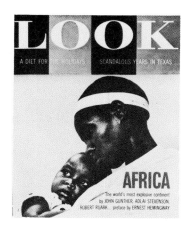

Art Directing the Picture Magazine

by Allen F. Hurlburt

Art Director, Look Magazine

THE advent of the picture magazines in the 1930s brought about far reaching changes in editorial and advertising design. Not only did they provide new vehicles for the talents of artists and photographers, but their influence altered the content and format of many other publications. Magazines devoted to fiction and service broadened their patterns to include picture stories and photographic reports, and special magazines in many fields now make use of the techniques of photo-journalism.

In the advertising field this influence has been widely felt in the changing approach to photographic illustration. In the early days of advertising, photography was largely confined to the studio but today many photographers, influenced by the photographic realism of the picture magazines, are taking "available light" photographs to give a more believable result to advertising illustration.

Photo-Journalism and the Picture Story

The main ingredient of the picture magazine is the picture story, which combines words and pictures to develop a complete narrative. The layout and design of the picture story differs in many ways from the design of normal editorial pages.

In the first place the designer is denied the neutralizing effect of large grey type areas and must utilize the varying sizes and values of photographs to achieve interest. He must use contrast of subject matter, contrast of size and contrast of value to create excitement and yet he must give the whole layout an organic and functional unity that will give the story continuity and order.

Though the art director is frequently involved in the planning stages of a picture story, his real work begins after the photographer has completed his assignment.

The pastel sketch, so valuable in other forms of advertising and editorial design, is of little use in developing a picture story. To be convincing, the photographs must develop naturally out of the situation that develops in the field.

Frequently the art director is confronted with several thousand exposures and must select from these the dozen or so pictures that will make a three-page picture story. Pre-selection by the photographer, producer, or picture editor will save some of the eyestrain, but often the seeking out of the right picture is the most important part of the story layout.

As in other areas of design, the merely pleasing arrangement of elements, the collection of pictures, is never an adequate solution to the layout problem. The self-conscious design that calls attention to itself is also wide of the target.

Only when the design begins with the basic editorial idea and becomes a synthesis of visual and typographic elements projected in dynamic form, can it serve its true function in visual communication.

The art director must also design beyond the limits of the story. He must concern himself with the relationships of feature to feature and feature to advertising, in terms of the total unity of the magazine.

In his quest for better results he must also concern himself with problems of reproduction and he is frequently called on to participate in the planning and development of new printing equipment and new printing processes.

Format of the Picture Magazine

Before the picture magazines entered the publishing field, most magazine format was based on the separation of advertising and editorial material. Advertising was divided between the front and the back of the magazine with editorial spreads sandwiched in the middle. What editorial material appeared outside of this central section consisted of short features and runover matter with very limited design and layout potentials.

Picture magazines introduced a new concept of format where major editorial features are distributed throughout the magazine and "jump-over" continued lines are virtually unknown. This means that the magazine art director and designer must contend with the fact that many of his major editorial units will face advertising and he must plan his layouts accordingly.

This new approach toward format has influenced the make-up of many publications outside the picture field and has led to a more complete integration of advertising and editorial material in. magazines. In turn, it has influenced the advertising designer to adjust his techniques to fit this close relationship.

Art and Illustration in Picture Magazines

The decline in the importance of magazine fiction and fiction illustration is only in part traceable to the picture magazine. Television, radio and moving pictures have played very important roles in the changing editorial pattern.

Though the major influence of picture magazines has been in photographic areas, these publications have exercised considerable influence in other phases of art. Through their emphasis on fine art features and through unusual approaches to art in illustration and graphic representation they have opened new areas to the artist and illustrator. Frequently the artist whose work is considered too advanced for the traditional magazines has found a mass audience in picture magazines such as *Life* and *Look*.

Picture Magazines and the Future

Even as picture magazines have influenced reading habits and taste, they are in turn influenced by changes in ideas and visual concepts from other sources. Successful pictures of twenty years ago are frequently today's tired clichés and photographers, writers and designers must be continually on the search for new and better ways of communicating through pictures and visual ideas. This is the challenge that the magazine art director must constantly face, and this is the great opportunity for the artist in magazines.

Fabulous Grizzly Adams *by Harold McCracken*

DAMNEDEST BEAR
HUNTER OF THEM ALL
By HAROLD McCRACKEN and Gene Caesar

For this story about a recluse who trapped wild animals — including grizzly bears which he domesticated — we chose an incident in which he and his "tame" bear came upon a female grizzly and her cubs. The two adult bears immediately started fighting while the cubs scattered. In the fracas, Grizzly Adama was pinned under the two fighting bears and was almost crushed to death. The sketch (above left) was submitted by Stan Galli, the artist chosen to illustrate the story. For the finished painting (above right), three changes were made on the original sketch. First, we decided to have the man struggling to get free instead of lying motionless. Secondly, we placed Adams' gun out of his reach to increase suspense. Lastly — and this is a purely technical consideration which an art editor has to watch for — we arranged the man's body almost completely on one page so that the action would not be lost in the center fold (indicated by dotted lines on the layouts). The next step was to make photostats for several layouts (only the accepted one is shown here). Several styles for title, blurb, credit line were suggested for the editor's choice.

DAMNEDEST BEAR
HUNTER OF THEM ALL
By HAROLD McCRACKEN and Gene Caesar

Art Directing
the Men's Fact
Story Magazine

by C. Edward Derullo

Art Director, True Magazine

Our part of the publishing field has its own peculiar problems and demands. For example, research for accuracy in illustrative matter is an essential in fact stories, both on historical or modern subjects. Whether by means of illustrations or photographs, the reader of non-fiction men's magazines expects authentic portrayal of the people and places in his stories. The illustrator—artist or photographer as the case may be—must therefore be chosen with considerable care. Ideally, he should match the author of the story in viewpoint, enthusiasm and knowledge of his subject.

The art editor must constantly keep in mind that it

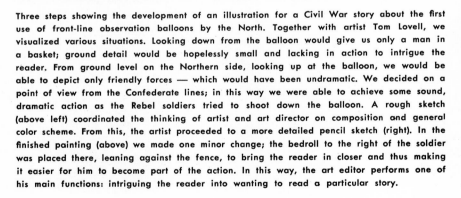

Three steps showing the development of an illustration for a Civil War story about the first use of front-line observation balloons by the North. Together with artist Tom Lovell, we visualized various situations. Looking down from the balloon would give us only a man in a basket; ground detail would be hopelessly small and lacking in action to intrigue the reader. From ground level on the Northern side, looking up at the balloon, we would be able to depict only friendly forces — which would have been undramatic. We decided on a point of view from the Confederate lines; in this way we were able to achieve some sound, dramatic action as the Rebel soldiers tried to shoot down the balloon. A rough sketch (above left) coordinated the thinking of artist and art director on composition and general color scheme. From this, the artist proceeded to a more detailed pencil sketch (right). In the finished painting (above) we made one minor change; the bedroll to the right of the soldier was placed there, leaning against the fence, to bring the reader in closer and thus making it easier for him to become part of the action. In this way, the art editor performs one of his main functions: intriguing the reader into wanting to read a particular story.

is the provocative visual impact of the picture (in the right setting of layout and typography) that stops the casual scanner of his magazine—keeps him there long enough to lead him into the story itself. But if the illustrations should "say" too much (and perhaps give the story away), or if they don't tell enough (and thus fail to create interest) the reader may turn the page and go on to something else.

At *True*, when a story is purchased, the art editor reads the manuscript and makes notes of important dates or events, or descriptions of people in the story, while also mentally classifying possible candidates for the job of illustrating it—artists or photographers who

have made a study of the subject or period called for. Subsequently, editor, managing editor and art editor confer and decide on the best illustrator for the job. In turn, after the illustrator has read the story, he discusses it with the art editor and they agree on suitable situations for pictorial development. Then the illustrator submits his sketches, some of which will be his own ideas, and some a combination of his own and the art editor's suggestions.

For any one issue, the art editor must consider the sketches in connection with the other illustrations, both from the standpoint of variety and value in visually strong impact. Often the final sketch selected may com-

bine the best features of several. Once past this hurdle, the finished illustration is—hopefully—no problem.

Productionwise, at *True* page layouts are made with pictures, titles, blurbs and other details indicated. After a layout has been approved and adopted, type or hand lettering is ordered. An accurate photostat paste-up is made (for position only) incorporating picture, title and blurb, and indicating captions and text. Then all the items, pasted down, are sent to the engraver. The engraver's plates, text and captions are locked in place after having been proof-read, and a complete proof from the printing plant is sent in for final approval before electros are made and the presses start rolling.

Art Directing the Chain Store Magazine

by Jan C. Mayer

Art Director, Family Circle

THE job of any magazine art director is to style his magazine so that its appearance will be distinctive, and to buy the kinds of illustrative art and photographs that maintain the style and quality he has set for his book. What is the difference, then, if any, between the approach of the art director for a national women's magazine that is sold on newsstands and that of the art director whose job is to style a supermarket-sold magazine of the same type?

On first thought, one might say that the two art directors have identical jobs and problems, for both kinds of magazines offer similar editorial fare. It would follow that both require the same kinds and range of illustrative art. But there are important differences, and the first has to do with the factor on which each kind of magazine depends for circulation.

The newsstand-sold book depends mainly on subscriptions. When a reader subscribes for a year (or longer), the editor and the art director are in the very agreeable position of not having to worry about reselling each month's issue to that reader. They're "set" for the duration of the subscription.

Keeping the Reader Sold

But how about the editor of the supermarket-sold women's-service magazine? These books—representing the largest single-copy sales in the country—offer no subscriptions; their job is to lure readers back to the store. So it's the task of the editor and the art director to *keep the reader sold* on the merit of each issue and to make him want to buy it every month in his supermarket. This means continuous selling and close attention to the seasonal likes and needs of readers. Here the art director meets a two-way challenge: He must stay down to earth with his readers, but he must also find endless ways of varying the pictorial presentation of everyday material that is often somewhat repetitive. He must do this over and over, month after month, with simple directness and with an imaginative flair that kindles interest in the current issue and sparks curiosity about the next.

Some of the newsstand-sold women's magazines cater to more sophisticated readers or higher-income-bracket readers than the supermarket-distributed ones; and here's a key to another difference between the art-directing jobs of the two. For although an art director derives fun and stimulation in competing on a more sophisticated level in the purchase of art work, his ingenuity meets a greater challenge as he is obliged to keep his sights trained on readers' real needs.

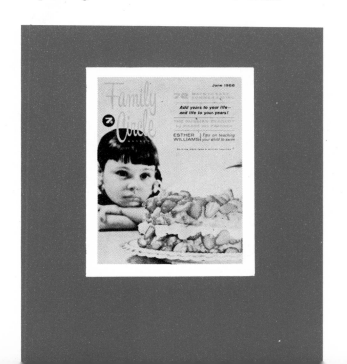

Aiming at Readers' Budgets

Some newsstand women's magazines feature luxury entertainment and expensive fashion, home-building, and home-furnishing ideas in their editorial matter, although fundamentally the median income of their readers is the same as that of the supermarket-magazine readers. The former often present what their readers dream about rather than what they can afford. Contrarily, supermarket-distributed magazines offer much service material that's down to earth in terms of readers' budgets. In *Family Circle,* for example, 60% of the editorial material features service—recipes and food preparation, clothing, home-building, home furnishing, and so on—all geared realistically to the buying powers of our readers.

A supermarket-distributed magazine is usually the only magazine in the store where it is sold. It is displayed, alone, on a new kind of newsstand—the checkout counter where food purchases are paid for. But although it doesn't have the competition of other magazines, it has to compete with all the colorful products displayed beside and around it. It's a package, vying with other colorful packages in the market; and just as the homemaker sees all the food items on the shelves each time she shops, she also sees the market-distributed magazine. How attractive is the magazine package? Just as she comes to prefer certain brands of food and to look for their packages, so she looks for the magazine package if it pleases her.

Having looked at these differences in the two kinds of art-directing jobs, other facets remain the same. The art director of any women's magazine must select illustrations that will persuade thumbers-through to stop and read the love story, the travel feature, the humorous piece, the service article. He must keep a change of pace throughout the book by varying the kinds of illustration, and this means that he must be able to choose the right artist for each job. He must help keep interest high from the front to the back of the book so that reader traffic will be good from cover to cover. And he must keep an editorial "family resemblance" throughout the magazine, despite the variety of its parts, so that the book has its own stamp and individuality that is recognizable and pleasantly familiar to the reader.

The AD's Special Problems

The magazine's editor and its art director face the problem of maintaining the quality of their product by changing its contents each month with a skill that will not affect that same recognition value that the soap manufacturer needs to keep for his product. Therefore, a cover with strong design that characterizes the magazine is important, but it must also permit change of subject matter to indicate clearly, month by month, that a new issue has just appeared.

Because supermarket-sold magazines are essentially service magazines and direct themselves to budget-minded readers, it is one of the art director's problems to evolve methods of presenting inexpensive cuts (in fashions as in meats) to such advantage that they might have come out of *Vogue* or *Gourmet*. Yet even the backgrounds and props for picturing them must be selected with an eye toward economy; for the magazine's aim is to show only what is within the reader's means.

It is true that the combined staffs of a magazine's food editor and art director devote more time and effort to preparing and presenting a meal than any busy homemaker would be likely to invest. But the homemaker isn't obliged to serve millions of guests. Our aim is to show food so attractively that our homemaker-readers will be impelled to buy those foods; and we also present foods geared to seasonal food-promotion needs of the various supermarkets.

LOOK

From Look's Motion Picture Awards announcement in the March 6th issue, on sale today: "For 15 years—through a world war . . . and Hollywood's cold war with television—Look has been presenting movie awards that reflect a period of great achievements, changes and hopes in the film industry. To mark the anniversary, Look takes both a backward and a forward look and finds no lag in Hollywood's creative vigor. In 1955, the industry broke away from old patterns of film making; it started a new working alliance with TV and produced some remarkably fresh and powerful films. Look honors those who paced the industry in the past and presents new awards to the best during the past year." * * * Each week 6,000,000 Look readers buy a ticket to the stars at their favorite theaters.

AWARDS

the *3rd Ingredient*

With camera and film, a photographer can make a picture. But not a memorable picture. For that, he needs a third ingredient . . . a rare, elusive ingredient. Some call it inspiration. Others describe it simply as talent. By any name, it's the quality that welds an emotional link between picture-taker and picture-viewer . . . the quality that LOOK photographers call on to illustrate the exciting story of people.

LOOK

Publication
Advertising
Promotion

by George Krikorian

Promotion Art Director, Look Magazine

TO observers of the art and advertising scene in America, a rather pleasant and over-due development seems to have taken place within the post-war period. And that is in the professional maturity of publication self-promotion and advertising—once one of the dullest, most unimaginative and least courageous forms of advertising—a development which is encouraging and exciting with promise.

Attacking the Twin Problems

The two fundamental purposes of publication promotion—greater circulation, greater advertising acceptance—present many opportunities for highly effective work. Many publications treat these problems with meager efforts bordering on apathy. Others have been attacking them with maximum effort, and thus with maximum results in sales and prestige.

Obviously, the extent of these attacks may depend on matters of budget, and the size of the publication. But in the main it depends on the ability, courage and *vision* of the promotion director himself. Men of ability alone are not rare, but men with ability plus courage and vision are. And when you have a man heading a team with these qualifications, a lot of other important things fall in line, not the least of which is his search for, and the eager acceptance of, the work of thinking art departments and his ability to get that

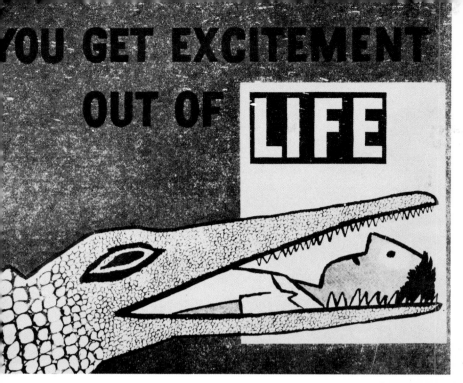

thinking *used*. It goes without saying that some of the best campaigns have died on the typewriter and drawing-board, because the guy above couldn't *see* it to *sell* it or couldn't *sell* it if he *saw* it.

The Coordinated Program

Many use stock prescriptions to help ailing publication circulation and advertising. In spite of cheers for these stock prescriptions to fit any and all problems, *effective promotion realizes that each problem calls for its own solution*. The realization of this is the beginning of the difference between static, pedestrian promotion and effective, imaginative promotion.

The successful promotion program, whether the publication is in a slump or is thriving nicely, is a well-coordinated program thrust in various directions for various purposes, highly geared and delivered with frequency. Important as is the *immediate* purpose for each piece of promotion, equally important must be a

93

Wise. You are if you look here for your job. There's more to choose from in The New York Times—more than in all other New York newspapers combined. See the jobs offered by employment agencies and employers today and every day in The New York Times.

strong family resemblance in all of a publication's advertising and promotion. Thus, over a period of time, coordination of all efforts will be evident to the audiences approached. The individual personality of the organization will have been strongly established . . . one promotion piece having complemented the preceding one and grown into a concerted effort.

This old and basic theory of advertising, which is the toughest single thing to create and *sell*, has become a "popular" expression today. It is called "creating an image" and has become quite the style just to discuss. Not enough people do anything about it. But the wise men have known about it a long time. They have dreamed it and developed it. They have coddled it and spanked it. They have made sales by it and have been fired for it. And, when it is presented to them as the thing to do in a busy office or at a cocktail party, they nod and beam and pretend that it's new to them, for in their hearts they know that this is the next best way to help it along.

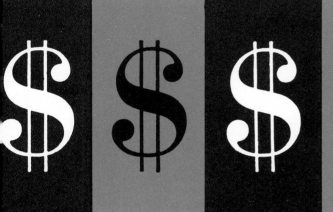

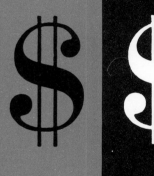

Art Directing . . . Trade · Company Publications

Part 6 *Designed by* Alberto P. Gavasci

Trade Publication Advertising and House Organ Design . . . Paradox for Ad and Client

by Lester Beall

Designer

WHAT are some of the problems of the designer of trade paper advertising? If he checks over any one of a number of *Art Directors' Annuals* published in the last fifteen or twenty years, he may very well get the impression that good design was and is an inherent property of all trade paper advertising. For during these years some fine examples of good design and good typography have been produced in this field. Closer examination, however, will indicate that this is due, in the main, to the radio and television broadcasting companies who have, particularly in the last ten years, produced some of the best in creative design to be seen in all types of advertising.* Nevertheless, even a quick glance at a few industrial or trade paper periodicals, will convince anyone of the fact that a very great percentage of the advertisements in these periodicals is of the very worst sort—design-wise, organization-wise and often thought-wise.

Opportunities for Trade Paper Advertising

This is a paradoxical situation when one looks at the problem clearly. In most industries the trade publications are very closely read and examined. It is even probable that in many instances these publications are perused more carefully by those interested than the general magazines. The opportunity therefore for the advertiser to impress himself solidly with his specific audience is enormous. Engineers, merchandisers, manufacturers, business executives, depend upon trade periodicals, in their specific areas, to keep them informed as to what is happening in their industry today and what can be expected tomorrow.

Industrial or trade advertising offers a further opportunity for those interested in the basic requirements of good advertising. The problem in this field is primarily to present or inform readers of new methods

*It will be interesting to refer to William Golden's comments on this, page 124. See also Herbert Lubalin on pharmaceutical advertising design, page 65—Ed.

and new products or new services. It is not a problem of generating a mass of ballyhoo based on ephemeral and tricky ideas that carry little basic information. The designer who approaches the problem of trade advertising should be well aware of this fact; for here is the chance to approach an honest problem devoid of the slickness and the near dishonesty that colors, in too many instances, some of our more commonly advertised products. The best trade paper advertising in many cases is not merely advertising, but an information service, a service that those in the industry involved, are eager and ready to receive. The fact that this situation is not fully realized and that instead most trade publications are filled with an air of confusion and an overall aura of mediocrity, is a problem that should be vigorously corrected by the advertiser and the advertising agency.

Good Design and the Cost Factor

However, it must be recognized that the cost factor often seemingly blocks the use of good design and good art. It has long been a practice in trade paper advertising to keep design and production costs proportionate to the space cost of the specific trade papers involved—in other words, keep them low. This is an illogical philosophy that functions only as a monumental limiting factor in the production of efficient advertising. The cost of space should never dictate production or art costs. If the cost of space is to determine how much or how little is expended on production costs, good design will always be relatively rare in trade paper advertising. Indeed, if one is to carry to a ridiculous, though logical conclusion, the philosophy of space costs determining art and production costs, one must assume that if even the best space were offered to an advertiser free, he could not from a doctrinaire point-of-view disburse any monies on design, art or production. Naturally, it is an accepted fact that in many instances the industrial advertiser does not

Harvest

Each year America's rooftops yield a new harvest—a vast aluminum garden spreading increasingly over the face of the nation.

The past season produced a bumper crop on all counts: 3½ million new antennas bringing the total number of television homes to 34,567,000.

The average television family spent more time watching its screen than ever—5 hours and 20 minutes a day.

Day and night CBS Television broadcast the majority of the most popular programs and during the past season extended its popularity by enlarging the network to 209 stations—a 75% increase in a year.

Today CBS Television delivers more homes for less money than any other network, and in comparison with its closest competitor, offers an even better buy than it did a year ago.

CBS Television advertisers invested $165,268,000 over the past 12 months—a 20% greater investment than was made on any other network.

By demonstrating television's ability to move our expanding national product into the American home *most efficiently*, CBS Television has become the world's largest single advertising medium.

THE CBS TELEVISION NETWORK

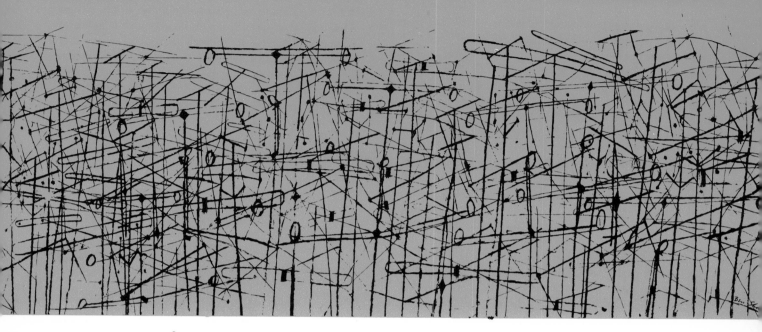

women !

...spend more money for more things than all other members of the family combined.

...spend more daytime hours with WCBS-TV than with all other New York television stations combined.

The place to sell more of your product to women, your best customers, is on WCBS-TV.*

*CBS OWNED
Channel 2 New York
Represented by
CBS Television Spot Sales

have an adequate budget. But it is nevertheless axiomatic that any expenditure on space that is not backed up by an efficient use of art and design, to aid in the projection of the copy theme, is wasted money.

House Organ Problems

Some of the same problems that exist in trade paper advertising are prevalent in the design and production of house organs. Also, in this field it is again true that some excellent work has been produced. The pharmaceutical houses in particular have been aware of the opportunities to do a fine job of public relations by the use of this medium. And long recognition of this fact has established the West Virginia Pulp and Paper Company as a leader in the house organ field. But this work is not characteristic of house organs in general. In many instances they are produced by members of an organization who have little or no background for the problems involved. Often the job of producing a house organ is in addition to other duties usually considered more important. In cases such as these, it is quite unlikely that the company involved can or will allot any funds to speak of for production and good design or good art. Even some of the more successful house organs are handicapped by a relatively small staff that is inadequate to cope with the many and varied problems involved. The business of gathering material for a house organ is of itself a very large one. Sometimes the editor must not only gather the material, write it or rewrite it, but must find himself at least partially engaged in some of the production problems. The designer, because of this situation, can prove to be of invaluable aid in the overall production. The good designer will organize his material in a cohesive and logical sequence that clearly projects to his audience the character of the industry the house organ represents. But, in addition, his knowledge of production processes and costs makes him frequently of inestimable value.*

Reflecting the Character of a Company

The house organ, as we know, is an excellent instrument of public relations. More and more corporations are becoming well aware of this. There are many facts of industry that can be projected more dramatically in the house organ than in general space advertising or direct mail promotion. One would expect because of the number and variety of industries producing house organs that a great variety in format and design would be evident. Many house organs, instead, utilize a *Life*-like format that in some cases adequately serves the purpose of informing, but leaves much to be desired

* See Tobias Moss' views on this point, page 64. Turn back also, to Salvatore Taibbi's examples on page 100—Ed.

in terms of originality or drama. On the other hand, the early success of the pharmaceutical publications has engendered a kind of antiseptic type of design that is becoming more and more boring as time passes. It has often been expressed that nothing succeeds like success. Hence it is only natural to expect this overall lack of originality in present-day house organ design. What was good once seems to be accepted as good for a thousand times. It is perhaps again an instance where there is great reticence to contemplate a change for fear of losing the audience. Yet, house organs by the very nature of their function should embody the most original and forthright expressions of the character of the industry projected. The designer, especially if he is fortunate enough to work with a creative writer, can contribute immensely to this acute expresssion of a company's character that is so important.

which do you want?

THE FORTUNES OF PEACE

You Get
Quiet Operation
at Low Cost

...when you use Torrington's
Extra-Quiet "LU Series" fan blade

*Especially designed to give quiet
operation in a wide variety of
applications. The simple one-piece
construction of the "LU Series" also
makes it available at an unusually low
price. Manufactured in 7⅝″-8¾″
and 10″ diameters. Pierced for all
anti-bearing motors.*

The "LU Series" fan blade represents only
a small portion of the unusually broad
variety of air impellers which Torrington
produces for heating, ventilating,
refrigerating and air conditioning. This
product range and manufacturing
capacity can provide . . . quickly and at low
cost . . . the fan blade or blower wheel best
suited to your air-moving requirements.
Torrington has extensive research and
test facilities which are available to assist
you in the solution of design problems
relating to air flow, sound and vibration.
No one has had more experience in the
design and production of air impellers than
Torrington. Nowhere else can your dollars
buy so much in terms of product quality
and customer service.

THE
TORRINGTON
MANUFACTURING COMPANY
TORRINGTON, CONNECTICUT
VAN NUYS, CALIFORNIA · OAKVILLE, ONTARIO

PROBLEM: GRAVITY

MARTIN
BALTIMORE

Designs by Lester Beall

9

Salesmen of Service . . .
The Public Utility Art Director

by Salvatore J. Taibbi

Art Director, American Telephone & Telegraph Company

THE art director's role in a public utility is a creative one. His present place as part of management is relatively new. Here he lends to the management function the eye and imagination of the creative artist. Here, at or near the policy level, he can contribute directly to his company's program the product of his native talent and years of training.

The range of his contributions, far from being limited, are challenging in their extent. When he takes part in sales activity, he usually is helping to sell service rather than a physical product which can be seen and touched. In addition, he is frequently asked to illustrate and present in attractive graphic form such abstract ideas as "Good Citizenship," "Loyalty to an Ideal of Service," "Community Stewardship" and the like. This means that he must constantly draw upon his imagination in a somewhat deeper sense than the needs of design alone would dictate.

Furthermore, the public utility art director is often called upon to create and develop ideas outside the purely public relations areas. For example, he works with engineers, accountants, business office experts and others in the operating departments. In these areas he must have the ability to translate into good and practical design the basic ideas of people unskilled in the creative arts.

Of course, in a public utility, as anywhere else, the art director is a combination artist, designer, production man, businessman, salesman and listener. Yet behind all these roles lies the basic artistic talent for which the art director must find an outlet. To put his talent to work profitably, he must be realistic, understanding and considerate. His ideals must aid his business associates. Every business concern, large or small, whether it performs a service, manufactures a product or retails an item has its own particular practices and policies. The art director must recognize and accept them—for they underlie the development or creation of ideas that tie in with the company program.

The success of every art project depends on the art director as an administrator. He must organize his art staff to perform at peak efficiency and must coordinate its work with allied production departments.

The creative arts he employs cover every medium and technique. To know every phase is difficult, but the art director must know his own job and the related fields in the graphic arts as well. He must keep pace with changing trends in advertising and editorial art and in visual aids. He must watch closely the developments in printing to broaden his views and increase his effectiveness. If he does these things the quality and quantity of output by his staff will remain high.

Developing a "New Look"—Gradually

Changes in art and production techniques are made gradually. The art director should not be discouraged if his creative ideas are not always accepted promptly. For example—Figure "A" shows the early stages of the cover and inside spread of an internal magazine *Current Developments* for public relations staff. The specifications were: "black-and-white, typewriter used for copy, and printed offset on bond stock."

Figure "B" shows the results of some of the changes. Cover was printed on a separate stock in two colors. Using the same typewriter, and justifying left and right edges, copy is more readable in two columns than in one column. Chapter heads, sub-heads and picture captions were set in linotype faces. Bendays were introduced to attain dimension and attention. Sizes of photographs were increased. Original art, rather than photostats or other reproductions, gave better printing results. Still using the offset process, the appearance and legibility were improved by using a better grade of stock. These added new features increased the cost and production time. However, the results are more stimulating, pleasing and effective. The request for copies has grown.

Exposure to the "new look" generates enthusiasm for more improvements. Figure "C" is the present magazine. The new look is evidence of the special handling, understanding, consideration and patience of the art director and all the people involved. The maga-

A — Cover

A — Inside spread

B — Cover

B — Inside spread

C — Cover

C — Inside spread

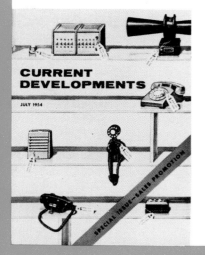

zine now uses two colors throughout, four colors on special occasions; better printing results are due to better grade of stock for color on cover. All copy set by linotype in three columns for better legibility and more pleasing effect. The layouts show more flexibility and proper play to illustrations and photographs. Naturally, the cost and production time increased somewhat. However, these factors were offset by wider reader acceptance of the new look and by management's increased use of the magazine. This is especially satisfying to those who work on and produce the magazine. Such encouragement stimulates the art director's interest and his enthusiasm to continue his suggestions for improvements.

Selling a Creative Idea

In many ways an art director should be aware of good business procedures. And there are occasions where sheer salesmanship is the only way to put a new idea across. He must think on his feet as well as with brush, paint and canvas. There are times when new ideas are submitted by people unskilled in the creative arts and it takes the convincing business mind of the salesman, as well as the creative mind of the artist, to develop those ideas to their full effectiveness.

It would be nice if there were set rules one could always follow in translating design problems to people untrained in art. But there are none! Each person and each design problem form a different situation. One can never apply the same formula twice to the same person, nor even to the same design problem.

The art of listening must be added to the art director's assets. We spend a large part of our lives listening to other people talk—and many of us do it badly. The art director is almost constantly in a talking-listening-demonstrating situation where the exchange of suggestions and ideas take place informally. He must develop an attitude of wanting to understand and appreciate the other person's ideas without prejudice.

For example, consider *The Bell Telephone Magazine*. It is a non-technical review, published quarterly. The magazine gives management people a broader view of the history, objectives, operations, and achievements of this business than they might attain in the course of their day-to-day occupations. It also gives an added sense of participation in the problems and accomplishments of this nation-wide public service. The art director is called into consultation by the

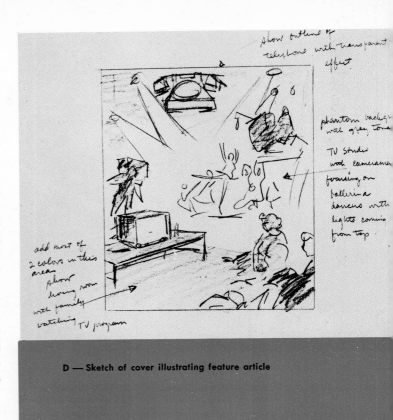

D — Sketch of cover illustrating feature article

editor to discuss each new issue. All magazine articles with illustrative materials are listed and viewed carefully as they will appear in the issue. A feature article has been selected and must be illustrated in two colors for the cover. A *talking-listening* situation takes place where ideas and suggestions are submitted by the editor and author of the article. Here, the art director must collate all the expressed opinions and interpret them to form an illustration. The art director *demonstrates* his ability as an artist and submits sketches, incorporating all suggestions, as shown in Figure D. With an approved cover sketch, the art director selects a capable illustrator to complete the painting. Figure E shows a color comprehensive of illustration which is submitted to the art director before the final painting. Figure F, the final painting and Figure G, the printed cover with the approved illustration.

The art director, like a public utility, gives a service. He is the symbol of a specialized service. He represents the traditions of applied art at its best: years of study, training and experience and the never-ending quest for new ideas. And he must blend all these factors into a service for his associates and for his company.

10

E — Color comprehensive of illustration

F — Final painting

Bell Telephone MAGAZINE

WINTER 1955-56

G — Finished cover

Dealer Publications . . .
Potent Media For Communication and Selling

by Alberto P. Gavasci

Consulting Art Director; President, A.P.G. Associates, Advertising

INTERPRETING visually management's overall objectives, and by working in close coordination, the art director's status and function has attained major importance in company/dealer communication.

The art director's concepts must command attention and form persuasive buying patterns. He must be able to assimilate data from the field and know how to translate them visually into potent advertising messages—into merchandising with point-of-sale impact. But at no time can he afford to indulge in artistic caprice, for fact must precede fancy.

Dealer Publications—a Case History

To illustrate the focal point of this article, I would like to refer to my experiences with the U. S. Gypsum Company, which engaged me as its art director a little over a decade ago. The task at the outset was a rather formidable one—that of transforming two dealer magazines—*Popular Home* and *Business of Farming*—from the appearance of gaudy glorified catalogs into publications with the quality-look of such national magazines as *House & Garden* and *Better Homes & Gardens*. To rate greater attention, these USG publications had to be invested with newsstand eye and buy appeal.

Mention should be made here, that wartime stringencies existed at the time and there was little material available for sale. So, these publications had a dual responsibility of creating desires for USG products, then holding potential demand in abeyance until items could be supplied.

Articles introduced USG products used in building homes and in remodeling operations. They presented ideas along with practical how-to-do-it featurettes. USG products were slanted into appealing pages, thus selling these products with quiet tact and reassuring demonstrations. This adroit editorial approach eliminated all necessity for shouting claims.

Again, it became the duty of the art director to act as a coordinator and interpreter between top style consultants, photographers, decorators, and architects—skilfully directing their talents into carefully planned

Advertising Age, July 23, 1945

U. S. Gypsum and Dealers to Keep Magazines Postwar

Urban, Farm Papers Maintain Contacts with Big Market

Chicago, July 19.—A new merchandising tool created during the war—company-dealer magazines for urban homeowners and farmers—has been adopted as a permanent part of the postwar sales strategy of United States Gypsum Company.

Immediate prospects of this leader in the building materials field and its thousands of dealers throughout the country were hard hit after war broke out and the government, in 1942, halted new construction. Labor was conscripted, deliveries restricted and dealers found it harder than ever to maintain contact with a large but indefinite market.

Farm Paper First

As a result, USG introduced its first magazine, "Business of Farming," in 1942 and urged dealers to send copies to farm owners and operators. This marketing contact captured quick favor and the following year the company started a companion publication, "Popular Home," for city and town dealers.

The 8½ by 12-inch four-color magazines, published eight times a year, now are subscribed to by an impressive number of dealers from coast to coast. They pay five cents a copy for "Popular Home," four cents for the "Business of Farming." Each publication offers the dealer an excellent means of local identification, full-color reproduction of products (important for such items as paint and roofing), a full line of products, and the service of an adequate publication staff, and relieves him of all the details of maintaining a consistent market contact except selecting the ads he wants featured, providing a mailing list—and signing the order for copies.

formats. "Name" contributors were secured to give the publications the prestige of national magazines. Features were executed in full color which gave them richness and allure. As a result, the magazines became a continuous showcase for USG output, issue after issue. They presold readers and conditioned buying attitudes.

Helping Dealers to Increase Sales

USG welcomed the revamped publications, whose circulations scored phenomenal increases. Here was a device that created and controlled a captive audience, an invaluable selling tool of unlimited applications— an impressive medium of contact with customers. The back pages carried a full-page advertisement with the dealer's individual imprint, thereby providing local identification. For a token charge of five cents a copy, U. S. Gypsum mailed *Popular Home* and *Business of Farming* eight times a year to names supplied by dealers. Often the cost of one such subscription produced sales that ran into the thousands.

The pronounced response to the re-styled publications caused U. S. Gypsum to make them a basic part of its postwar promotion program—for here was a strategic technique of getting the company story and products inside homes, and also keeping contacts with dealers alive and active.

In today's keen competition, where millions of dollars are spent fighting for consumer preference, it is well to consider the use of such company publications. Properly designed by understanding art directors, they can command the attention and importance enjoyed by national magazines . . . above all, they can deliver maximum value for the advertising dollar.

Furthermore, this engaging editorial approach builds up the character of a company and the personality of its products. Recipients of *Popular Home* and *Business of Farming* represent a vast and loyal audience, that eagerly looks forward to each successive issue as a source of new ideas to incorporate into their homes. This means activation of a steady stream of sales that flow into dealer establishments—who are mindful and appreciative of this assistance and frequently tie-in window and floor displays with themes of articles.

Their complete professionalization graduated these publications into a position of great influence and authority . . . one capable of swaying millions of readers to spend hundreds of millions on USG products. Here is a precedent in mass-penetrating sales communication that other firms can profitably adopt and pursue through the years. Of course, the priceless ingredient in this formula is a management-and-merchandising-minded art director.

(a) Magazine before revamping

(f) Cover of *Popular Home* supplement in 4-color, full of point-of-sale impact

(c) Before restyling

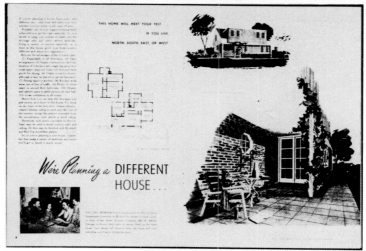

(b) Magazine with new eye- and buy-appeal quality

(e) Art director's choice of top illustrator
Mischa Kohn to interpret architectural
drawing of "House of American Heritage"
coordinated editorial and art

(d) *Popular Home* magazine with the quality-look of national publications

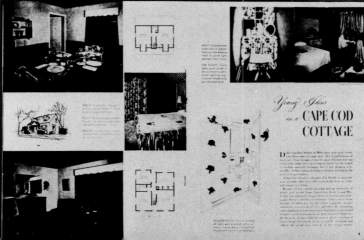

Books and the AD . . . Adventure in the Graphic Arts

by Merle Armitage

Editorial and Art Director, Western Family Magazine, Los Angeles,

Consultant for Look Magazine

IF Americans do not produce the best books, physically speaking, in the world, they probably produce the most. The statistics on book volume in this country are difficult for the layman to believe—it is not counted in thousands, but millions of copies, if all types of books are included. The center of book publishing is New York, although there are great publishing houses in Boston, Philadelphia and Chicago, and a few in other cities such as San Francisco, Cleveland, Atlanta, Cincinnati, Richmond and elsewhere. But essentially, the home of the volume publishers is New York. Although it has not a single printing firm with presses of the high-speed volume necessary for a national magazine run, New York has some of the best book-printing and binding establishments in the world.

While it was not always true, with few exceptions the function of publisher and printer are entirely separate in the United States. In its barest terms, the procedure of a book publisher is to contract with writers (usually on a royalty basis) and to edit the manuscripts selected for publication, to contract with printers and binders for their production, and then to sell them—through book dealers, and sometimes direct to the readers. Books sold through well established book stores account for the major sales of "trade" books, although the book clubs service thousands of subscribers, particularly in remote sections where retail outlets are scant or non-existant. A minority purchase direct from the publisher. The various book clubs have greatly expanded the number of book buyers and book readers in this country while the low-priced paperbacks, sold also through drug stores and many other outlets including even some supermarkets, have run their sales to large figures.

Design Considerations

The publisher usually decides what sort of format is required for the book including the paper to be used, its page size, the binding and the overall costs. Eventually the manuscript goes to the designer, who may be on the firm's permanent staff or may be a free-lance artist or art director. The designer usually sets the style of the book—he must decide on the type face and its arrangement on the page, the type and placement of chapter headings, the style of endpapers, the design of the title page, binding and dust jacket.

Jackets are often an amusing facet of American book publishing, for far too often they are designed by men who have never considered the design of the book as a whole, nor even read the manuscript. The dust jacket, as its name implies, originated primarily as a protection from dust and dirt in the dealer's shop. Gradually, however, it came to be realized that the jacket should serve the functions of a package design at the point of purchase. It should not only call attention to itself from the numerous other "packages" in a window display or on the bookseller's shelves but should induce the browser to stop and examine the book, and perhaps to buy it. As such, the jacket should play the dual role of a point-of-purchase display and an attractive package that expresses the book's contents or use—its flavor, as it were. Thus, the jacket should be an integral part of the book's overall design; visually depict the "product" and help to sell it.

The Production of a Book

The designer having made his dummy and set the style, the book (in manuscript form) goes into the publisher's production department for manufacture. All the mechanical details are ironed out so that, when the printer receives the manuscript, it is completely specified as to type, type sizes, width of line, leading, number of lines to a page, and so on. The printer usually sets galley proofs first, for correction and possibly some last minute editing. Author's alterations (often second thoughts) are among the many headaches of publishing for it is expensive to make corrections when type has been set. In fact, publishers charge

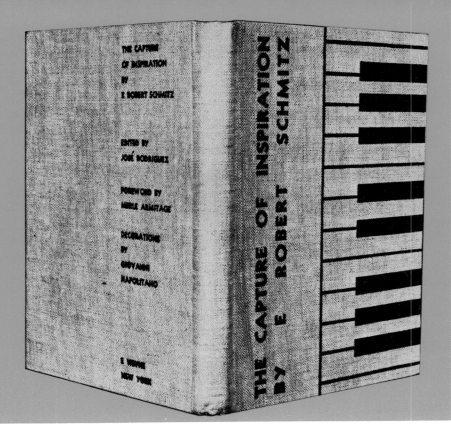

THE
CAPTURE
OF
INSPIRATION
BY
E
ROBERT
SCHMITZ
E
WEYHE
NEW
YORK

DECORATION BY GIOVANNI NAPOLITANO

FOREWORD
BY MERLE ARMITAGE

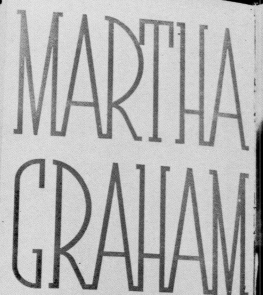

MARTHA

1937 • MERLE ARMITAGE

Edited and with a Foreword by
Merle Armitage • Articles by
John Martin • Lincoln Kirstein
Evangeline Stokowski • Stark Young
Wallingford Riegger • Edith J. R.
Isaacs • Roy Hargrave • James
Johnson Sweeney • George Antheil

Margaret Lloyd • Louis Danz •
Martha Graham • Biography by
Winthrop Sargeant • The Martha
Graham Repertoire • Paintings by
Edward Biberman and Carlos Dyer
A Portrait of Louis Horst •
Affirmations by Martha Graham

AUDITORIUM BUILDING LOS ANGELES

GRAHAM

MARTHA GRAHAM

EKSTASIS

the author for the cost of such "AA's" above an agreed percentage. The next stage is page make-up; here the designer and the production department take a last look at every detail, to be sure that instructions have been followed or that the planned design is working out satisfactorily.

If the book is to be printed by letterpress, electrotypes may be made of each page for ease of handling and economy in producing future editions (printings). It may be noted parenthetically that, in most cases, the first edition of the average book just barely clears the publisher's investment and its costs. If offset printing is used, after the galleys have been corrected reproduction proofs are pulled of each page on a high-gloss paper. These are then pasted into signatures, photographed on to the plates and then wrapped around the cylinders of the lithograph presses. Many combinations of book printing are now employed. For example, if very fine quality of illustrations is desired, sheet-fed gravure may be employed, although the balance of the book may be letterpress. Binding is done either in the plant of the printer or by one of the great independent binderies, which now employ machines for speed and accuracy in the volume book business.

Contemporary Design

The book designer is to the publisher and printer what the architect is to the builder and contractor. Indeed, very few books today escape the hand of the designer, who has brought a new dimension into the book world. But there have been many controversies about this, and many schools of thought. For example, some designers and publishers seem to want to return to modes of the past in their concepts—which is rather illogical, as it means to package a contemporary book in a "period" format. In the great epochs of the past, moreover, painting, music, architecture and books have always been an expression of that time, that environment, that way of life. The intelligent designer or publisher will do himself a great favor if he allows the design of the book to be a reflection of its contents adding, of course, the aesthetic knowledge resulting from the advent of contemporary arts and crafts of every field, from architecture to industrial design. Our time is *now*, and to be an honest reflection of our time, our books must also be freighted with the visual elements that say *now* gracefully and convincingly.

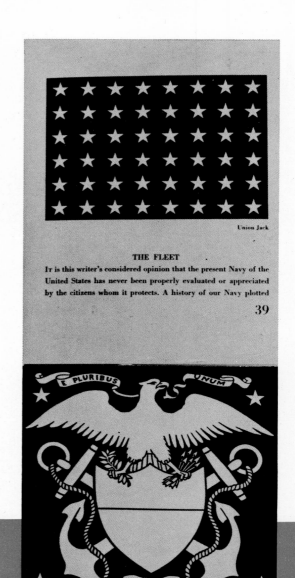

Union Jack

THE FLEET

It is this writer's considered opinion that the present Navy of the United States has never been properly evaluated or appreciated by the citizens whom it protects. A history of our Navy plotted

39

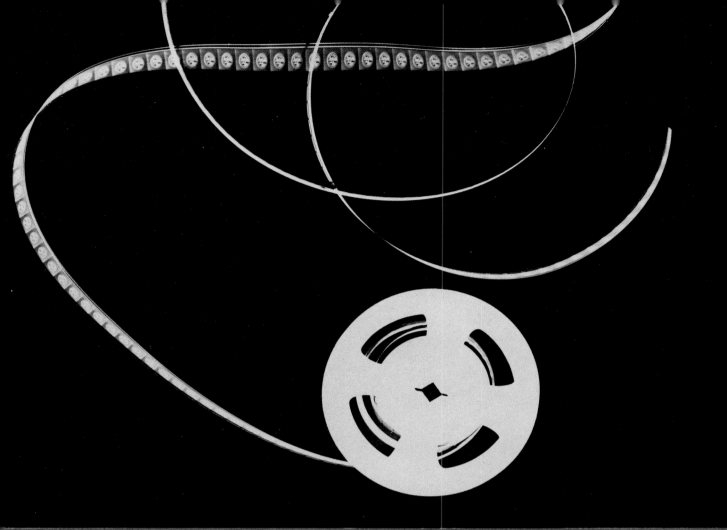

Art Directing . . Television . . Motion Pictures

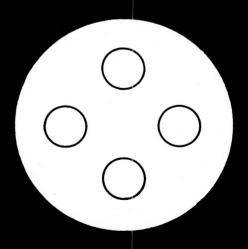

The Television Commercial . . .

Newest Opportunity for Art Direction

by William R. Duffy   *Senior Television Art Director, McCann-Erickson, Inc.*

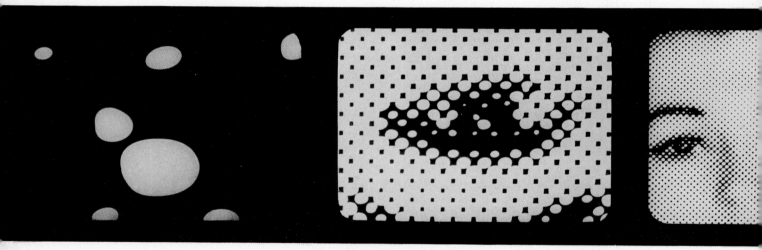

Stephen Frankfurt

Jack Sidebotham

112

TELEVISION is, first and foremost, a visual medium. It is similar to and yet dissimilar to any other advertising, entertainment or communication medium. It presents a new field to the art director in which his job is huge, his scope wide — his potential unlimited.

The basic function of the television art director is a creative one. He is an idea man with a practical working knowledge of his medium and the overall techniques of advertising, psychology and research. He must know thoroughly and believe strongly in TV as a sales medium. He must keep abreast of rapidly changing production methods. He must be able to work with the writer in creating a whole campaign — as well as one specific commercial — and maintain, throughout, a strong visual approach.

The television AD designs layouts for lettering, artwork, displays, packages, settings, lighting, costumes, make-up, animation, props and product photography. He is responsible for the construction of artwork and scenery used in commercials, selects the source of finished work and handles the cost estimating and final purchasing. He must follow through and supervise the work in all stages and, on its completion, give it his final approval. Thus, in television, the art director may truly be called the "tastemaker of tomorrow."

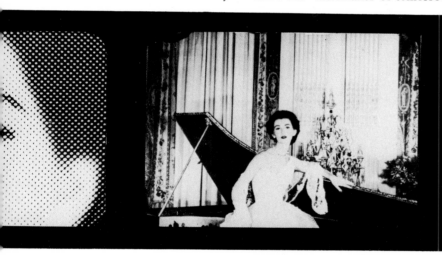 

Stephen Frankfurt

His storyboards, rough or comprehensive, serve as a guide to the finished commercial. By themselves, the individual drawings that make up a storyboard may have little meaning. It is only when they are read — like music, as a sequence of notes — that they illustrate the fluid image and prove the basic rule of the TV art director — "Commercials are not just written, they are designed".

Storyboards

The functions of storyboards are many and varied. They show the client what he may expect from his commercial as a finished product. They act as a pattern to follow in designing specific art work, lettering, special effects, settings, lighting, costumes, animation, styling. They also function as a definite guide for the producer and director in cost estimating, scene composition, animation execution, visual color and pacing. In short, they are the blueprints by which the original idea is guided,to completion.

Television is a complex medium that calls for a wide range of activities not generally required in other mediums. The budgets and deadlines are usually much tighter, further complicated by the absence of hard and fast rules of procedure.

Teamwork is an essential factor in the successful solution of any given problem. A good TV art director learns to work closely with the writers, producers and others concerned. While the personal contribution may be great, the personal recognition is relatively small — TV is not a one-man medium.

In television, the AD is not confined to his drawing board as much as are most art directors in other fields. His time is roughly divided between creative and client meetings, film screenings, on location and at studios (live, animation and film), in control rooms, at display and construction companies, and at prop and costume warehouses, or general window shopping. But this, too, varies between agencies. Some AD's handle many more of the parts of a commercial than do others. It has been said, as a matter of fact, that the ideal commercial-creator would be an art director who could write advertising copy, then turn his cap around and go out and produce it.

Background and Future

The television art director should have, ideally, a background in the fine arts, advertising art, display, typography and lettering, illustration, architectural drafting, cartooning, design (set, package, industrial and general) and decoration. He must have an understanding of construction and dimensional artwork, and should be sufficiently flexible to meet the varied, changing requirements of the medium. In addition, knowledge of and interest in allied subjects such as the theatre, music, the dance, radio, photography, films, advertising and marketing, engineering, research, psychology, writing, salesmanship, business administration and public speaking will be valuable assets.

The future possibilities of television art direction are unlimited. With the growth of TV as a sales, entertainment and educational force, the role of the AD is becoming more and more definite and important. The advent of color TV serves to increase both his work and his potential. As the cost of color TV sets decreases the audiences available to advertisers can be expected to expand proportionately. It should be kept in mind that color calls for TV art direction with a high degree of concentration on color harmonies, color psychology, color as a sales impetus. The opportunities are boundless. Who else can handle the task but people who have been trained in just these specialities—the art directors?

There is a choice of futures in any one of a number of directions within the TV field — in advertising agencies both large and small, the major networks or in the smaller stations here and abroad, with art services, producers of live shows or film and animation, in scenic and display studios, with the advertising staffs of leading companies, with editorial and news services, or as a free-lance with any or all of them. In other words, the TV art director can go as far as he chooses, by working hard — as a pioneer, a salesman, a producer, a businessman — and as an artist.

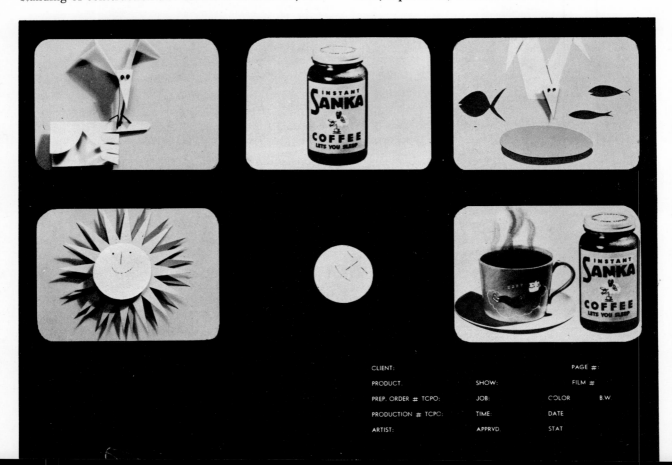

IT PROBABLY will be 1966, the end of television's second decade, before anyone figures out exact job specifications for television's art directors.

Right now, at the end of the first decade, it's still pretty confusing. Perhaps this is because there are four specialized fields in art direction for television and many people, inside the TV business as well as out, have only a vague understanding of this job function or its tremendous potential.

Potential? Television, because of its visual mood factor, certainly will require more—as well as more astute—art directors to fill its needs. During the first ten years of TV, the art director was something of a hit-and-miss character—almost anything you did in television was a hit, so he just couldn't miss!

But as television has begun to grow, in stature and in production quality, the job specifications start to fall into place. Eventually, the maturity of the medium will demand an analysis of the art director's functions in four directions.

The four directions are occasioned by the fact that television automatically divides itself this way. Program and commercial are separate operations and, by production technique, film differs from live television.

Art Directing for TV...Four Big Potentials

by Harry Wayne McMahan Special Consultant to the Industry; Author of The Television Commercial and Television Production

So job specifications—and employers—will be quite different in each of the four directions. Now this is complicated still more—in a still-growing industry— by the fact that no two networks, no two stations, no two advertising agencies handle television in the same way. But, let's generalize:

Art Director, TV Film Program

His qualifications are approximately the same as those for Hollywood feature movies. He is concerned with the pictorial quality of literally everything in the final picture except the faces of the actors. This means: the settings, the furniture and other interior decorations, the wardrobe of the performers and possibly even the title lettering for the show opening.

He reports directly to the producer and the director and works closely with the key staff in the pre-production planning stages. It is his responsibility to keep the physical appearance of the production in line with the writer's mood, the director's staging needs (even to the actors' exits and entrances) and the camera-lighting problems of reproducing the tonal values of the picture (both in color and black-and-white).

His staff may include a set designer who develops the sketches of the settings, the scenic artist who executes these sets, and the costume designer. His employer generally is a film production company or one of its suppliers.

15

Art Director, TV Live Program

His staff will include all the equivalents of the film art director, and he may also have control over the make-up department. He is also staffed with a graphic artist who handles all art measuring less than 30" x 40" in size (union rule!), such as maps, signs, photographs, etc.

His employer generally is a TV network (or station) or possibly an independent art studio. If a TV station, he is expected to know commercial production as well.

Art Director, TV Commercial (General)

Whether live or film, he is expected to have the above qualifications, plus an experience in advertising application, a knowledge of advertising techniques and aims. His employer could be the TV station (doubling in program work) or, more likely, a film production company specializing in commercials.

Art Director, TV Commercial (Agency)

In large advertising agencies, film work may be separated fom live TV, but generally the commercial art director requires knowledge of both techniques.

His problem, right now, is that most advertising agencies think a commercial TV art director is simply a man (or woman) who makes the sketchy storyboards that go with the commercial scripts. Actually, this is only one phase of his work.

The agency commercial art director in TV, to be fully competent, must have all this knowledge, plus:

1. Working knowledge of camera lenses and their characteristics.

2. Working knowledge of typography and its advertising application.

3. Comprehensive knowledge of modern fashion, decor, "taste."

4. Working knowledge of animation and the design and development of cartoon characters.

5. Comprehensive knowledge of editing and visual transitional techniques in both live and film TV.

Altogether, it's a fairly large order. But television itself is a fairly large order. In ten years it became a billion-dollar advertising medium in an era when agency billings tripled. By 1965, it is estimated all billings will double again, with TV in the forefront. Many agencies have more than half their advertising dollars in this new medium and some agencies predict a possible 90% of their billing in TV. Manpower obviously is needed, and the TV art director holds a key to the needed improvement in the medium.

The textbooks haven't been written, the schooling is only half started; but mark this word: another ten years will see the television art director the most sought after, the best paid of all his advertising fraternity. And it won't be a minute too soon!

Still Art by Stephen Frankfurt, teaser for
Lincoln Division, Ford Motor Company

THE art director of a television network or station is responsible for the design, the supervision and coordination, and purchase of all art work and lettering required for his programs and for the "on-the-screen" promotion of programs. He is also available as consultant to advertising agency personnel with art and design problems in their "package programs" and commercials on the station or network. He uses art rendered in all media, but is free from the limitations imposed by the various reproduction processes in other branches of commercial art.

TV Design Problems

But there are some peculiar problems inherent to designing for television. The medium is incapable of really differentiating between subleties of tonal and color contrast because, for one thing, the average home receiver is almost never "perfectly" tuned. Speed is essential in the design and execution of much of the art for television. The producer of a TV program is frequently unable to plan his art requirements very far in advance. Often all art for a show is designed and finished on a few days' notice; for news programs, it is usually just a matter of hours.

The TV art director is seriously handicapped if he lacks at least a working knowledge of animation, if he doesn't think in terms of design-in-motion. Tricky animation, however, can never eliminate the fundamental need for good design and good taste — and these are just as essential in television as in any medium.

Graphic Design in Television

by Georg Olden   *Director of Graphic Arts, CBS Television Network*

In the preparation of graphic art for television, the same general procedure applies as in the making of film strips and slide art. After the design is completed, the art is rendered on illustration board. The lettering is done on a separate transparent "cel" overlay and placed over the art. This combination is then photographed as a unit, either in transparent or opaque form depending on the TV transmitting equipment.

A notion persists among some artists and art directors that television design and typography are complicated, and require secret formulas which only the specialist has the right to know and apply. Many articles have been written listing do's and don'ts, and speculating on the elements constituting good television design. Actually, there is little need for confusion for, as in most areas of design, simple logic supplies many of the answers.

First of all, let's analyze, from an advertising point of view, the basic problem of static television design. Unlike space advertising with its multifarious variety of sizes and shapes, television advertising has to contend with an inflexible 3 : 4 space ratio. It takes great ingenuity to develop new and interesting presentations when one has to work within just one space relationship day after day.

17

Another characteristic of the medium the art director must remember is the "cropping" tendency in (1) television transmission, (2) kinescope recording, and (3) in home receivers. A maximum margin must be left around the finished work in order to allow full copy to appear on the viewing screens regardless of conditions. But there is no great difficulty here. Any television station will gladly supply the art director with the proper specifications or dimensions within which he must design his finished piece. In the final analaysis, all that is required of the TV designer is common sense and adherence to a few simple rules, plus the same basic ingredients that apply to producing good art in general—taste, imagination and ability.

Typography for TV

As regards type legibility, let there be no question about one point: *any modern type face can be used for television.* These faces will be as legible on television as they would be under equal space conditions in any other medium. If a display face is successful in terms of legibility and eye appeal when used on a car card, it will be equally legible on TV. As a matter of fact, our modern type faces have been so carefully refined in their historical development and in their contemporary design that they represent the most adequate treatment of a given shape in terms of the purpose for which the face was designed.

Some faces have been designed for maximum readability, whereas others have been designed primarily for effect. The injudicious use of these faces in any medium produces the same result as their improper use in television. The same rules and the same common sense apply in all cases.

On live television, one of the most widely used devices is the practice of electronically super-imposing lettering, picked up by one camera, over an image (live, film or artwork) picked up by another. The technique of superimposition cannot yet retain full sharpness and clarity to the image picked up by one camera without subtracting definition to a corresponding degree from the other. Even when a choice of lettering is sound and the background is free of distracting contrasts or "busy-ness", the presence of an art director in the control room (where the "mixing" of the two pictures is done) is almost essential to guarantee a successful, legible, properly balanced superimposition. In the absence of art supervision in the control room, however, this general rule can be followed by the technical director: a 70-30 relationship, with emphasis on the lettering.

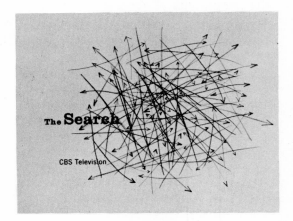

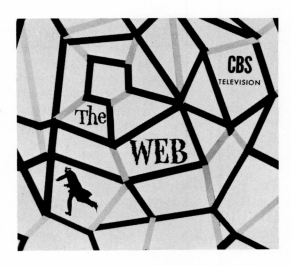

Designs by Georg Olden

118

Principles of Good Design

With reference to design principles, the one thing a TV art director must learn and transmit to the copywriters, producers and directors with whom he works, is that the announcer is the television equivalent of body copy in space advertising. If this fact is ignored, the impact of the visual material will be destroyed by overloading the promotion piece or commercial with unnecessary copy which could be delivered *audibly* by the studio announcer.

We have learned to limit the design elements in posters to the most basic and simple ideas which can be caught at a glance. Posters are actually a harder medium to work with and to design than is television graphic art because they receive no assistance by way of running copy delivered by the announcer. And yet, posters are effective in their very simplicity. TV graphic design, too, can become even more effective through the addition of movement and elimination of all elements which interfere with the immediate visual point—that which catches the eye of the viewer and holds his attention with sufficient power to allow the audible commercial to get its message across.

As arbiter of the artistic product of so influential a medium as television, it is imperative that the art director should have not only impeccable taste but a profound respect for all phases of visual creativity. This requires an understanding of all the visual arts and familiarity with other media of graphic presentation, in addition to knowing the techniques—the limitations as well as the advantages—of TV broadcasting.

THE advertising business has been defined as "15% commission and 85% confusion." Perhaps an unfair attitude to take toward the profession as a whole, but as a description of TV it is too close for comfort. The general confusion which permeates the industry seems to reach into all its branches — from the ratings right down to the actual video techniques — and thus many people tend to overlook the fabulous successes TV has already scored to observe that maybe they buried the body of AM before it got cold.

Lighting: Two Schools of Thought

A typical instance is the current lively discussion over TV lighting. Motion picture lighting has been tried, as have stage techniques, with equally unsatisfactory results. The results are best summed up by a spectator's remark overheard at a recent symposium on lighting by a group of TV engineers, "The more light they turn on, the worse it looks."

There are at least two main schools of thought on TV lighting — exposure vs. mood. The question seems to be like the chicken and the egg controversy —

TV Lighting and the Art Director

President, Calkins & Holden, Inc.

...Or How to Choose a Necktie

by Paul Smith

which should come first? The engineers say, "Let there be light! We want exposure!" The directors say, "How about mood? Dramatic effect?"

Obviously, both men are striving to do their best based upon a great deal of experience — but unfortunately they are striving toward different goals. How are we to reconcile them to decide what to do?

In advertising photography we had the same problem. Maybe we can take a hint from the experience of the commercial photographer. For years most commercial photographers adhered to the "light up the set" technique. They had $50,000 invested in fancy Salzman and Klieg lights and by Godfrey, they were going to use them! Besides, if the set were lit up like a sailor on shore leave, the photographer's problem was simplified. He could shoot fast, stop down, get good detail — and who could criticize him? A photo is a photo — the camera doesn't lie.

This was the psychology that caused the tremendous repudiation of photography by advertisers in the early thirties in favor of art, which was only reversed by — guess who? — the mood boys! When the camera began to use its imagination again, the advertisers began to buy photography again.

A TV picture, after all, is about on the level of a photostat or a 55 line screen newspaper half tone. While we are heartily sympathetic with the engineer who wants to avoid what he calls a "noisy picture," the fact remains that some fine mood shots are done every day in newspapers and reproduce very well. The same goes for TV. It's all in the way you do it.

In the first place, "mood" shots can be either high or low key, weak or strong contrast. The secret is in picking the ones that televise. No good photographer would deliver a "chalk and soot" print for a newspaper ad any more than he would recommend a high-key pearly confection for the same medium.

The secret is in maintaining proper value relation within the gray scale. Strong contrast . . . sure! But fill in the shadows with a little reflected light. High key . . . sure! But put some "local" accents in the composition so the customers can figure out what the picture is all about.

Naturalistic Lighting

There are many more purely technical lighting problems which remain unsolved. But there are plenty of non-technical problems, too, ones that *can* and *should* be met. Take the very simple but annoying fact that a shot that looks swell on camera number one can look lousy on number 2 from a different angle. This can be solved in many cases by the use of so-called naturalistic lighting — the kind you find out-of-doors. Here is one of the most useful formulas for the TV director and should enjoy much wider use than it does at present. It is pleasing and "correct" from almost any angle — side, ¾, back, etc., as proved by the thousands of distinguished photographs taken every year using it. Look through any issue of *U. S. Camera*.

About the only angle from which naturalistic lighting is uninteresting (and this is significant) is the angle that has been recommended for years by the manufacturers of cameras — namely, with the main source of light directly behind the camera — i.e., with the subject squinting directly into the sun! The engineers wanted to make damned sure that a "safe" angle was recommended and, in consequence, millions of family albums are bulging with snapshots taken from this unhappy point of view. Is there a moral here, I wonder?

Naturalistic lighting can be simulated in the studio with great ease. All that is needed is a high level of general illumination from above (the sky), a good strong key light (the sun) and a front-fill light to give some luminosity to the shadows. It is a pleasing, flexible lighting scheme. It looks good from almost any angle (very important in multi-camera shots) and gives good definition of form.

One of its simplest and most effective variants is that used to televise prize fights and wrestling. A good high-level light from above, with the reflection from the canvas providing the fill light for the shadows. Successful and simple.

The Gray Scale

Another fundamental principle is, of course, the use of the gray scale. Artists have known for centuries that one of the secrets of composition is simplification of "values" — i.e., restricting the gray scale of a picture to a limited few . . . and these in logarithmic, or optically even, steps.

For TV, because of the limited response of the medium, it is wise to employ as few tones as possible. Four or five basic values will suffice for any picture but the secret is the optically even steps. If you want to test the soundness of this theory, you might, as an experiment, use it to select your necktie in the morning. Here is how you do it. Taking your suit and shirt as the starting point, always pick a tie that is either half way between them on the gray scale, or is an even step darker or lighter than the other two.

You will be astounded at the way it works. Most people pick a tie for color. This is a mistake. Pick them for "value" and they sing. The same goes for a picture whether it is a painting, photo or TV image. It is the value relation that makes or breaks it. Keep the tones simple and *even* in separation.

In this connection, we might observe that most engineers prefer *too many* value steps in a picture. This is perfectly natural, because their mind is upon the fidelity of the image they produce through their technical wizardry, rather than upon the emotional values of the image. Because it is possible to get a complete gamut of tones, they believe it is *desirable*. To do so is, of course, proof of their engineering skill. We are all apt to see beauties in our own profession that are invisible to the layman. After all, surgeons refer to a "beautiful ulcer."

12

Remember a limited value scale makes the picture. There are only thirteen notes on a piano but a slide whistle has a million! The use of values, more than any other single factor, controls the mood of your show. They, plus composition, determine whether it will be gay, somber, sinister, sentimental, or what have you. Watch them carefully.

The simplest way to control your value scale is in the local color of the set, using lighting only for accents and modeling, but this formula will be cold and uninteresting if any mood at all is desired. Even so it is better than an arty set where value scale is neglected.

The best formula is probably a compromise between having the grays "local" on the set and costumes — and having them modified by lighting. To do this it is better to avoid both the light and dark ends of the gray scale in the actual value of sets and costumes. Thus complete modeling is obtained by the play of light and shadow upon them, and it is imperative that modeling lights be used here, because general high illumination would result in a flat uninteresting picture. Confining the grays to the middle portion of the scale also helps the flesh tones of the picture because it doesn't kill them with contrast.

Showing Products on TV

Another problem that needs some concentrated attention is the presentation of products on the TV screen. Often we see video pictures of bottles, cans, boxes, articles that would make an agency art director wake up screaming and that no client in his right mind would O.K. for a newspaper or magazine advertisement.

Highlights that destroy form, color translated into faulty gray values, halation, reversal, bad forms, all bear witness to some overworked TV director's movie or show business background — and his ignorance of standard advertising practice. Elementary devices such as the use of a luminous "tent" on shiny objects to even off specular reflection, or matte-surface versions of packages to kill glare seem to be unknown to some.

Or look at the typography of television. The quality of printed matter appearing on TV screens in the form of subtitles, screen credits, commercial messages, etc., is often in the worst show-card tradition or else harks back to the "ladies, please remove your hats" vintage of the old silent days. In some cases it is plain amateurish. Of course the frantic rush and overpowering expense of present day programming is in part to blame. It took the movies twenty years to learn something about subtitling. Recently there have been some promising efforts in this area. Let's encourage them.

Utilizing Visual Know-How

What steps can be taken to remedy some of these conditions? Are there changes that can be made in the present TV production structure that will utilize the visual know-how that has become second nature to advertising and at the same time take some of the load off the shoulders of the over-worked TV director?

At present the set-up is something like this: the TV director blocks out the show. At camera rehearsal he tells the lighting director what lighting he wants. On a big dramatic show the lighting director usually makes a lighting plot specifying what areas are to be lighted and what moods and special effects are wanted. Usually lighting is roughed-in before rehearsal begins.

The director blocks and marks separate scripts for the announcers, the technical director, the floor manager, and for the audio, film and sound effects men. He orders the sets, props, obtains clearance on music and continuity. He makes up cue sheets for camera men, audio, sound and film men, etc. Meanwhile, he has to write up the reports on the previous week's show. All of this he has to do before the show ever goes on the air, when his job really starts!

Many stations have seen the handwriting on the wall and have installed TV art directors. A few TV directors, are or have been artists and can do a good job, but they are already overworked. Their function is becoming more and more executive and the creative end of their work has to take a back seat to the more important business of actually running the show.

At air time the TV director works from the control room. He sets up all the shots, calls all cuts and switches on each camera, cues all actors, gives all musical cues, audio cues, applause cues, cues props in and out, calls lighting changes, sound effects, film cues — and for every command he gives he must think ahead far enough to give a "ready" signal a safe interval before he gives the actual one.

In addition, he selects which picture of the various cameras is to go on the air and meanwhile keeps track of elapsed time and edits or adds to the show off the cuff, if it is running under or over!

No wonder TV directors eat phenobarbital like popcorn and exchange sedative prescriptions like housewives trade pie recipes!

The answer is obvious. What is needed is a man who can share some of this load. Such a man must have training in visual presentation, he should be an expert in visual selling and in interpreting the client's and agency's viewpoint. He should know how to present products and people visually in a professional way. He should be able to bridge the gap between the agency and the TV director and in so doing take a heavy load off the latter's shoulders.

Where shall we find such a paragon, such a full-panoplied genius? We've had him all along! You guessed it . . . the agency art director. Let's face it . . . we either must use him or start from scratch and train somebody to think exactly like him to fill this need. In so doing we will not only greatly lower the incidence of nervous breakdown among TV directors but, perhaps more important, cure a rapidly spreading malady among TV viewers — galloping ennui, aggravated by a persistent twitch of the thumb and index finger, the ones that turn the dials to switch channels . . . and open pocket books.

The Art Director in Television Network Promotion

by William Golden

Creative Director, Advertising and Sales Promotion, CBS Television

BEFORE television, the printed advertising output of a radio broadcaster was voluminous, but predictable. It had a tidy, seasonal aspect. There was a time for mailing pieces, for trade paper ads, for sales presentations. There was even a season for crises.

Its function was to affirm the vitality of broadcasting as an advertising medium, to provide a background that would help salesmen to sell its time, programs and facilities to advertising agencies, and to reflect a corporate personality.

The advertising and sales promotion department furnished advertising for the network, to local stations owned by the network, to some affiliated stations that lacked adequate creative and production facilities, and to groups of stations which were represented by a subsidiary Spot Sales organization. It furnished to all of its affiliates, once a year, mats of ads for every show on the network for use by stations in their local press.

The advertising content of our "product" consisted, primarily, of three basic ingredients. facilities, programs, audiences. The problems seemed to be identical year after year. Like much product advertising it was a matter of telling the same story in new forms each year.

Promoting Television's "Product"

Television is a very different thing. It uses all these things and more. Its growth is so rapid that it has not yet fallen into a fixed pattern. Whatever happens, happens fast. There is little time to solve a problem because it doesn't exist for very long. And unlike radio, the major effort of a broadcaster is addressed to the audience rather than to the advertiser.

The need for advertising to advertisers exists with the same force as it did in radio but here again the problem is different. Radio in its early days had to be *sold* as an advertising medium. The comparable period in television was much shorter. As soon as there was a substantial number of receivers on the market, television's appeal was fantastic. Advertisers didn't need to be sold on television. Its impact was all too obvious. What they were most interested in was how *economically* they could use it, and so network trade-paper adverising quickly became more competitive.

Consumer advertising absorbs an increasingly greater proportion of the television network's advertising effort, time and budget. Having made a substantial investment in a program series, the sponsor and the network are more sensitive to the size of audience the program attracts. There is no disposition to give a program time to build an audience as there was in the early days of radio, with its relatively low production costs. And so programs are apt to change with greater frequency, and each change usually means a new advertisement of the "premiere".

Designs by William Golden

Newspaper Advertising

Because truly effective nationwide advertising in newspapers can easily cost more than the program itself, it is necessary to prepare these ads with great economy and to place them strategically. Off-hand it would seem to resemble closely the advertising of the motion picture companies. But the very different production pace of the TV program product, and the different length of life of the product, affect the advertising solution of the problem.

In order to reduce his production costs, an advertiser tries to reduce his production and rehearsal time to a minimum. If he has a program series that does not have the same cast, writers, and story line each week, he must get his story cleared, cast it freshly each time, produce it with a different set, and a new group of performers.

To prepare a newspaper ad for which electros can be shipped all over the country, our minimum (and usual) plating deadline is five days before the performance. More often than I care to remember, we have arrived at the deadline hour lacking either the title of the show or its cast—and sometimes both. Rarely are rehearsal photographs available, since the photographers have had no one to photograph. If they could get the cast, the set would not have been built. Or the leading lady would be in New York and the male lead in Hollywood.

If the program title is well known it is feasible to make a drawing to interpret the mood of the story, and hope to feature the cast in type. But even here, it's a good idea to sneak a peek at the shooting script. In condensing a story to an hour or half-hour, there is a pretty good chance that the scene you remembered so well has been cut out.

It seems difficult enough to make *advertisements* under these circumstances. But whenever we begin to feel sorry for ourselves our sympathy and admiration go out to the people who have to produce the *program* from scratch in less than a week.

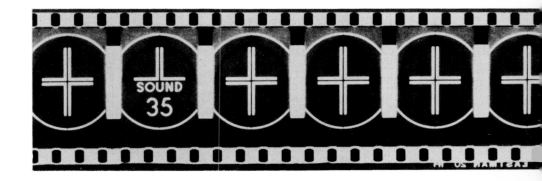

Movie Advertising, I Love You

by **William H. Schneider** *Vice President and Creative Director, Donahue & Coe, Inc.*

THIS is a mash note to the trollop of the art directing trade, motion picture advertising. Although this lady of ebullient charm and easy virtue gets wolf whistles and snide asides from the fraternity brothers on Madison Avenue, I say she is more interesting by far than her haughty sisters who get to go to the ball. Moreover, she has a heart of pure gold. And now gentlemen, permit me to drop this heavy metaphor, and pick up a cudgel.

The collective opinion of art directors concerning motion picture advertising can be summed up in two words—"It Stinks." And the publicity seekers of the art and copy mills can usually grab a couple of paragraphs in the trade press by airing this threadbare premise. So, since contumely usually derives from misinformation, let's get the record straight.

"More Fun For The Art Director"

Lest I seem less than objective (which I am) in this onrushing thesis, I hasten to state my qualifications as an authority. During my total career as an art and copy laborer for advertising I have spent roughly twenty percent of my time working on movies for such companies as Metro-Goldwyn-Mayer, Paramount, Twentieth Century Fox, United Artists, Columbia and Republic. The rest of my working days were spent selling everything from gasoline to food products. So what odious comparison can be drawn by a man so strategically situated? It's very simple, my dear Watson. Motion picture advertising is more fun for the art director. In order to cram proof of this broad statement within publication limits, the professor will adopt the question and answer technique, acting at once as interlocutor and end man.

"Mr. Interlocutor, why is motion picture advertising more fun for the art director?"

"Well sir, Mr. Bones, in the first place, it's the only field where you can visit the client's factory, and see people like Marilyn Monroe at work. If you doubt me, compare this with a trip through a canning factory or a shoe factory, or perhaps you would like to name your favorite factory. Down boy—even the most violent partisan won't dare dispute your claim."

"How do you go about making a movie ad?"

"You start off by reading a script, and even the frequent dull ones are more fun than the usual product background the art director has to read. Like a report on the health-giving properties of somebody's double-dipped, vitamin-tipped bubble gum, for instance."

Pictorial Content

"Can you tell us about the pictorial content of a movie ad?"

"Thank you sir, that's a good question. They give

you a set of 'stills'. This is trade terminology for photographs. You go through a couple of hundred and pick the ones you want to use. Or if you have something special in mind, you send a sketch to the Coast, and Miss Monroe will pose it for you. As you may have noted all the models in movie ads are real famous. Now, compare this simple easy procedure with the problem of getting some mean little monster to get that 'Gee Mom,' look as he surveys a plate of breakfast food."

"How about buying illustrations for motion picture ads—do you get to do that?"

"Yes indeed. I have bought some very fine illustrations from men like Albert Dorne, Jon Whitcomb, David Stone Martin, Norman Rockwell, and others too numerous to mention. Moreover, we are buying more and more good illustrations all the time. With just a tiny shove, I would say this will become a trend."

"Doesn't it tire you to put those tired, trite headlines into the ads?"

"In all honesty, a resounding 'yes'. But when I feel particularly weary I relax by looking through the magazines at the tired, trite headlines for automobiles, and food, and soap, and in a short time, Virginia, I am lulled into a dreamless sleep."

"O.K., but then do you not get tired of putting kissin' pictures into the layouts?"

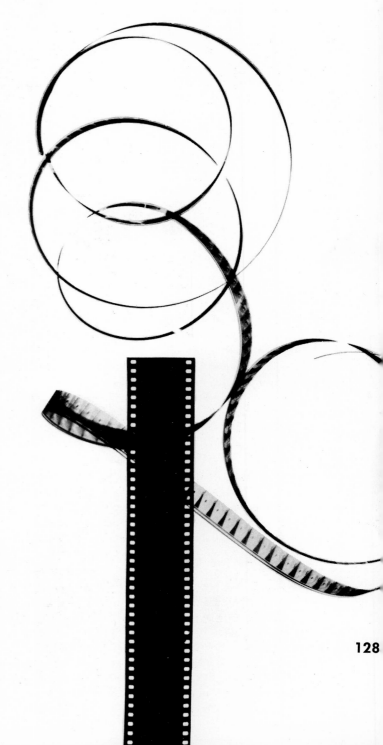

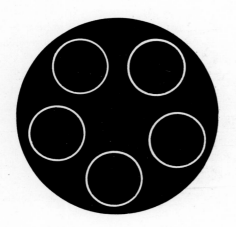

William H. Schneider

"I do, forsooth, but I will continue to do so until people get tired of kissin'."

"Then let's take another tack. Why do you louse up the ads with all that awful type—those big titles and all those names?"

"You touch me where it hurts, my friend. I agree those names are harmful to the appearance of the ads. But the legal profession has made a fetish out of getting every last player into the ad, each in his proper size (large) and they have now got the set designers into the act, and soon the script girl will be there and then every bit of white space will be used up and perhaps we can start all over again. On the other hand when you have a title like *Caine Mutiny* or a star like Clark Gable it makes sense to play them big. Or, to slip on an old tweed cliche—I've always heard that the art director loves nothing more than a 'challenge'. Believe me, sirs, to make typographical sense out of a long list of names, each calculated in percentage points of the other, is a feat to challenge the most ingenious layout artist."

The Challenge of Movie Advertising

"Speaking of challenges, what is the fundamental challenge of motion picture advertising?"

"Fundamentally, there is but one challenge and that is to sell tickets. This feat is calculated to keep the mind nimble when you consider the fact that a major company can turn out thirty or forty pictures a year— and each one of these is a distinctly different advertising problem. The mix of story, stars, directors, locale, and appeal changes radically from picture to picture, which is a contrast to your pancake and pie crust mixes. On the latter you dream up a theme and play variations on it until the client, after a year or so, says 'Hold! enough!' For each of these pictures you must create a line at the box office or the campaign is a flop. This simple test is as rigorous as the point-of-sale test of any retail store promotion. But our Pearl White of advertising suffers many perils in achieving her goal. For instance, the critics. You work hard on great ads for a movie and then the critic will warn the patrons not to go, on pain of asphyxiation, and they do it on the same page, yet!! This doesn't happen to the automobile advertiser. Then, too, you can open on the day of a blizzard or a hurricane. Or you can do a high class campaign and get the carriage trade (small) while the leather jacket and popcorn trade (large) stays home. And to accomplish your box office bonanza, you usually have about four or five ads ranging in size from a hundred lines to about five hundred. Confidentially, General Foods uses more space than that. I could go on, sir, but I feel these challenges may suffice the most chivalrous of art directors."

"And now, Mr. Interlocutor, I come to the sixty-four thousand dollar question. (A roll of drums as I go

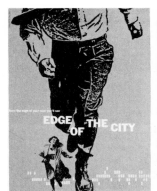

Designs/Saul Bass

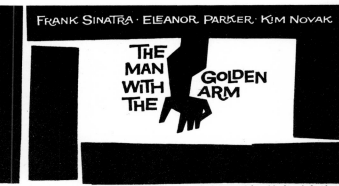

Produced & Directed by Otto Preminger, Released by United Artists

into the thinking booth.) Do you believe motion picture advertising can be improved?"

"Of course it can. Let me give you a premise, a promise and a prophecy. The motion picture business is exciting and glamorous because it is show business. But to date, it hasn't attracted its quota of bright, young creative talent because it still retains the bumptious aura of Barnum. This seems to deflect the bright young men who would rather work with enlarged Ben Day dots and photographs of grown men sipping drinks whilst perched in trees. But if they would like to practice their civilizing missionary influence the movies will welcome them with open arms (premise over—promise coming up).

"Genuine art and copy talent will find more money in the movie field than in general advertising—ditto for stimulation and opportunity.

"Prophecy—the continuing competition of television is resulting in films of higher quality and higher I.Q. which will be reflected in the advertising. Movie attendance is increasing—which means bigger budgets for better pictures—which in turn puts a minimum on selling ingenuity and creative talent. The fairly certain advent of pay television, with its concomitant struggle for gigantic, nationwide viewing will open new fields of entertainment exploitation. Ergo, you can find a lidless future in this field if you are as bright as you think you are."

Copy Photography for This Section by Adpix

THE INDUSTRY IS WAITING FOR PICTURES THAT SELL TICKETS

006664

Art Directing . . . Retail Stores

Part 8 *Designed by* **Ralph Daddio**

Photo/Cicero

Ringing the Retailer's Cash Register

by Ralph Daddio

Advertising and Sales Promotion Director, Kresge-Newark, Inc.

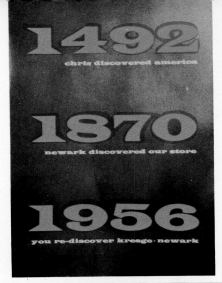

THE retailing industry is an important factor in the nation's economy, with some 2,600 retail stores and 115,000 specialty apparel stores contributing more than 20 billion dollars in annual volume of business. It employs many thousands of personnel and hundreds of art directors to help tell, and sell, the consumer through printed media. The two most important types of retail operations are the specialty store and the general department store. The former deals in a specific merchandise classification such as women's fashions, men's, children's, or home fashion needs. The latter, on the other hand, carries a complete assortment of merchandise in all of these classifications.

To better understand the problems of the art director in retailing, let's first take a look at the structure of the store management organization and its functions. Generally speaking, top management usually consists of four divisions:

Merchandise Division—responsible for the purchase and moving of merchandise toward the consumer.

Sales Promotion Division—is responsible for moving the consumer toward the merchandise through the use of various advertising media.

Operating Division—controls and supervises all selling and non-selling personnel.

Controller's Division—maintains and controls dollar budgets essential to a sound business operation.

DIVISIONAL ORGANIZATION CHART

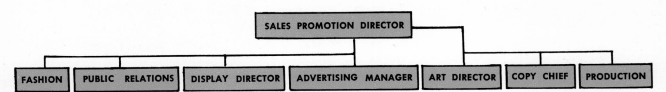

The Sales Promotion Division is headed by a director, who is usually equipped with merchandise know-how coupled with a strong copy sense, or art sense, or a combination of both. He works closely with the merchandise divisions in planning sales and promotional efforts on a long range, six-month seasonal basis, keeping in mind the events that traditionally repeat themselves—for example, January White Sales, February Furniture Sales, Spring and Easter Fashions, Mother's Day, Father's Day, July White Sales, August Furniture Sales, Fall Fashion Presentation, Anniversary Sale, Christmas Presentation.

The art director in the retail store must be aware of all trends in advertising and the graphic arts to visualize, design, and interpret merchandise themes or ideas. He coordinates the visual design from newspaper to storewide posters, streamers, sign toppers, elevator cards, menus, carcards, outdoor advertising, and point-of-sale displays for all promotional events. With competition vying for the same merchandise, from the same or comparable sources, the art director's responsibility is doubly important in understanding merchandise thinking and timing to insure the success of any given presentation. The art director is

DISCOVER
a world of savings!

KRESGE · NEWARK
86th Anniversary
SALE

2 Courtesy Days: Friday, September 28th and Saturday, September 29th

Photographer/Harold Halma

DISCOVER
a new world
with Chris and his
modern Isabella

a world of luxury in a Karastan rug!
a world of quality at Kresge · Newark!

DISCOVER
a new world
with Chris and his
modern Isabella

a world of beauty in jewelry by Coro!
a world of quality at Kresge · Newark!

DISCOVER
a new world with Chris
and his
modern
Isabella

a world of glamour in Roman Stripe!
a world of quality at Kresge · Newark!

constantly challenged to produce an effective selling
ad in the shortest space of time—and this calls for
professional handling from the original communication to layout, copy, art, production, engraving and
final release. It is not uncommon in the face of competition for an ad to be created one day prior to its
appearance in the newspaper, resulting in plus dollar
sales to the store that moves the "fastest with the
bestest." Most retail advertising is geared to ringing
the cash register the day following the advertisement.

In most stores newspaper advertising is the major
medium for telling and selling the buying public on a
day-to-day basis. Consistency of advertising format is

133

1

1. Harold Halma
2. Tod Draz
3. Bernard Phreim
4. Jane Turner
5. Joe Kaufman
6. Bill Charmatz
Art Director/Ralph Daddio

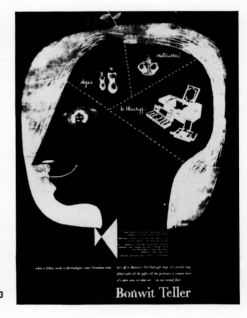

3

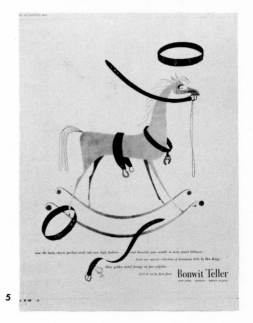

5

134

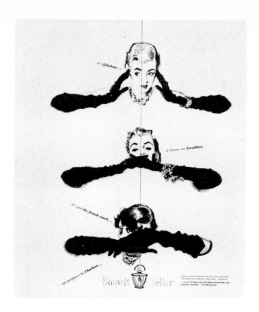

2

4

135

6

essential to consumer recognition. The layout design, signature cut, art technique plus typography play an important role in sustaining this "look".

In developing the advertising format, art directors are sometimes assigned to redesign the store logotype or signature cut. This opportunity opens creative possibilities in establishing the overall format of the ad. Once the original layout design is conceived, the art technique is the next step in developing the advertising format, which can be interpreted by one of many ways: black-and-white illustration, line and wash drawings, dry brush, photographs, combination photographs and art work, reversed art and type, and surprint art and type.

The art director must understand the capacities and limitations of newspaper reproduction in directing the preparation of art technique for a maximum printing result. The use of a minimum of three tonal values in proper relationship to each other will insure the best printing results. Creative typography is another integral part of graphic advertising design. In most stores the typography is supplied by the local newspaper. However, there are some that obtain their type either wholly or in part from outside typographers.

Direct mail is another important medium used by many retail stores, used to supplement the store's advertising where newspaper circulation is limited and more consumer coverage is desired. In other instances, direct mail is used to remind customers of special sales, events, fashion shows and the like. The special direct mail lists, maintained by all department stores, may run anywhere from 25,000 to almost 500,000 customers. The retail art director is responsible for designing and producing any and all direct mail pieces. The presentation may take any form or shape, from a postcard to a single sheet to an accordion fold to tabloid to broadside. Four-color art and photography plus black-and-white illustration are widely used in letterpress or offset processes with suitable paper stock. The larger stores produce a minimum of six direct mail booklets per year, with the Christmas catalogue receiving the strongest emphasis.

With the constant challenge of producing effective selling messages, leadership is an important factor in organizing a team to execute visual presentations to original specifications. The art director is a personnel administrator, handling a staff of many personalities. His responsibility is to stimulate and inspire; to direct and supervise layouts, artists, photographers, photo retouchers and production personnel, plus all free lance resources. He is an informed artist and designer, aware of current trends in advertising art, typography, and production, and he coordinates these elements into a well-designed format that will consistently reflect the merchandising and service policies of the store.

Jane Turner

The Art Director Moves Merchandise

by Juke Goodman

IN retail advertising, no two stores work in the same way. So to convey an advertising message, whether it is to be institutional or for merchandise promotion, an analysis must be made of your public—what people you are trying to reach and what type of merchandise you are trying to present to them. Only when these factors have been determined will you be in a position to decide the best type of layout and best art technique for the ad. Thus, you would hardly choose a dreamy Dali painting if you were selling practical household equipment, for example, (keeping in mind the potential customer as well as the type of merchandise) but such an illustration might help to sell an exclusive perfume. The art director must be merchandise-minded.

The layout is a mirror reflecting the visual image of an idea. So an art director must develop the faculty of criticizing his own work, analyzing it, making any necessary changes, reworking each layout until it can stand on its own. It is best to anticipate all the possibilities within a given space.

Selling Merchandise or Service

In essence, the art director in a retail store is confronted with three selling situations. The advertising with which he is primarily concerned must sell: (a) the store and its services (the institutional ad); (b) a specific department of the store, and the service or merchandise it offers; (c) a specific item of merchandise. The retail store of whatever kind or size offers its services and facilities to its customers, Mr. and Mrs. Public, but its existence is based on selling. The art director's task is to help move the merchandise—to sell the store's service—through all the visual means at his disposal.

Different Approaches to Layout

The approach to a layout may be taken in various ways:

1. Layout visual is made; then copy and art ordered to fit. Result—ad.
2. Copy and art complete; then layout is made. Result—ad.
3. Art complete; then layout is made; copy is written to layout. Result—ad.
4. Copy complete; then layout is made; art is prepared to conform to layout. Result—ad.

How Some Store's Layouts Are Prepared

Macy's, Abraham & Straus, and others, first make their space break-up, then tentative rough layouts are made and sent through the various channels for OK's on space, merchandise, copy and layout. Then the component parts are reassembled, and sometimes a more complete layout is made without the finished artwork. Copy and art are then ordered to conform to the rough layout. The copy may be sent out on galleys, and when the art is received, a photostat or sketch is made in the correct size for the actual ad. This is a speed-up method, which avoids delays caused by missing elements.

Bonwit Teller, Saks Fifth Avenue and others make a rough layout first to illustrate the merchandise to be used in the promotion. When this tentative layout is approved, art and copy are ordered to conform to the space allowed in layout. The art director may even give the copywriter a character count, indicating the exact number of words (actually the number of characters going to make up words) needed to fill up the copy block allowed for in the layout and based, of course, on the size type to be used.

Lord & Taylor works differently. Their emphasis is on art display and a minimum of copy, to put over an idea. As the art plays the major role, the idea must be very carefully conveyed to the artist. In fact, the artist often will sketch in the figures to show exactly how the page will look, and this rough may be OK'd before the sketches are actually ordered. Most of Lord & Taylor's artwork is rendered actual size and the copy or lettering is put on the art. Thus, the finished art really represents a finished ad from which a complete plate can be made.

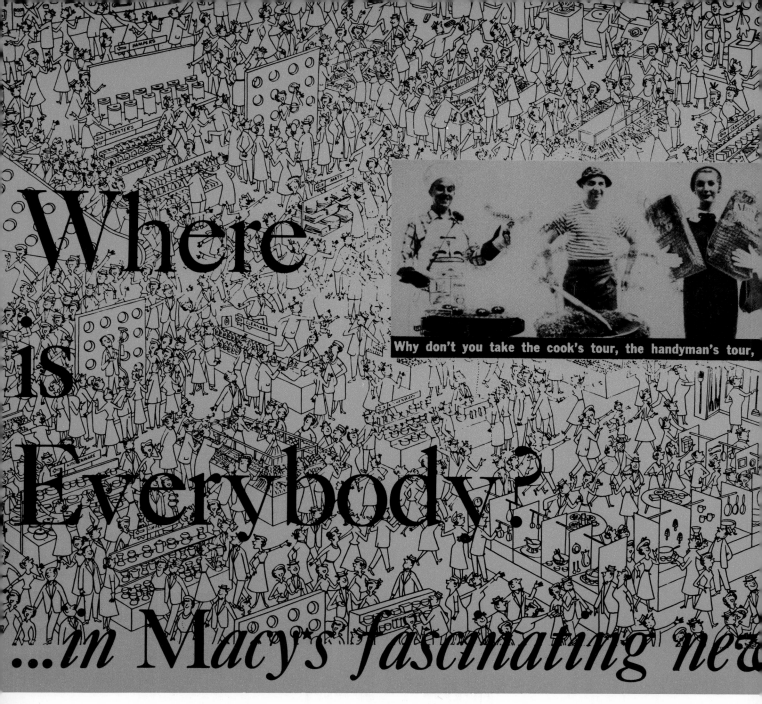

Where is Everybody?

...in Macy's fascinating nea

Why don't you take the cook's tour, the handyman's tour,

An Ad Is An Ad Is 100

TODAY is Thursday. It could be any Thursday in April, June or November. Actually it's Thursday, December 8, . . a busy day in one of the busiest creative factories, Macy's advertising department.

Over 100 pages of advertising will pass through our hands today. Each page has at least 3 items or groups of items . . . a total of 300 items in all. That means there are 300 items requiring personal attention . . . 300 items, each with its own set of copy, layout, art work, buyer's comments, merchandise problems. And . . . we see these 300 items only once: one proof, one look, one set of corrections . . . a prayer and then off to the newspaper.

Fighting the clock and the calendar is our constant concern. Creativity we take for granted. We think fast, act fast, and constantly hope that we don't have to second guess. We rarely have the luxury of trying an ad another way. When we do have to second guess (and for many reasons we often do) we turn on a dime and prepare what is practically a new page . . . or two or three or even five pages . . . on a day's notice. Because it is a retail business, this situation arises constantly.

Mathematically, we can turn out our volume of pages, but that isn't all we do. We pre-plan campaigns

AIR CONDITIONERS

OIL CLOTH

usewife's tour ... visit the brand-new Mecca of every gear-and-gadget-happy American

Housewares Basement

by Morris L. Rosenblum   *Creative Advertising Manager, Macy's, New York*

and handle all other forms of graphic material from TV commercials to labels. Our organization consists of 12 copywriters, 12 layout people, an executive organization, a complete photo studio, a staff of retouchers and artists, and a production department.

Pre-Planned Layouts

How do you go about creating good selling advertising on this basis? It's quite obvious it can't be done haphazardly. The advertising must be carefully planned and well organized ... and still manage to look spontaneous and contemporary. Many of our ads

must, of necessity, have an established format. Pre-planned merchandise layouts save time and also give the younger designers and writers a direction in which to work. Over and above the individual formats, we have evolved a philosophy about Macy's advertising ... a sort of all-encompassing tent. It constantly reminds us that we are the largest store in the world and we must look like the largest. It reminds us that we deal with a mass market whose interests are varied, so our copy and art must reflect the interests of a mass market. However, it doesn't mean talking down to or up to them, but talking *at* them.

Long-playing hits by Phil Rose of California, in wonderful cotton knits and corduroys that cut merry capers at college, at home. They're madly colorful Roman-holiday separates inspired by the Italian songs in Columbia Records' new Long-Playing album

HOLIDAY IN ROME

How do we achieve this in graphic format?

1. By keeping every ad simple and direct in the way a good poster is simple and direct.
2. By using photography wherever possible. Where photography is not possible, because merchandise is not available or can't be photographed, we try to simulate photography. There are exceptions, of course ... rare cases where we feel that, as an accent, a line drawing or loose wash or cartoon is more effective.
3. By retaining a classic type face, rather than a contemporary or fashionable one, as our predominating type ... in our case, Caslon. This helps maintain the feeling of stability.

A Day with an Advertising Department

Let's look in on the advertising department at Macy's this Thursday. We'll start in the photo studio. They began early this Thursday morning, mixing chemicals and developing last night's exposed negatives. (Six photographers shooting all day expose a lot of film.) The photographers are backed up by a complete staff of stylists, prop men, dark room, technicians and clerical help ... about 16 or 17 in all. We need them, because there's no quota on the number of photographs a day. What has to be done gets done, fast and well. One studio may be shooting a room setting, another a group of European fashions for a publicity release, another a set-up involving 150 toys. It doesn't matter whether it's black-and-white or color, a single shot or a complicated montage ... we do them all. Every piece of merchandise is checked in to the studio very carefully, every prop is checked in, every item is carefully watched and returned. Downstairs, in the art department, 6 to 10 retouchers (depending on the day's volume) are busy completing the job. They work carefully to the layout and with the layout artist.

It's still Thursday, still early in the day. Let's watch the rest of our organization. As I have said, 100 or so pages of advertising will pass through our hands today. Right now, the copywriters and layout artists are finishing copy and layouts for next Friday's and Saturday's ads. By Friday night, before they leave, they must complete all Sunday layouts for the following week. This may be as many as 40 or 50 pages.

At about 2:30 of the same Thursday, we look at the first of the proofs ... about 40 to 50 pages in various stages of completion. We take our last look at Friday and Saturday pages (*this* Friday and *this* Saturday) and our first look at all the ads that will appear in Sunday's papers. We study them carefully for policy decisions, for merchandise information, price corrections, details of engraving and typography. How often we would like to move a headline up a pica or over a pica ... but then we think of the clock and we don't change anything unless it's absolutely necessary. Because, as I've said ... one look, one proof, one set of corrections ... and away they go.

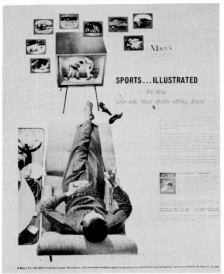

Parenthetically, the newspapers do an amazing job of typography and engraving for us. About 95% of our type is set at the newspapers and they make all our engravings.

All our ads are O.K.'d by our Bureau of Standards for merchandise facts, by our Comparison Office for price and policy, by buyers and merchandise vice presidents for merchandise information. True they have looked these things over in the pre-planning stage and on their schedules. But this proof is the one time they get a chance to check all the details and facts. The advertising managers, art directors, copy-writers . . . everybody looks at these proofs. The production department gets the last look. They collate all the information from all these sources. They confirm the corrections and send them off to the newspapers. The next time we see them, they're in print.

However, before the ads go off, we sometimes find that headlines were badly written or the concept of the ad was wrong, merchandise errors were made or man-ufacturers can't deliver merchandise. There are so many, many reasons why ads have to be redesigned on Thursday or Friday for that Sunday's papers . . . and we take this in stride, too.

Planning Ahead

It's still Thursday and sometime today, usually in the afternoon, our executive group will have three or four long-range planning meetings. At these meetings we'll start anticipating the demands of a new season, a new fashion, or a new special purchase. We may find, for example, that an item in yesterday's paper sold very well and we suddenly decide to repeat that item in an-other paper tomorrow. This, too, we take in stride.

All the while this operation is going on, our sched-uling department is preparing a brand new schedule for the week after next. This is a world all its own. Newspapers, markets, dollars and cents, merchandise problems have to be planned and carefully plotted by paper and by day. Then when this schedule is com-pleted and sent out to the organization, the whole cycle starts all over again.

The Excitement of Retail Promotion

How do I fit into this picture? Actually I am the catalyst that gets things going. I see almost every ad at some stage or other. I help plan promotions. I create the formats. I sit in with the merchants and help them interpret their merchandise situations in terms of good solid promotional events. I watch to make sure all our advertising is within the policy, scope and philosophy of Macy's. And, perhaps the greatest fun of all I help train young people.

Now this, I am sure, sounds very hectic and it is hectic. But it's also exciting . . . exciting in the sense that what you do today is in the papers tomorrow. You walk down on the selling floor and watch the people flock in and hear the cash registers ringing. Suddenly you realize that the ad you've designed, the pictures you've drawn, the words you have written, all put together look good to you and the customers too! You realize that what you are doing is not designing advertising but selling. The customers believe you. They trust you . . . they come in and buy, or even phone or write. That's our kind of satisfaction.

A great difference between our sort of advertising and national advertising is that we in department stores are not only the creative staff, but we're also our own clients. We are concerned about each promotion because it represents us as well as the buyers, depart-ment managers, and merchandise vice presidents. It is a strange phenomenon indeed that we are not only ad-vertising agency or service department but our own clients as well.

And while this Thursday at Macy's may sound hec-tic, I'm sure it's no more hectic, no more interesting than your business. Just different.

Posters; Displays; Direct Mail;
Industrial Design...and the AD

Part 9 *Designed by* **Ladislav Sutnar**

Posters...Oldest Medium of Visual Communication

by Garrett P. Orr   *Associate Art Director, Outdoor Advertising, Inc.*

■ The basic history of the poster is as old as civilization itself. Ancient Egypt, Babylon, Athens, Rome, Pompeii all made use of this excellent medium of mass communication. An exhaustive study of the history of the use of the posted notice as a means of communication, advertising and propaganda would fill volumes. The earliest posters were carved in stone or painted on a convenient wall. In the eighteenth century, the invention of the lithographic process by a German, Alois Senefelder, made possible the development of the poster as we know it today.

■ During the nineteenth century posters came to be considered an art form in their own right, dignified by the pencil and brush of many of the popular artists of the day. Among these were Toulouse Lautrec, Gustave Doré, Puvis de Chavannes and Boutet de Monvel, to name a few of the more famous.

■ The first World War gave a powerful impetus to the development of the poster as a mass propaganda medium. Its effectiveness in recruiting, selling bonds, encouraging conservation and influencing public opinion was recognized by both sides of the conflict. Indeed, the technique developed by a German artist of this period, Ludwig Holwein, still influences American poster design.

The Outdoor Advertising Industry

■ The physical appearance of the poster has gone through great changes from the crude posted notices to the individual standardized panel in use in America today. A great deal of credit is due to the outdoor advertising industry for this development.

■ In place of the itinerant sign painter and the odd job bill poster there are now hundreds of individual outdoor advertising companies or "plants" all over the United States, servicing hundreds of thousands of outdoor advertising structures. Many years ago leaders in the industry realized the need for an organization to elevate billposting to a dignified place in business and to bring about a recognition and better understanding of the medium's national scope, vigor and character. The resulting organization was the first national association of advertising men in this country. It is now known as the Outdoor Advertising Association of America, Inc. Its membership includes 90% of the plant owners in the United States.

■ The Association recommends standards for outdoor display structures, advertising service, business practice, market coverage and public policy with the express purpose of making outdoor advertising effective on a national scale.

■ The Association places special emphasis on the maintenance of good public relations in the plant's own community. Members have agreed to locate their structures "in such a manner as to recognize and respect the public interest in natural scenic beauty, parks, parkways, and their immediate approaches, and historic places, so as to respect rights and interests of owners and occupants of property in fact residential".

■ Furthermore, the Association strongly urges a rigid maintenance policy for the advertising structures of its members so that regardless of where they appear they are freshly painted, often landscaped.

■ The Association has also established a copy policy

14

The opening symbol of this section represents an arrow hitting a target [an ancient Chinese mark for center]. Here it stands for the two-fold function of art direction in advertising: first, to attract attention and to arouse interest in a product or a service; second, to convert that interest into buying action. — *Ladislav Sutnar*

which specifies that "no copy will be displayed which induces a violation of federal or state law, is offensive to the moral standards of the community, (or) is false, misleading or deceptive".

■ Recognizing the industry's public responsibility, the national Association has adopted a public service advertising policy in support of many public welfare causes. This cooperation is a sound business policy, which profits not only the outdoor industry, but the advertiser who buys posters. The very purpose of outdoor advertising is to sell the advertiser's product, or idea. It is most important that a favorable atmosphere be created for the presentation of his message.

Elements of the Successful Poster

■ It is up to the art director or designer to present that message effectively. The successful outdoor poster must do three things:

1. *It must catch the eye.*—No matter how convincing its message, if a poster is not seen it is wasted effort. It must have eye appeal designed to compete successfully for attention with surrounding buildings, store windows, vehicular traffic, traffic signals and other outdoor designs.

2. *It must be remembered.*—The prospective customer must feel that its message is aimed directly at him. The word message must be brief and to the point. If a human interest situation is involved, it must be familiar to the viewer. It should convey a feeling of personal relationship between the viewer and the poster and ultimately, of course, between the viewer and the product advertised. Concerning sales, if a poster is not remembered it may as well have not been seen.

3. *It must build up an impulse to buy.*—In the final analysis this is the vital test of a poster. All other factors are aimed at this one point, Sales, with a capital S. It is almost impossible to put down any set rules

for putting successful "sell" in a poster. However, if the poster has eye appeal, has remembrance value and convey's a convincing message applying directly to the consumer, it usually follows that it will stimulate sales.

■ In the vast majority of posters, the picture is of first importance in reaching people and appealing to them, for pictures speak a universal language. Pictures and word copy should tend to read as one—be easy to grasp—and register with singleness of effect. There may be occasions, however, when an all-lettering poster will do a better job. The decision as to treatment will depend on the specific problem involved.

■ The component parts of a poster should be organized and combined so as to form not more than three main elements. In these three elements, the designer must often fit a sales message or caption, an illustration to dramatize this caption, a picture of the product, the name of the product, the name of the advertiser and, at times, a trademark and slogan. Wherever possible, an attempt should be made to reduce not only the number of component parts, but the number of elements. Almost without exception, the resulting poster will be more forceful and have more selling quality. However if a number of "musts" have to be included, simplification may be accomplished by the use of panels, by overlapping one element over another, by letting the product carry the name or by combining related elements.

Pictorial Elements

■ The illustration must attract the eye and tell its story in the same breath. This rules out subtlety and frills. Simplification and the elimination of unnecessary detail is of the utmost importance. If possible the silhouette should convey the intended meaning. Frequently a straight profile will express better than any other view. This point is well illustrated by the contrasting front and side views of a person drinking from a glass. If silhouette value is strong, even though the viewer does not have time to take in all the details of the picture, he will get your story.

■ Pictorial elements should be made as large as possible. Full length figures have a tendency to look small on a poster. The art director should employ the "close up" technique as often as the situation permits. A portion of a head or the head and shoulders will frequently tell the story. Let the picture suggest something larger than the drawing itself. This will result in a far more dramatic and powerful poster.

■ The illustration must contrast with the background so that as a mass it is identifiable from a distance. Background detail should be played down so as not to distract the attention from the center of interest. In fact, flat backgrounds are usually best. Dark backgrounds call for predominantly light figures and, of course, light backgrounds are best for predominately dark figures. The use of color is also important and helpful in achieving this silhouette quality.

■ The range of colors in poster advertising is unlimited. The use of color in posters is a study in itself. However, strong bright complementary color schemes with plenty of contrast are more effective than pastel harmonies. Excessive variations of tone, too much delicacy of patterns, use of tints or indefinite hues should be avoided. Probably because of the great amount of ultra-violet light outdoors, warm colors seem to have the best outdoor carrying power.

The AD's Visual Approach

■ The art director usually makes numerous rough "thumbnail" sketches in small size until he is satisfied with the arrangement and design of the basic elements. He frequently ends up with several different, but sound visual approaches. He then carries these selected roughs to a degree of finish which will enable the advertiser to make a final choice. Normally these are color sketches, often comprehensive in form.

■ Following the advertiser's approval of the design, the art director must then consider what artist he will employ to make the finished art. Much will depend upon the nature of the subject matter. Some artists specialize in food, beautiful girls, animals, character studies, and so forth. The artist usually renders the painting in 16x36 inch size—for easier reproduction.

■ Since the design will not be reproduced in actual size—the standard poster is 8 feet 8 inches high by 19 feet 6 inches long—the artist must make compensation for this enlargement when he makes finished art.

Lettering

■ In most cases a second artist or "lettering man" must be employed to do the lettering. Letterers are available who specialize in poster work. However any

Development of a 24-sheet outdoor poster: [This picture story of the creation and production of a Nabisco poster originally appeared in *Printers' Ink*. Photos made by Alton Ketchum of McCann-Erickson, Inc.]
1 — Herb Noxon, McCann-Erickson AD gets schedule 18 months in advance from Nabisco account group head, v.p. William Conine. —
2 — Year's poster program features various products. — 3 — Briefing session with copywriters starts the search for ideas. —
4 — Good posters begin with a good idea. —
5 — Rough designs are sifted. —
6 — Spector of a tight schedule. — 7 — Next come sketches of people for use in campaign. —
8 — More sifting of designs follows.

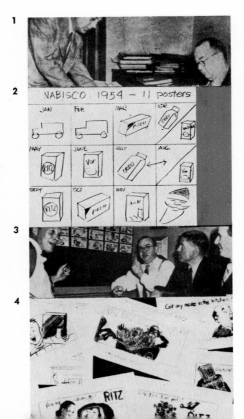

competent letterer will be able to do a good poster job if he keeps certain fundamentals in mind. Good straight sans serif lettering of a little better than average weight or thickness is best for poster copy. Script, Old English, or fancy lettering are undesirable because of poor legibility.

■ Lettering must be legible for quick reading, reading at a fair distance, reading from fast-moving vehicles—hence the need for simplicity.

■ Staggered or trick lettering is not suitable for posters. Straight horizontal lettering is best. The size of letters varies with the importance of the message. However, lettering which will reproduce to less than four inches in height on the posted panel will not be readable at any distance.

■ Currently there is a trend to lower case lettering on the theory that the eye is more accustomed to lower case type and will therefore read it more easily. Naturally the most important section of the message should be given the key spot in placement. It should be borne in mind that the average reader reads most easily from left to right, so if there are two or three blocks of word copy, they should be arranged to take advantage of this tendency—thus, in general the trade mark, signature or product will be most effective in the lower right hand section of the poster.

■ Lettering frequently serves as an element of design. For example: it may be slanted to indicated speed, it may be shown in perspective as long as it retains legibility, it may be given a third dimensional effect or be printed in fluorescent ink on a dark background.

Producing the Poster

■ The poster art director must be familiar with methods of poster reproduction. He should know the requirements of each method and their respective advantages and limitations.

■ If 300 or more posters are to be printed from one design, the method usually used is lithography. There are two methods of lithography: hand lithography for simpler designs which feature line art and fairly solid color masses, and photolithography if the art is more complex and there are critical shadings of color.

■ The theory of lithography is that water and grease will not mix. The printing plate first comes in contact with a series of water rollers so that it is entirely moistened except where grease crayon designs have been applied. As the plate continues its revolution on its cylinder it comes in contact with ink rollers which apply ink to the greased portions but not to the moistened areas. The plate next comes in contact with the paper sheet and the ink image is transferred to the paper. A separate plate is required for each color.

■ In hand lithography a lantern slide is made of the original art. The slide is then placed in a projecting camera and the design is thrown on sheets of paper

9 — Agency account group acts as jury, eliminating 10 but keeping 20 designs. — 10 — Sketches in color are made to submit to client. — 11 — Comprehensives for 12-month campaign are shown Nabisco advt. director at first meeting. — 12 — At second client meeting lower sketch is approved for finished art. — 13 — Roy Spreter [right] while painting the poster discusses color values, expression with AD Noxon. [Outdoor ads are only medium reproducing by enlargement. Painting must be blown up 8 to 10 times its original size.] — 14 — After two months at lithographer finished poster is checked outdoors before release to the various plants.

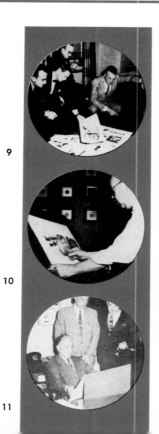

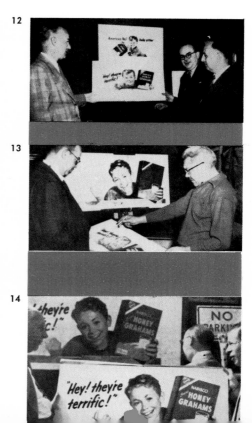

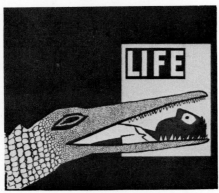

Life magazine series of posters on a theme such as "You get information out of Life", "You get surprise out of Life", "You get excitement out of Life." Artist Raymond Savignac, Art director Hugh White.

arranged on a panel in the same order in which they will appear on the actual poster panel.

■ An artist traces the design on the paper with special grease crayon. He then sprinkles the tracing with lithographer's powder which sticks to the crayon marks. The paper sheets are then placed in a transfer press where the tracings are imprinted on grained zinc plates, separate plates are made for each color in each section of the design. These plates are etched to develop the design and are then ready for the press.

■ Photolithography, the method in widest use today, enables the lithographer to make a truer reproduction of the original design. By this process the design is photographed directly on the plates. Color break-up is achieved through the use of filters. After printing, the sheets are sorted, folded, wrapped and sent to the plants for posting.

■ For smaller quantities, the silk screen process is most commonly used. In this process, the areas which are not to be printed are blocked out with a stencil or glue so that only the uncovered areas of the screen permit color to be forced through onto the poster sheets. Silk screen is most successful in flat color reproduction, although variations of the process permit color blending at added cost.

3 Sheets—Bulletins—Spectaculars

■ Although the 24 sheet poster is the most widely used form of outdoor advertising, there are other important classifications of the medium upon which the art director will be asked to apply his talents.

■ Advertisers often use the 3 sheet poster to supplement 24 sheet poster programs. The 3 sheet usually is printed in three sections and assembled on a sheet metal panel surrounded by a narrow wooden molding, the outside measurements of which are 8 feet 7 inches high by 4 feet 10 inches wide. Like the 24 sheet, it is usually reproduced by lithography or silk screen.

■ Big brother to the 24 sheet poster is the painted bulletin. These differ from 24 sheets both in size and character. The bulletin is larger than the 24 sheet and is generally much longer in proportion to its height than the poster. Bulletins will vary, but the average painting area is four units of height to one of length.

■ As the name implies, bulletin copy is painted on the surface of the structure rather than being posted on it. Original or finished art for the bulletin should be done to scale. It is called a "painter's copy" or "painter's guide". This is usually made ½ inch to 1 inch to the foot. Blue prints or tracing with a color key are then usually made and these, with colored photographic prints of the pictorial material are sent to the plants where the bulletins to be painted are located.

■ The same basic principles of design apply to painted bulletins as apply to 24 sheet posters, only more so. As in poster design, a brilliance of color is demanded.

One of a series of posters for a safe driving campaign, designed by Walter H. Allner. — Another poster by Leo Lionni for Family Service Association of America series.

DON'T PERFORM   DRIVE CAREFULLY

which way out?

for family counseling call

AFFILIATED WITH FAMILY SERVICE ASSOCIATION OF AMERICA

The number of colors which may be used is almost unlimited. However, because bulletins must be hand painted, simplicity is of great importance. Complicated color blending and use of any unnecessary detail should be avoided.

■ Both 24 sheet posters and painted bulletins are frequently illuminated for night time value, but the most spectacularly illuminated outdoor advertising is called just that—the "spectacular". A spectacular is usually considered to be a large permanent sign individualized with special lighting and action effects. A good example of a spectacular would be one of the large flashing signs in Times Square, New York.

■ The semi-spectacular is basically a painted bulletin to which can be added in varying degrees, neon lights or bulbs within the panel or on top of the structure, three dimensional effects, illuminated plastics, animation, reflector material, and in selected locations where there is not too much competing light to spill over onto the face of the bulletin, a combination of fluorescent paints and special lighting which combine to give an effect known as "black light".

■ The design problem in connection with spectaculars or semi-spectaculars is somewhat similar to that of the motion picture animator or the television art director. The designer's palette is light and motion. Instead of producing finished art for the lithographer, he works with blue prints for engineers and electricians.

Principles of Good Design

■ In the final analysis, however, whether he is designing 3 sheets, 24 sheets, painted bulletins or spectaculars, the basic principles of good poster design apply in every case.

The design must have:

An Idea. The most important element, regardless of art or technique is the idea. It is the means of putting across the sales message and making it remembered.

Interest. The design must attract the eye and hold it long enough to convey the message.

Simplicity. The whole design must be able to be seen at a glance. Eliminate unnecessary detail.

Brevity. Word copy should be short enough to be read by passing motor traffic.

Legibility. The message will be lost on a large segment of the possible prospects if the word copy and pictorial situation does not carry for a considerable distance.

Familiarity. The viewer must identify himself with the situation and the product.

Color. To compete with the surroundings, color should be pleasing to the eye, but vivid in hue and strong in contrast.

Originality. This is what you are hired for.

Closing the Sale Visually...
The Point-of-Purchase AD

by W. Stuart Leech   *Art Director, Einson-Freeman Co., Inc.*

■ Most successful point-of-purchase advertising grabs you by the coat tails, leads you into the store and says: "Pick up and take me home—I'm the best buy for your money."

■ The art directors who work on this sales promotion material are a breed of cats all their own. They have a solid art background and a combination of good taste, judgment, merchandising ability and organized business sense. Their work requires a sound working knowledge of a prodigious list of arts, crafts, cardboard engineering, motion devices, plastics, and display devices and materials.

■ Point-of-purchase advertising has problems all its own—State laws and regulations (what is food for one location is poison for another); motion; lighting; practical distribution of material; construction problems and a host of others.

■ Yet with all the problems that face the point-of-purchase art director, this field is probably the most exciting and interesting for the AD. Each problem is different and presents a new challenge.

■ The most creative and fertile minds achieve the finest results. However, there is no substitute for team work; the art director alone is not enough. He must have a friendly handshake in every phase of his work.

A Case History

■ For example, let us take a large beer campaign for a southwestern territory. The emphasis is on Texas, with distribution in three or four bordering states. The problem is to create a campaign that will help the retailers, a campaign that will give blanket coverage where it will do the most good in increasing store traffic and sales. The retailers will want something new—something that will sell the beer faster than ever before. It must be, in fact, the magic carpet that will move a Niagara of beer from their shelves.

■ After conferences with the client as to his needs, desires and budget, the wheels start turning. The research boys have made hundreds of polaroid shots of bars, stores and markets of this area, and have classified them. These files are studied and checked for promotion aids now being used; methods of decorating windows and stores; new locations for display material; how merchandise is sold in that area, and so on. Notes are made and local laws are consulted. For example, no beer advertising material may be used within six feet of the front window in one state, while anything may go in another.

■ Statistics show our biggest outlet will be in super-

Creating a display: — 1 — Rough visual. —2 — Corrected layout. — 3 — Production dummy. — 4 —Final reproduction. Design W. S. Leech.

markets. However, we must also cover bars, package stores and small grocers, and we must not forget the Negro and Spanish-speaking markets.

■ The big problem is the theme. It must be something that will stimulate sales and tie the entire program into one package . . . something that our competitors are not doing or have not done in recent years. It must be colorful and above all, it must attract the eye.

■ Reams of sketches are made; gimmicks are devised; motion and light are pre-planned. Plastics, mobiles, floorstands, counter cards, shelf-talkers and a dozen other possibilities are considered—always with the thought that the budget could have been larger. After weeding out the sketches to his final choice, the client (bless his heart) picks a theme—and is enthusiastic. Sketches that cover all the vital situations are retained, artists are decided on for the finished art. All goes well and everybody is happy.

The Campaign Takes Shape

■ The next few weeks of production art find the art director as busy as the proverbial paper hanger. Artists are given assignments, models are chosen, photographers and lettering men are all busy. Cardboard engineers design and construct the physical form the displays will take. They are made to open with the least effort and the greatest speed. Of course, the displays must fold down into parcel post size, and this is sometimes an engineering feat in itself. Sculptors are preparing molds and wire formers are making samples.

■ Motion displays are tested, changed and retested. They, too, must fold flat with only the thickness of the motors to worry about. Some displays must be battery operated, some may use plug-in motors. The weight of the moving part, the location in which the unit will be used, and the price are generally the deciding factors.

■ During all this process of creating, the art director tries to interpret the likes and dislikes of the client. Many people object to the color green on beer or liquor displays—it suggests a raw or immature product, they say. When in doubt, use red—it is always an eye-catching, compelling color and is rarely in competition with the color scheme of the store or shop.

■ To expedite production, photographs of all art and lettering are blown up to reproduction size. They are mounted on cardboard constructions and serve as a guide for the plate makers. These photographic dummies give the exact location of the art and the lettering. Now, for the first time, the art director gets a general black-and-white impression of how the final display will appear. A second set of construction dummies is made for the die cutter and easel-making operators. Thus, both the reproduction and the display finishing operations may be started together.

■ Before it is realized, days have flown by and the campaign is beginning to take on a more concrete form. All phases of art and materials have been finished and the final presentation is to be made. Thousands of dollars have been spent and the psychological moment has arrived for the client's nod of approval. And this is often the art director's moment of glory.

■ So it goes. Tomorrow you will be working on watches, the day after you'll dream up something for cat food. I tell you it's a busy but never a dull life.

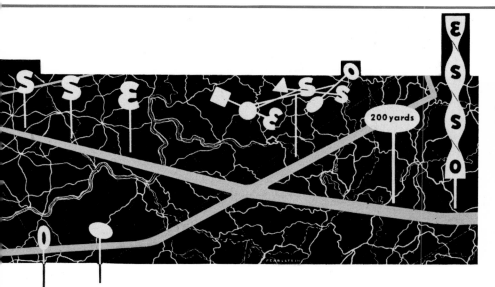

An example of a three-dimensional p-o-s system for a chain of service stations. It is composed of interchangeable units that allow variety in display, with motion supplied by wind.—Designed by Goldman and Pearlstein.

"addo-x" dealer kit designed by Ladislav Sutnar; a portfolio of dealer aids related to point-of-sale; [above and to right: authorized dealer sign, a streamer for store window and wall, and a counter display.] The portfolio also emphasizes company's new trademark and the seal "a West European quality product", both designed by Sutnar.

The Complex Problems of P-O-S Advertising

by Paul R. Lang

Vice President and New York Manager, Ketterlinus Lithographic Co.

■ When the art director sits down to confront a tough point-of-sale problem he must think of many more factors than size of page or number of colors. In nine cases out of ten he is not dealing with flat surfaces, nor with definite dimensions, nor even with one specific material. He must, in fact, consider the suitability of cardboard, of plastics, metal, wood, wire, silk or numerous other substances. And he must keep in mind the complexities of today's fast-changing patterns of merchandising and distribution.

■ So, when an art director is asked to create a point-of-sale display he has a wide field to choose from; in fact, there are almost no restrictions except that of price. He can design a flat piece, a piece in three dimensions, a large piece or a small piece. But, in any case, it must be practical in the sense that it must be planned for folding and shipment, often guided by parcel post requirements as to dimension when shipped.

■ He must also consider where the display is to appear—first, in regard to the type of retail outlet, and then whether it is to be used in a window, on the floor or on the wall of the store, on the counter, pasted on the door, or hung in the air above the merchandise. He must consider the function of his particular piece of point-of-sale advertising. Is it to be simply a poster to serve as a reminder, or is it to educate the customer about special features of the product? Is it to concentrate on selling the merchandise, or is it to induce action such as through an offer of a premium for his purchase? All of these may be functions of a display and the art director must design his piece accordingly.

Budget Considerations

■ Then, he must think of the budget—which brings up questions such as the sheet layout which, in turn is controlled by the size of the lithographic presses. He

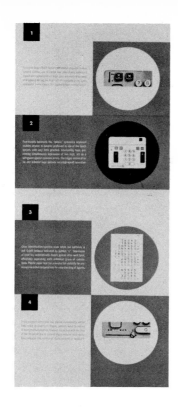

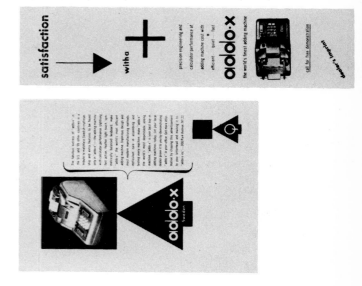

thus becomes involved in press runs, number of impressions, costs of mounting, press plates, color values, and so forth, all of which must be determined and computed in advance. In fact, the budget dictates the nature and materials of the display; the quantity required may determine the method of reproduction—as letterpress, silkscreen or gravure are also used.

■ The art director must also know a good deal about light, motion and sound, about batteries and electrically connected motors. Nowadays point-of-sale displays flash on and off, have arms in motion, tap on the window, or speak words via tape recordings. If his display is to do any of these things, the art director must be ready to design one that will function accurately, effectively, and also meet such requirements as mentioned above—budget, shipping, setting up in the retail outlet and so on.

The Display in Use

■ Indeed, an important question is who sets up the display—an installation service, the company salesman, the dealer or his salesman? If the art director designs a display that is so complicated that, after it is folded flat for shipment, the ordinary salesman

would be unable to set it up after receipt, it will very likely never be used!

■ The first problem concerns the dealer. Four factors are involved in the dealer's evaluation of a display.

Here they are:

1—Is it attractive? — 2—Does it sell merchandise? — 3—Does it help to sell related items? — 4—Does it fit the available space in the window or inside the store?

■ The art director who creates point-of-sale material is probably more aware of the problem of immediate sales than is the art director of almost any other branch of advertising. He must first sell his design to the client and, second, he must be concerned with whether the display piece will sell the client's product in the retail outlet—the point where the purchase is actually made. The acid test is *sales*. His skill in design, his art know-how, his ability to select the right artist or photographer, are all tools to enable the art director to create an effective and attractive selling piece. But if the point-of-sale display does not *sell* for the client, it has little reason for being.

Designing for Direct Mail

by Mahlon A. Cline
Art Director and Typographic Consultant

■ Direct mail nowadays covers a wide field of printed material; so the demands on the art director's creative ability, his understanding of the thousand and one details—design, art, type, paper, printing—must all be coordinated in order to design successfully.

■ The term "direct mail" means something different than other forms of advertising, however, because its design must be planned for a specific size and directed to a specific audience. The difference is that the physical characteristics are not predetermined. So the art director must look at all aspects of the problem— determine the single dominant idea, study the copy, and project these elements into a visual message. Let's consider the essential points of direct mail design:

1—Consider the physical form of the mailing piece — 2—Consider the design aspects — 3—Consider an efficient procedure to adhere to.

■ In planning and developing the physical form of a direct mail piece, the art director must be familiar with all forms of direct mail advertising—must know the purpose of each—for he may be called upon to

design such things as: anniversary cards, announcements, annual reports, blotters, book covers, booklets, books, broadsides, brochures, bulletins, calendars, catalogues, financial statements, folders, house publications, illustrated letters, labels, letterheads, mailing cards, menus, package inserts, programs, and others.

Check-List of Basic Elements

■ After the general format has been determined the design aspects are ready for consideration. Here is a brief list as a guide for checking the basic elements: 1—Purpose — 2—Design (a) illustration; (b) color; (c) typography; (d) paper — 3—Production (a) reproduction method; (b) printing processes.

■ As to purpose, the questions often asked are: "is it suitable?"; "does it reflect the characteristics or quality of the client?" The aim should be to produce the required result—which may be that of sales, or to influence and move buyers to action. Or the printed piece might aim to inform and develop better public or employee relations. Size, shape and materials are important to the all-over aspects for a specific job.

154

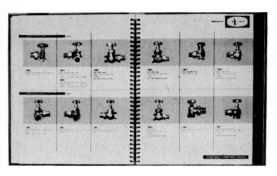

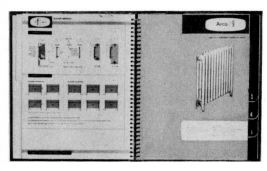

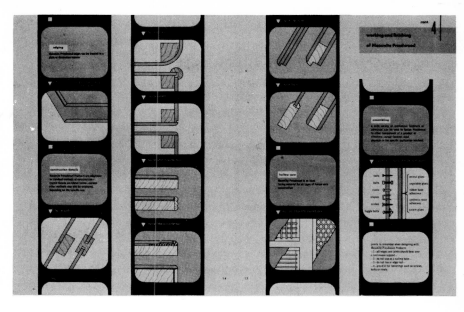

Various industrial catalogs with an orderly design pattern to make information easy to use; radiator heating equipment presentation [American-Standard], and "film strip" showing "presdwood" [Masonite]; designed by Ladislav Sutnar for Sweet's Catalog Service.

■ The art director/designer must also consider the elements of illustration, color, typography and paper. These, as we all know, are basic to any design problem; but in the light of our special application there are a few points that must be considered carefully.

Illustration—To gain the reader's attention, to explain the construction of a part, to show drama or humor, to show style, to show products in use, or to chart growth of a company—these are a few of the objectives of an illustration which may determine its shape, size and cost.

Color—Attention to color is a major consideration because of its potential effect on sales. Color has a decided influence on people; color can attract attention as well as sustain interest throughout the folder, booklet, broadside or catalogue. And it can provide a perfect tie-up with the other forms of promotion—packages, labels, posters and window streamers. Color adds realism and has a practical value of identification for trademarks and products. The psychological effect of color is known—color may be suggestive of danger, heat and cold, purity, cleanliness, happiness, dignity, excitement and so on.

Typography—As another tool of the art director, the type elements have a direct relationship to other units. The essential factors of typographic arrangement are those of legibility, harmony and emphasis. Typographic style is determined by the general con-

cepts of the advertising campaign or direct mail piece itself—such as being newsy or strictly formal in character. And type contrasts are an important consideration for, through type, infinite variations can be achieved by the use of bold type, condensed or expanded, change in size or style, roman or italic. But the typographic design of any printed piece should maintain a balance of legibility and harmony.

Paper—In his paper selection the art director realizes that without proper surface, texture and appearance the mailing piece he has planned cannot be successful. Paper and its combination with the other elements—illustration, design, color and typography—must be thought of as an essential to obtain the best possible result. Points to be considered are availability, appearance, texture, bulk, size, weight, color, surface finish, grain and cost.

Printing Processes—The art director has, somewhere along the way in his design planning, considered the final reproduction of his piece. He knows the advantages and limitations of letterpress, offset, gravure and silk screen. Each process has its place, each is right for the given job—or at least it has certain advantages. Modern developments in the graphic arts have removed many of the production distinctions among the processes, but the art director should make an effort to keep abreast of trends and further advances so as to take full advantage of them.

Creating a "Stopper"

by P. K. Thomajan   *Advertising Consultant*

■ Arresting the attention of the speeding reader . . . really bringing it to a standstill . . . this demands a degree of authority and ability. A stopper is a coveted achievement and represents the *ne plus ultra* in advertising technique.

■ Usually it is an overt originality. There's a bit of nuclear cerebration in the makeup of a stopper . . . a dynamic fission of elements that detonates vital essence. Here is a very special combo of TNT-PDQ.

Simple and Brief

■ A stopper can be as simple and brief as IBM's one-word symbol—THINK—which has become supercharged with positive associations. Nothing can touch a stopper for touching people to the quick and quickening responses.

■ Who can ever forget World Peaceway's advertisement that appeared before World War II showing a naked baby lying helplessly on a monstrous butcher block? Such appeals have a potent aplomb from which there can be little evasion.

■ A stopper can take the momentous and make it *omentous*. Adroitly, it *eyetalicizes* significant issues. A stopper of stoppers was a posterette issued by the Red Cross blood bank. This consisted merely of a large drop of blood suspended in white space . . . containing the sole word . . . GIVE.

Give it White Space

■ Considerable white space is essential to give a stopper ample room in which to swing and develop an orbit of influence. The juxtaposition of diametrically opposite elements . . . mighty and minute . . . can produce an effective stopper. A graphic instance is Rusling Wood's classic . . . "Yes, I am a Nut". A variant would be a tiny isle of text in an ocean of white space.

■ Stoppers can have a perverse way of upsetting apple carts and then, to use the vernacular, *picking up the beans.* They can have a touch of magic with their ingenious way of materializing surprise effects. Such as . . . a man's hand suddenly protruding from the center gutter of a magazine . . . caught in the act of giving a gift package of a certain brand . . . to the reader. Then . . . imagine a tie ad consisting of a large bust of an historic celebrity posed on a pedestal . . . wearing a modern tie. Accompanying this . . . a plaque with the words: "Museum Ties for Men of Taste." Of course, one of the very modern classics of this genre is the pause-provoking ad titled: "Which One Has The Toni?" . . . posing an intriguing picture and a subtly obvious question . . . leading to a ready answer.

Successful Stoppers

■ An astute stopper should be able to make the reader take a second look and rate a second thought. A suc-

15

Stopper examples: — 1 — "Yes, I am a Nut, so if I am a nut, I am rather proud of it"; advertisement of Rusling Wood Inc. mural advertising. — 2 — Bufferin medicinal advertisement. — 3 — "I dreamed I was a Work of Art in my Maidenform Bra", one ad of a well known series. — 4 — Hanes stopper for seamless hosiery. — 5 — 'Smirnoff unique promotion of vodka.

1

2

cessful stopper has a forthright fortuitousness. It is a real natural enjoying a happy confluence of all aspects.
■ Good stoppers cannot be produced with a temperamental snap of the fingers. They require a certain subconscious interval in which to formulate . . . before they are ready for conscious manipulation. Sheer bravado in conjuring deliberately arbitrary effects can often backfire with rather disastrous results. However, a bravura flair, something quite different, has a great deal to do with making a stopper click . . . such as the spontaneous felicity of Jose Ferrer delivering a line from *Cyrano*.
■ A stopper can be a diverting visual-verbal *tour de force* . . . take a figure of speech and cut figure 8's by executing it literally . . . as instanced by various Ohrbach ads. Copy with counterpoint can artfully cue a stopper . . . such as . . . "A Whale of A Sale with Minnow Prices."
■ Angling is so very important . . . such as showing a rear-view mirror projecting from the outside edge of a page imaging a glamorous car coming up . . . then the words: "A passing reflection of an approaching GM model." There is vision and design in a well-composed stopper. It can command the right-of-way.
■ The Smirnoff Vodka ad showing a beach-tree with men perched in its stark limbs stands out as a unique stopper . . . a fine flight of fancy expertly anchored in a basic theme. A posteresque stopper would be one showing a giant cactus displaying a packet of common pins, identified by a jack-knifed name. One look . . . one thought . . . and all is said and done.
■ One of the earliest stoppers, which dates back several decades, was a full-color full-page Jell-O ad, that showed a carton of this product lying across a railroad track. Intense drama and a focalization of interest was created by an approaching locomotive and the excited driver of a horse and wagon . . . rushing back to rescue the precious Jell-O. A good stopper is never dated and can be re-run without looking tired . . . witness the famous Y & R ad titled IMPACT . . . which made its debut a quarter-century ago.
■ There are no pat formulas for stoppers . . . These ideological phenomena boldly defy the cliché approach. They are entirely uninhibited and stem from quirks of fancy abetted by reflex reactions to the spirit of a situation. Stoppers have a way of pulling out all the organ stops . . . resulting in reverberating performances. Exposure to a full-fledged stopper gives one an agreeable sense of contact with a kinetic entity.
■ Certain stoppers loom as directional landmarks on the advertising scene. They are the ultimate in communication . . . for they make it consummate.

EDITORIAL NOTE

Stoppers have a legitimate and strategic value in advertising because, as Mr. Thomajan says, they are not just superficial tricks. They emerge from the subconscious only after intensive study of a specific advertising problem.

This eye-opening approach, is definitely related to the surrealists' program of startling the observer—through combining inanimate and living things which have never before been brought together. Dali's art is based on this sort of juxtaposition, though as a gimmick in painting it has very little intrinsic validity because a creative painting must live not only tomorrow but forever. However, when Dali functions naturally as a sensational illustrator he makes compelling stoppers that are valuable in today's visual communication.

57

3

4

5

Let's Look At Industrial Design

by Donald Deskey

Senior Partner, Donald Deskey Associates

■ When the industrial designer has been retained by a client, he becomes a component of a task force whose function it is to set up and operate a product or package design plan. The objectives of this plan are determined by management, along with time schedules and budgets necessary to implement and to accomplish it. And it must be based on the fullest use of the imaginative and creative powers of the entire staffs of both the client and the industrial design consultant.

■ If the industrial designer is to fulfill his role properly, he must integrate himself into the management team. The common objective of stimulating sales and increasing profits through better-designed products sets the pattern for a smooth, cooperative operation. Industrial design has developed into an agency for the performance of certain tasks for reasons similar to those that brought the advertising agency into being. Good design is as important to the overall well being and the profit picture of a company as is the most efficient production method and engineering know-how.

■ Today's industrial designers must have an acute and practical awareness of the needs, the problems and complex modus operandi of business and industry. Their contributions to sales and profits are not based upon a two-dimensional solution of a design problem, but involve thorough and intensive study of many factors that go to make up a product or package.

The Answers Must Come First

■ So it is essential that the industrial designer under-stand, and be able to interpret into the design concept, the cost and production factors involved in developing such new product or package. He must link the creativeness and freshness of the concept to the needs and limitations imposed by merchandising definitions.

■ It should be remembered that each time a manufacturer changes a design, whenever he introduces a new package or product, he takes a risk. Questions like these arise. What material should be used? Will the design sell? Should it be marketed through new or established channels? What directions should advertising and promotion take? What will it cost and how shall it be priced? Sound answers must be forthcoming if the manufacturer is to remain in business. And the answers must not come after the product has gone to market, but before!

■ It is the industrial designer's role to become a ready and reliable tool for management's use to provide these answers; to make recommendations that will reduce these risks to a minimum. Because of his sepcialized training and experience, because he is constantly observing and predicting trends, analyzing demands, and compiling factual information based upon research, he is in a position to provide the kind of objective advice management needs.

■ The area of operation of the industrial designer, although it touches the work of the art director of the advertising agency, differs radically in its basic requirements. The art director, in whatever field he is employed, is concerned primarily with the visual arts.

158

Examples of industrial design: — 1 — Simple useful objects; waste basket and hamper of plastic vulcanized fibre. — 2 — Package design; whiskey decanter. — 3 — Industrial equipment design. — 4 — Interior design; Bigelow-Sanford Carpet Co. office. Work by Donald Deskey.

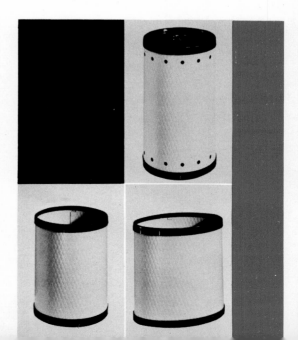

To the industrial designer, however, the design solution is evolved or developed on a basis of carefully integrated research, rather than pure creative effort. This is not to say that the art director is not as aware of the value of marketing research as a means of determining design but, for the industrial designer, research in the fields of marketing, production, distribution and cost give him a much more accurate guide to the ultimate design solution.

Planning and Consumer Research

■ The amount of time and money that can be spent on research in relation to design solutions for products or packages is in direct proportion to their importance in the markets for which they are intended. In comparing the end product of the industrial designer with that of the agency art director, we find a much longer life span. The product itself outlives the advertisement.
■ The industrial designer and the art director have one very important thing in common, nevertheless. They are both very much aware of the value of consumer research and motivation studies as guides in their work. But here again, we find a difference. While the art director, concerned with a campaign of advertising through a variety of media, might plan ahead for several months, or a year or more, the industrial designer, on the other hand, sometimes works for as long as five years on a new design before it is introduced to the market. Design programs frequently stretch into several years. Target dates vary according to product. This can also be true in package design, though redesign in packaging at frequent intervals has now become an accepted merchandising technique.
■ An error on the part of the manufacturer or of the industrial designer in not properly gauging the degree of acceptance by the consumer (or the distributor or the retailer) may be disastrous in terms of sales. What the consumer or the eventual user wants, and how he plans to make use of it, is of more importance than what the designer thinks the product should embody.
■ Thus, the industrial designer fits himself into a planning group whose purpose it is to analyze the product in relation to its competitors, to assess its advantages and disadvantages, and prescribe sales and merchandising possibilities. To this end he and his staff coordinate their efforts with the client's organization and all aim for the same objective. This applies to the development of new products, or to the redesign of existing products to meet new competitive situations, new marketing trends. Whatever the problems, the industrial designer must key his work to consumer demands and client needs.
■ In addition to being a permanent and reliable source of creative thinking of wide experience, the industrial designer offers a vast array of facilities and services that are not readily available elsewhere. Research on new materials, methods and processes; experimental laboratories; shops completely equipped to turn out working models or prototypes of products being designed; marketing and merchandising research and services — these are but a few of the extended functions of the modern industrial design organization.
■ The industrial designer lives largely in the future, but must have an acute awareness of today. He enables his clients to set trends, thereby establishing or maintaining positions of leadership in their respective fields. Though his essence is that of creativity, his long suit is practicality and a business-like approach to the design problems of his clients. Product planning and development demand the kind of catalytic technique, the highly coordinated type of treatment on which the industrial designer has been trained to focus.

2

3

4

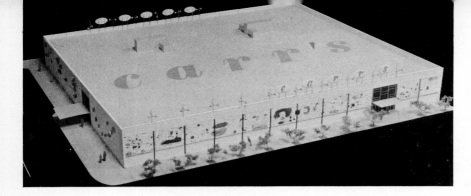

The AD and the architect:—In order to create a complete environment for self-service retail selling for Carr's Department Store, it was necessary to establish controls for lettering, color and display techniques that will support a merchandising philosophy and provide an understandable framework for the otherwise overwhelming quantities of material on sale.—Graphic designer and AD Ladislav Sutnar collaborated with Katz/Waisman/Blumenkranz/Stein/Weber, Architects Associated.—[Some problems involved are shown below]:

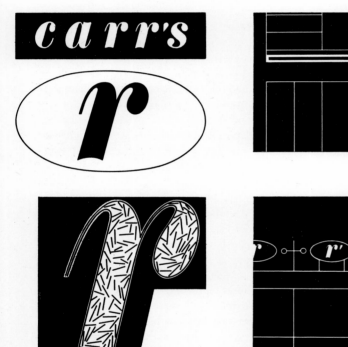

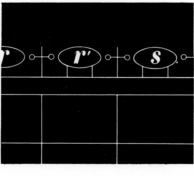

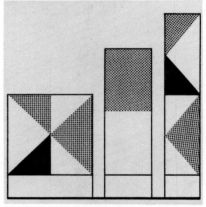

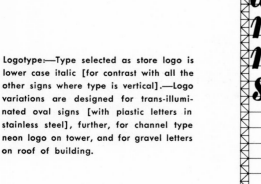

Logotype:—Type selected as store logo is lower case italic [for contrast with all the other signs where type is vertical].—Logo variations are designed for trans-illuminated oval signs [with plastic letters in stainless steel], further, for channel type neon logo on tower, and for gravel letters on roof of building.

Another reason why logotype letters slant is that the eye, aided by the italic, recombines the letters even when they are separated in ovals floating above a roof parapet or when on a thin steel tower, mounted vertically.

Use of color:—Basic fixture panel and wall are black, white and gray; [in order not to compete with the color of merchandise]. —For departmental identification strong primary colors are used. [Each color is consistently repeated, from hanging sign to counter price tag. It is also added to the fixture end panel].

Signs and type faces:—The major areas [all departments] are identified by large triangular hanging signs.—All permanent information, merchandise categories, exit signs, directories have their own sans-serif alphabets. Sign backgrounds use departmental color system.—[Below, type for departmental and other signs].

Symbols as identifiers:—To minimize writing and for an added interest groups of symbols are suspended from the ceiling. Groups are used in juxtaposition.—Instead of listing specific merchandise, these create, like pictographs, an abstract conception of the departments—[Below and right, a few symbol groups].

Cutouts of playing children identify young people's shop; [these are combined in circles and crosses revolving overhead]. Exciting geometric shapes describe the bargain section.—A hammer represents hardware; a tailor's dummy, etc., connotes fashion apparel group.—Lettered signs are more effective when used sparingly.

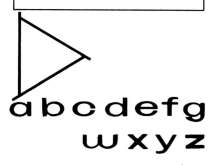

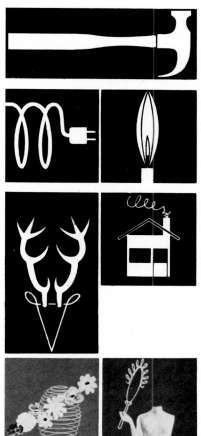

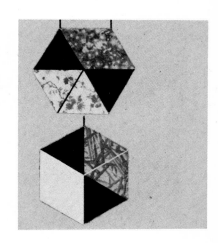

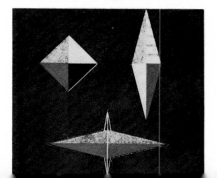

Art Director and Architect... New Avenues of Design Control

Richard G. Stein

Katz/Waisman/Blumenkranz/Stein/Weber—Architects Associated

A new requirement in the design process now makes desirable the inclusion of the art director's skills in the production of certain building forms.— Problems of identification, conveying of information, the discipline of visual and graphic components of buildings face the architect. The skills required for their solution are more than a typographer's and more than a letterer's.—They must recognize scale of building, they must be aware of the range and characteristics of available materials and the visual modifications necessary to work in them. They must consider color as it relates to three dimensional space and to other building materials.—They must acknowledge the relative permanence of buildings and not seek dominance.

—The art director by training and inclination has a foundation for this work. Many building types can benefit from his participation.—Merchandising buildings depend heavily on the graphic dissemination of information, everything from logotype to price tag. —Commercial buildings need coordination of building name and number, directories, stair and exit signs, door signs, color control in public spaces and more. —Schools and hospitals need their identification outside and inside, their governmental insignia, their door numbers and designations and sometimes a Latin exhortation or two.—Housing projects have a major problem of directing visitors through a whole maze of buildings often with not much apparent organizational order, and of disciplining the directories, apartment numbers, exits, incinerators and elevator doors.—Factories have many of the above needs in addition to a visual orderliness related to processing and to the safety of the workers. —Highways and their bordering facilities create the necessity for identification seen at 60 miles an hour. —The new avenue is wide and long.

Typical secondary entrance address panel, a part of a housing project building identification program; — designed by Ladislav Sutnar for "Castle Hill Houses" in the Bronx, New York; planned by Katz/Waisman/Blumenkranz/Stein/Weber Architects Associated, 1956.

A case study of some of the problems that call for a graphic designer's contribution in regard to self-service retail selling, (from store logotype to price tag, etc.) illustrated on the previous two pages. — Designer and AD Ladislav Sutnar.

16

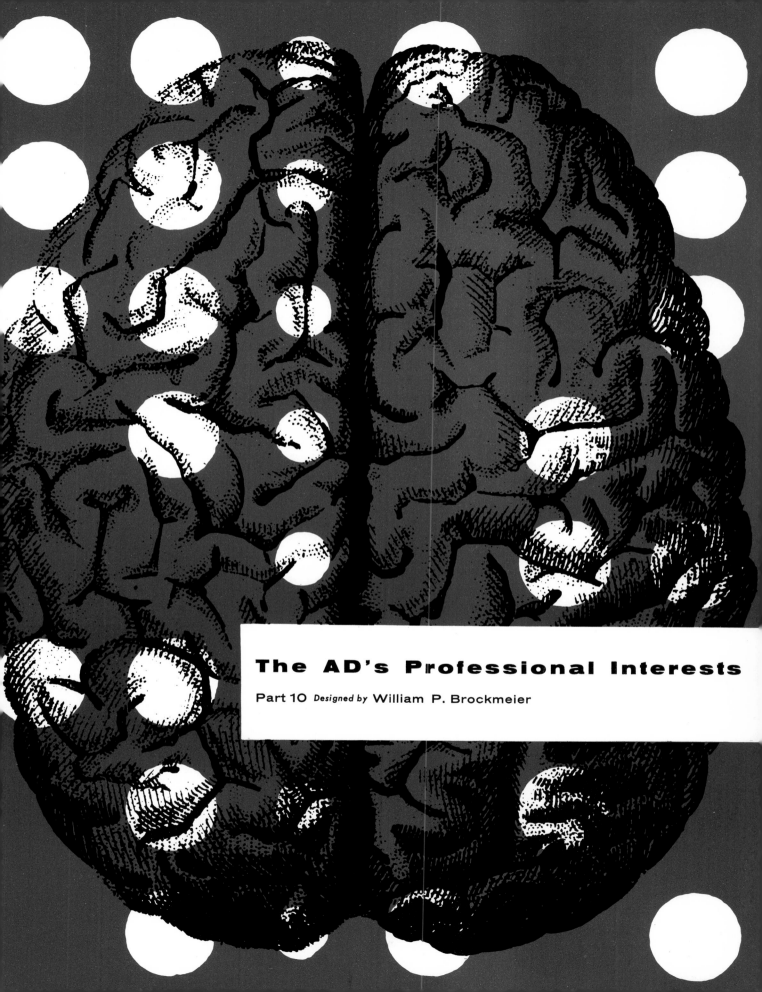

The AD's Professional Interests

Part 10 *Designed by* William P. Brockmeier

Why Research?

by Julian M. Archer

Vice President and Director of Art, Fuller & Smith & Ross, Inc.

AN advertiser asks, why?

Too often the account executive finds himself in the embarrassing position of being unable to justify campaigns to his client, simply because justification lies only in clever layout, copy and art, or vague references to its similarity to other successful campaigns for other advertisers with other sales problems.

Because the conception of advertising is basically visual, the art director is in a large measure responsible for the successful relationship between account executive and client, and should apply his full weight in counseling against advertising without substance.

Research Supports the AD

Consumer research surveys, the newest of advertising's tools, give hope of supporting the art director and giving art and copy once again a reason for their creative existence. While still in its infancy, its understood use and application gives the art director the opportunity to pinpoint and develop new and different visual sales concepts that effectively put to use advertising's newest implement.

The art director's contribution to the effectiveness of an ad is supported by the findings of research. Given the complete research picture the art director, after conferences with copy, media and contact, is in a position to interpret and put into effect specific approaches that are strengthened by his experience, logic and reasoning. Advertising matter with this co-operative background is a sound sales help, bears the mark of professionals, and takes care of the client's embarrassing "Why?"

* Reprinted from *Art in Advertising*.

Misuse Can Postpone Effectiveness

While there is very little danger of research not assuming its proper place in advertising, there is a very real danger that its effective use will be postponed by real or fancied misuse. There are those in advertising who purposely misinterpret findings to promote their own preferences in layout, art and copy. To minimize this danger and to implement and not stultify advertising's end product, research should recognize the advisability of utilizing professional advertising advice in the preparation of interviews and questionnaires, and their proper interpretation by qualified experts in art, copy, contact and media. On the other hand, advertising should recognize its responsibility to research. The future and value of consumer analysis and reaction depend entirely on its careful and intelligent application. Management must watch its use to make sure that research does not become a straight and narrow highway for the unimaginative, but a signpost to help the aggressive and imaginative. Copy, art and contact should exercise terminal responsibility and keep research from becoming sterile by constantly feeding its needs with new and stimulating advertising. Unless such cooperation exists, copy and art will find this potentially useful weapon a dangerous creative handicap and research will find itself researching research and in the process leveling all space advertising to ineffectual mediocrity.

The use of the agency's complete intelligence should be exploited after consumer response has been tabulated and studied. Only then can the client be assured that the answer to his specific sales problem has been tailor-made and the investment of his advertising dollar has been a sound one.

164

What Have We Got To Do With Science?

by Karsten Stapelfeldt

Designer and Illustrator

WHENEVER the talk gets around to the relation between Art and Science there is apt to be a variety of reactions, ranging from plain ennui to starry-eyed volubility or scornful rejection. As for myself, I get a fascinated and creepy sensation as if I were to hunt butterflies in a bog. And as I look at it, both the talk about such relations and the hunting are ancient and respectable sports that have bagged some rather remarkable butterflies. Science has become eloquent and theories of art have multiplied, but the bog has not grown any more solid. Science, moreover, furnishes much of the myth and magic which formerly were associated with art and poetry. Anyone who has a son or young friends interested in electronics or nuclear physics may have seen evidence of this. Art, with a capital "A", meanwhile, has become more tenuous and remote and often finds itself in the role of Cinderella, wtih no fairy prince in sight.

It is not surprising, therefore, that in a book about the profession of art directing there should arise the question: What has science got to do with it? And it isn't as if poor, old science had to be dragged into the discussion by the hair. Science, with a capital "S", jumps in with both feet, looks around with brash eyes and says; here I am! And here we are, the artists and art directors, and what have we got to do with science?

Before I begin, and before the bog gets too deep, let me say this. If there is ever to be such a thing as the Science of Art, this is not the place to discuss its problems. The only question that we can deal with here is: Where and how does the art director come in contact with notions that are a part of our scientific life?

The Role of Research

First and uppermost, there is the field of market research and research into reader response. This area of applied sociology or social psychology has grown tremendously in the past few years and promises to continue growing. While research has for years been an integral part of the advertising profession it is now not only the ad agency which does research. Magazines are engaged in it and, above all, the client hires research.

When I listen to my colleagues, even those interested in research, I feel that its possibilities are still not quite realized by our profession in general. One hears such comments as "It will blow over" or, more thoughtfully, "How can a researcher tell what an ad should look like?" I am not entirely unsympathetic to this question, but in view of the facts it would be good not to whistle in the dark. Let me point out one possibility. More and more independent research organizations are springing up which work with the client, not the ad agency. That some of these organizations are already in a position of being able to dictate advertising policies to the ad agency hired by the client is common knowledge. These research groups are staffed by highly trained specialists. "Well", one might ask, "what has that got to do with it? They still need pictures and layouts, don't they?" All right, but what sort of pictures and layouts? Suppose the researchers find that the illustration which you can buy for $200 will do as well as, and possibly better than, the one which is worth $1,000 or more? Suppose the research organizations hire their own art staffs? These are only some of the questions which come to my mind. Maybe it won't make much difference in the long run, but if this should happen it would certainly mean some readjusting for the art director.

And what about the ad agencies doing their own research? They have been doing it right along. They also can and do hire their very own bright boys and girls who are qualified to do a thorough job. But the time is coming when only a large operation warrants an enterprise with research assistants, electronic computers, and God knows what. We must remember that from a scientific viewpoint the field of social research is still in its infancy. Theories dealing with social behavior are in a state of flux and development. To quote Dr. Lyman Bryson*: "There is no systematic outline of a theory of communications." In this state of affairs, the specialized research group can bring an energy and authority into its work for which most agencies or magazines are not equipped. The social scientists, by and large, have not yet availed themselves of the tremendous laboratory which the field of mass communication is offering, but this is bound to change. We can expect that research into reader and consumer response will eventually concern itself not only with verbal communication but also with its visual aspect.

What does this mean to the art director? Rarely can he be more than an amateur in the field of the social sciences. But that is already a great deal. What is needed is a spirit of curiosity to find out why people behave as they do. And it isn't so bad. Fortunately for us, the social scientists of our day are prolific and often very readable writers, and the meaning of such things as motivation research is really not so difficult to find. Since motivation research is the slogan of the day I ought to devote a few words to it.

Some Aspects of Research

In dealing with the functioning of communication the evaluation of consumer or reader response is the only plausible approach. Copy testing has been and still is the most widely used instrument for evaluating this response. Its methods have grown with modern advertising techniques and most of us are somewhat familiar with them. These methods are designed for practical use in procedure and cost. Their findings employ statistical analysis along quantitative lines.

Experience has shown, however, that this is not enough and that quantitative analysis may actually be misleading. But it must not be forgotten that this approach is still basic and useful. The analysis of reader response now includes a consideration of the area of appeal. This is the only area where the social sciences can find an application at the present time. In other words, when we find that a product cannot have the same appeal to each and every person reading an ad we must find the particular group of readers to whom it appeals most, and especially *why* it does so. It is at this point that the methods of psychology become useful. The motivations of the reader become the subject of study. And it is one of the accepted notions in research today that what the reader says explicitly about his motivations is only partly representative of his real motivations. It is necessary to emphasize this, because there still lingers in the minds of some people

* See Mr. Stapelfeldt's bibliography (page 170).

connected with our profession the idea that there is something dubious about looking for hidden motivations. Research can tell us what people are, what they do, why they do it. It can also tell us—and this is often more important—what and why not. There isn't much else that research can do. The next step is up to the artist and the writer.

Does Research Mean Restriction of Creativity?

Restrictions are of various nature, and the first step in their consideration is to divide them into those which are indubitably valid and those which may change with time and place. For instance, an ad appeal which was potent at the end of the last war may have considerably less force at a time of free consumer spending and greater availability of goods. A campaign which observes necessary restrictions in England or Canada may not need these restrictions in the United States and vice versa. Now, the evaluation of the factors of time or of culture is best made by people trained in the objective study of human motivations. Intuition, no matter how perceptive or experienced, must remain suspect as a general mode of procedure. A viewpoint which neither violates the dictates of common sense nor ignores the potential fallacies of individual judgment would seem the only adequate one in the business of mass communication.

Actually, it is unlikely that scientific research will add to the long list of restrictions which beset the creative mind in our profession. Indeed, it is quite possible that an objective study and revaluation of these restrictions may tend to modify many of them. When motivation is explored not as a given absolute but within its setting of time and environment, the result may well be that the limitations which are set upon originality and inventiveness become more flexible.

The IBM Magnetic Drum Data Processing Machine

67

Points of Friction

Let us throw a light from still another angle. We deal with the problems of everyday existence by means of common sense and rationality. The work of getting together an ad, a magazine or a program is finally accomplished through these acknowledged ingredients of everyday behavior. We may ignore the astonishing deviations from the standard of common sense of which everyone working in the field of mass communications can cite examples. We may ignore them, because they belong either to the nervous agony of production among high-strung individuals or they are part of a ritual, a façade. The final result must largely be the result of common sense and of applied techniques, and the interpersonal communication during this process must of necessity be on the verbal level.

But this verbal level and the ideas associated with it become unreliable when applied to the study of response in mass communication. Human motivation is by and large neither verbal nor rational. This is not something new which may have been invented by Dr. Freud, but a problem with which man has concerned himself since ancient times. The historical analyses of human motivations have wrestled with this problem. And though there have been great makers of philosophical systems which emphasize man's rationality, these systems emphasize to us today only the fact that the interpretation of man's nature has tried many paths, most of which could be found to be inadequate only after they had been tried.

We may say that while we function on the common-sense, verbal level we are aware that the real motivation underlying our actions remains irrational. Now, for those who must function and be productive, the upper, verbal level is necessary (with the important modification of which I shall speak later). To reach the lower level of motivational interpretation is something for which most non-scientists are not trained. In general, the foremost danger which faces the amateur in search of hidden motivations is that of false value connotations. The values of the unconscious are not those of the common-sense, social communication. The trained social scientist cannot perhaps be completely objective, but he has learned to deal with such factors. His contribution must therefore be regarded not as a necessary evil but as a positive step forward.

Creativity and Mass Communication

There is, however, one modification of the common-sense, everyday routine which is of some interest. We do communicate on a verbal level and function with the illusion of rationality. But when we sit down to write a piece of copy, or when we undertake to make a design, our own unconscious motivations are apt to come into action. The brilliant piece of copy or the original design are often not the result of the conference room or the bull session. Nor are they the result of craftsmanship alone. Experience plays a role, but not necessarily. And experience, too, consists largely of an unconscious store of aptitudes.

What this ultimately leads to is the question: What is talent? Why is it good? The maker of a fine sonnet or of an unusually sensitive painting has little place in mass communication, as we know. But the functioning of creative talent in mass communication is in itself a fertile field of study for the psychologist, and one with which little has as yet been done. Is the talented individual creative because his unconscious functions freely in consonance with that of the greater number of his fellow men? If this is the Era of the Common Man, what is it to be original? The problem of standards in mass culture, influenced by mass communication media, is a very interesting one. Some excellent, practical work is being done in this field by magazines, and it is to be hoped that eventually there will come out of this work enough material to furnish guide lines toward possible answers.

It seems like a trite observation that we live in age of transition. For what age has not made this claim, and sometimes made it eloquently. To anyone who remembers, if ever so dimly, the spirit and the "feel" of the years before the first world war our time presents an entirely new universe. To some it may seem that the influence of science has risen and that of art has declined. But the wide dissemination of pictorial material, which is something unequalled in any previous time in history, makes a revaluation of the role of art necessary.

Minor Points of Contact With Science

There are two areas in which some art directors will have contact with science. One is in the field of science fiction illustration. I don't think that any particular problems are found here, as this is mainly a question of competent illustration of subject matter whose scientific content may be of a very tenuous character.

The other field presents more of a challenge: The art directing of illustrations for teaching purposes and for the popularization of scientific material. The quality of art used in text books and science magazines is definitely rising. One need only to look at a copy of *Scientific American* to see the possibilities. It is a small field compared to that of magazine and ad illustration, but it demands a thorough understanding of visual communication, a lively interest in the subject matter, and at times a measure of idealism to offset the lower financial reward.

Psychology and Art

So far we have discussed the points where the art director is apt to come in contact with scientific problems. Some of us may be interested to find out where modern psychology has concerned itself with problems of art and of the artist. A sketchy minimum is all that is possible within the framework of this essay, and I shall confine myself to the brief indication of two trends, psychoanalysis and gestalt psychology.

Psychoanalysis

To Sigmund Freud belongs the credit of having initiated a completely new approach to the scientific investigation of the human psyche. The orthodox Freudian approach interpreted artistic creativity as the sublimation of repressed sexual desires and of the Oedipus complex. The limitations of this approach, due to its mechanistic character, have been recognized by now, and remarkable work has been done on the problem of the nature of the creative personality and on the possible laws of aesthetic intuition. The relationship of the artist to art and of both to the culture in which they live are admirably discussed by Otto Rank.

The criticism that has been raised by adherents of strictly scientific method in regard to the psychoanalytic approach is this: that its interpretation of artistic symbolism is not open to proof. I must leave it to the interested reader to investigate for himself the pros and cons of this question.

Gestalt

A knowledge of some ideas of gestalt psychology may be of more immediate interest to the artist and to the art director. It can be applied to an understanding of the dynamic elements in layout and design.

Gestalt can be translated as: shape, form or figure as a sum total of characteristic qualities. The gestalt theory is mainly a theory of perception. Its core is the idea, by no means new, that the whole of a phenomenon is greater than the sum total of its parts. It is a theory that has applied itself to the processes of memory, learning, instinct, intelligence, and of values. It has been applied to logic and has found counterparts in the physical world, where gestalt means a self-regulating entity whose parts are determined in accordance with the whole (such as static electric currents).

For the art director it is of interest that the foundations of our present knowledge of visual perception have been laid by the work of the gestalt theorists.

69

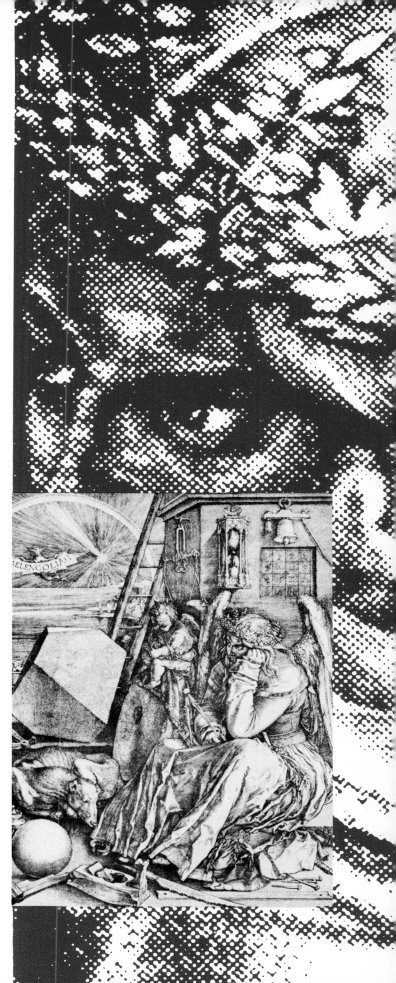

Die Melancholie
by Albrecht Dürer

Their findings seem to be made to order for the artist. Arnheim's *Art and Visual Perception* can be recommended as the most complete statement of the gestaltist's approach. Moreover, this book contains an excellent bibliography on art, vision and the psychological questions concerned with them. In the words of Arnheim, gestalt has something of an artistic look at reality, and vision is not a mechanical recording of sensory elements but ". . . a truly creative grasp of reality— imaginative, inventive, shrewd, and beautiful . . . the mind always functions as a whole. All perceiving is also thinking, all reasoning is also intuition, all observation is also invention."

The Social Sciences and Art

The problem of the relation between the art director's work and the social sciences is not a pressing one in everyday experience. Most of us will continue to work successfully without any concern for it. When I think of the host of gifted and competent workers in our profession I feel little inclination to play Cassandra and to prophesy radical changes. By and large, art directors do not suffer either from serious smugness nor from a hidden sense of impending doom, and that is all to the good. As painfully condensed as the preceding look at science's role is—and a whole book would hardly do it justice—it is meant to point out that there are windows open on what goes on outside. An intelligent person can hardly fail to ask himself questions of why? and how?, no matter how acceptable his work has become. Science can make some sense of this why and how.

Some sense, of a different nature, can be made of these questions if we remember that art, too, has answers which satisfy not only the artist but those who look at his work. Science, or it least the science we can see through our windows, is pragmatic. It is pragmatic on purpose and not only by necessity. The true artist is pragmatic by necessity and not always on purpose. This difference of perspective is important to remember. It seems that today the traditional idealism of the artist is confined to those who painfully seek new paths or to those who have consciously absented themselves from the arena of everyday combat with necessity. The answer to this is that Art for Use can strike a high level of performance, as shown in history and in our day.

My own opinion is that the art director or anyone who works in the visual aspect of mass communications might keep two things in mind, no matter how cut and dried his problems become between nine to five.

One: It is the ideal beyond necessity, beyond the utilitarian aspect, which produces the performance above the average.

The other: America is becoming more and more art conscious. The plutocratic museum of the Nineteenth Century has made way for the democratic museum of the Twentieth. The level of art teaching in our schools is constantly increasing. Thousands of people paint for fun who would, in another day, have regarded such an occupation as something slightly sissy. Millions see reproductions in our magazines which a generation ago would have been the delight of the connoisseur. The last tinge of aesthetic snobbery may yet linger for a while, but the groundswell of genuine interest is there. If leisure time and its frank acceptance by our culture increase at the present rate, there is no telling what our artistic climate will be a generation from now.

This, too, will influence the artist is mass communication, perhaps more so than the ideas of social science. At least I hope so. Also, I hope that the reader who is interested in the questions of science vs. art will avail himself of the special literature on the subject. The following, brief bibliography may serve as an introduction to such reading.

Science does not have all the answers. But answers can come only after the problems have been clarified. It is conceivable that the profession of art directing may realize the share it can have in this process.

BIBLIOGRAPHY

Arnheim, Rudolph—Art and Visual Perception, A Psychology of the Creative Eye. University of California Press, 1954.

Bryson, Lyman (editor)—The Communication of Ideas. Harper & Brothers, 1948.

Focht, Mildred—What is Gestalt Theory? (Columbia University Ph.D. Thesis), New York, 1935.

Freud, Sigmund, The Basic Writing of—Translated by Dr. A. A. Brill. Modern Library, 1938.

Mead, Margaret—Male and Female, A Study of the Sexes in a Changing World. Wm. Morrow, 1949.

Mises, Richard von—Positivism, A Study in Human Understanding. Harvard University Press, 1951.

Panofsky, Erwin—Meaning in the Visual Arts. Doubleday Anchor Book No. A 59, 1955.

Rank, Otto—Art and Artist, Creative Urge and Personality Development. Tudor, 1932.

Richards, I. A., with C. K. Ogden and James Wood—The Foundations of Aesthetics. Lear, 1925.

Riesman, David, with Nathan Glazer and Reuel Denny—The Lonely Crowd, A Study of the Changing American Character. Doubleday Anchor, 1954.

Smith, George Horseley—Motivation Research in Advertising and Marketing. McGraw-Hill, 1954.

Wickiser, Ralph L.—Fine Arts. Revue of Educational Research, 1952, 22, pp. 141-160.

The Creative Vs. The Scientific Approach

by Eugene Heiffel

Consulting Art Director

HONESTLY, now, when you read the heading with that little "versus" in it, didn't you subconsciously think of a fight? We know we did when we first saw it. Well, we were all wrong. A mental wrestling match is more like it.

What is meant by "creative"? This is a book about professional art directing. Naturally, then, when we talk about creativeness we mean as it relates to the art director. Others in the agency who contribute to creative activities will understand that no exclusion is intended. And in the same spirit, we hope we are not putting the art director on the defensive.

If any one thing makes the art director's position uncertain, it's that word "art." It can be so confining in some cases, so boundless in others. Come to think of it, many terms used in the advertising business are like Chinese writing. Chinese writing, as you know, is based on graphic symbols. These symbols stand for whole words. Likewise, the way we use the word "creative" in our business, it might be a symbol for a whole category of words—words like idea, imagination, originality, invention, freshness, perception, conception, projection and some others that you can think of. And all of these words are associated with "creative" but have different meanings for the people in the art, copy, media, sales, marketing and research departments.

Idea Creativeness

To avoid having this discussion get too far afield, we'll channel our thoughts mainly toward *idea creativeness*. We'll put the emphasis on the visual side.

To get together on it, suppose we agree the word "creative," when applied to advertising, means the power to generate ideas that penetrate the mind and produce sales. And since we are talking about art directors and creativity, let's get this straight—the difference between the fine arts creative person and the creative art director is just this: the fine arts guy doesn't have to think of the man in the street; the art director can't forget him!*

Haven't you noticed how often a lack of creative talent is expressed by emulation? How frequently emulation is commonly confused with creation? Especially, how much advertising is subject to emulation? The best and the worst advertising is on view to all. The choice is a matter of taste and judgment. Advertisements aren't meant to be esoteric. To see the passing parade, just turn the pages of your newspaper or maga-

* Refer to Henry M. Havemeyer's "Chart", page 44, and to Nathaniel Pousette-Dart on "Creative Imagination"—Ed.

71

zine. Neophytes engaged in producing advertisements are seldom concerned about the end purpose of the ads they emulate. The very fact that the advertisement was acceptable to an experienced advertiser makes the ad an idea source (in the eyes of the neophyte) that's safe for emulation. The tremendous volume of advertising produced without benefit of talent, intuition, taste, imagination and conception is thereby increased. The lack of creative talent is the big reason for trite, stereotyped, uninspired, wasteful advertising. Neither standardization nor formulas can successfully substitute for great creative ability. The lack of it results in methods that standardize a low order of originality and conception. But more about that later.

The Creative Art Director

Before we become involved with subsequent ideas, let's explore the phenomenon of the art director. Let's see how the tiny spark of creative instinct can grow to be a brilliant flame of visual salesmanship. Sounds a little on the conceited side, doesn't it? We might have said "genius"—another of those words with so many meanings in the advertising jargon. But genius belongs in the profession of art directing, at least according to opinions of these familiar greats: *Michelangelo:* "If people knew how hard I work to get my mastery, it wouldn't seem too wonderful after all." *Carlyle:* "Genius is an infinite capacity for taking pains." *Alexander Hamilton:* "All the genius I have is merely the fruit of labor." *Paderewski:* "Before I was a genius, I was a drudge."

How often do we hear: "Gee, I wish I had your talent for drawing. You do it so easily. What a lucky guy to be so gifted." A compliment in a way; an insult in another; a misapprehension to be sure. Enough to make you good and sore when someone says your talent was a gift.

The tools of creation are knowledge, imagination, experience and skill. They aren't gifts that are found under the Christmas tree. They are the rewards of hard labor. How are these tools acquired? Listen to this: All children are born with a talent for drawing whether they grow to become merchants, copywriters, account men, salesmen, bankers, editors, lawyers or poets! But children lose interest in drawing when they become inhibited by formal instruction in draftsmanship. They taper off and it isn't long before the walls are redecorated and restored to their pristine beauty. And the drawing phase of the child passes on to the doodles of the years of maturity. But not so with the embryo art director. Moved by the genes of his species, he keeps right on drawing.

There comes the day when we see our embryo art director sitting in the corner of an advertising agency's art department, another step in his evolution. He's bewildered, but he feels at home. He doesn't realize it, but he's fated to change from the introvert we knew in art school to the extrovert he must become to be a successful art director. The lamb must face the reality of the rough world of competition.

Our art student must now become a student of advertising—a simple statement, but what a variety of experience it includes and how much time is involved! Did you know it takes years and years of apprenticeship to learn the bare essentials of art directing? Many people think of art directing as principally layout and art buying. If you go into a doctor's office, you'll see prominently displayed a very authoritative-looking diploma and a license. No such proof of academic experience is provided the art director. There's no degree indicating the years spent by the art director in acquiring his knowledge of the anatomy of advertising, or the techniques of reproduction, or the requirements of the various printing processes, or the things to know about typography, photography, movies, slides, television, or many other subjects.

How did our embryo art director acquire that knowledge? The only way—the hard way. By taking special courses, usually nights and week-ends. By actual experience in print shops, at the typographer's, visits to the engraving plant, the gravure presses, the litho houses, the electrotype foundry, the photographers, the poster plants, the movie-makers, the broadcasting and the TV studios. Hours and hours, days and nights, and years and years devoted to learning about the production potentials and the problems of using the tools of the graphic arts, related to advertising. But this is routine; all art directors must follow this road to become capable enough to project visually the ideas of others.

Why should an art director go further? Well, just for one reason. He can't stop there! Remember, we're talking about the born art director. The years spent in art schools, and the time devoted to the technicalities of the graphic arts are requisite parts of the art of visual projection. They are necessary to the "how" of advertisements. The creative art director is mostly concerned with the "what" of advertisements. It's the "what" of advertising that contains the precious so-called creative ingredient expressed in pictures and words—words that help the picture project the idea, pictures that support the words. Pictures minus words rarely completely project the idea; words minus pictures seldom get read.

Your creative art director learns about this in a hurry. What does he do? Being born creative, he naturally acquires the tools for word-smithing to facilitate the projection of his ideas. He doesn't feel obliged to limit himself to the graphic just because of that little word "art." He applies himself to learning to use words. He writes to facilitate what he draws and he's beginning to realize advertising isn't creative in the sense that the fine arts are. He studies the so-called scientific side of advertising.

Research and the Picture Era

The first statistical experience he has is with market research. Not inclined that way naturally, he's unduly respectful of the mathematics involved. He relaxes when he discovers the arithmetic tells him quite dispassionately, the where and the who he's advertising to. He studies the analysis of the reports and finds them more interesting and less formidable.

Now, picture a whole group of art directors listening to a research authority talk about readership analysis. They are all experienced, well-placed art directors with important agencies. In this case, a series of talks is being given under the auspices of the Research Committee of the Art Directors Club. On the walls of the lecture room a showing of advertising layouts by the students of a prominent art school is on exhibition. The ads are well done. However, the art directors pass them by. Know why? They learned long, long ago that *layout is incidental to the basic idea.* The day when the layout alone claimed their attention belongs to their apprenticeship. The attractive arrangement of the elements of the ad in their proper sequence is routine now. It's the *context* of the advertisement that counts—the what, not the how. They're interested in reader-reaction to color versus black-and-white, bleed, covers, illustration, size and weight. They want to hear how readership reports can help them create more effective advertisements. They know their job is bigger than just making layouts and buying art. They are the new breed of AD that's the natural manifestation of the *Picture Era.*

Think of a typical family in the evening—your own, for example. Your wife is out with her mother enjoying the movies. You're looking at television. Junior's eyes are fastened on a comic book. Your daughter is goggle-eyed over the Ektachrome showing of a bridal wardrobe in a magazine. Grandpa's specs are beamed on the photos in a news weekly. *Pictures, pictures, pictures,* everywhere. How much time do you have for reading? Especially the advertisements? If you weren't professionally interested in advertising, would you be inclined

73

a.

b.

c.

A. 1940   B. 1929   C. 1952

to read long copy? You know you wouldn't and neither would many others. That's why businessmen, and you and anybody else trying to communicate a message to the public wants to know: what will get through? We all sense the terrific competition and naturally wonder if anybody's listening. We know they're looking, but are they doing more? Are they reading? We hire psychologists to try to find out what they will read. We dispatch interviewers to ask the so-called reading public what they read and remember. There is a constant checking and testing going on to try to chart a dependable course worthy of the tremendous advertising budgets involved. Unfortunately, the response is from the head instead of the heart. Psychology is a science that treats of the mind. Advertisers have an inordinate respect for the mass mind. We find, however, advertising ideas that reach the heart and stir the emotions will get results even when they don't meet all the specifications developed by questionnaires.

Trade Papers and Annual Reports

Take a good look at trade paper advertising; certainly this medium has selective readership. Notice what's happening there. It's the place where surely long copy should be. Reason why, informative, diagrammed and factual copy belongs in the trade press! What's going on? The battle for the eye has to reason with the *Picture Era* here also. The reader of the trade journal is supposed to be avidly interested in the information the book makes available to him. His job requires it. But are the ads' long copy read the way they used to be? Notice the resemblance to general advertising these days? Why is this? Abundance of ads; limited time.

Remember the cold impersonal dignity the annual report used to have? Look at it now—illustrated, interesting, warm, and human, besides including the facts and figures legally required. And the brochure that gives all the product details it can with pictures? Look at all the exploded views, transvisions, cross-sections, and all the modern techniques of visual aids. The communciation of ideas by way of consumer media is predominately pictorial because of the simple, obvious, practical reason that it is a part of the *Picture Era*. It isn't just style; it isn't just emulation. It's here! The changing world brought it and the genius of the creative ad man has applied it to advertising. To say that pictures are bigger and copy is shorter these days is superficial over-simplification. It's more than a whim or a fashion. It's a step forward in the art of communication that we call advertising. That's why more comprehensive, detailed, objective copy is being reserved for more specific media. Think back over the years.

Better still, look at the visual corroboration as it's paraded before your very eye in the successive *Art Directors Annuals*. See for yourself how true this is. Notice how the exciting changes in advertising reflect the demands of a changing world. And these changes are skillfully and consciously integrated to stay within the limits of mass familiarity. No sincere creative art director strives for a degree of originality that excludes the man in the street. He keeps his advertising fresh by the originality of his adaptation of the familiar experience. To go beyond the limits of the familiar is to find ourselves alone with our originality. So research is given the job of helping to determine the limitations.

Readership Studies

Almost everyone will agree that advertising is an intrusion on the public's time and attention. Just how much that intrusion is resented or welcomed depends on many factors. The reactions to these factors by the people are as fickle as only human nature can be. Anything that can make the public's reactions more or less predictable is an invaluable guide welcomed by all concerned with advertising.

The barrage of advertising is so constantly increasing that advertisers suspect the consumer of donning the armor of indifference. So they look to scientific research to find the weakness in that armor. They seek surer points of penetration for their advertising ideas. Recently, a world-renowned publication, not carrying advertising, asked its subscribers if they would rather have the subscription price raised or remain the same due to the inclusion of advertising. They voted overwhelmingly in favor of advertising. People like advertising when it's *interesting*. They resent being poked in the ribs by so-called hard-hitting advertising. Two great road blocks in the way of originality and freshness are regimentation and emulation. It's fine to put a little catsup on some foods once in a while, but catsup on all your food all the time! Ugh!

Ask a creative art director what he thinks of readership studies and you'll discover he considers them a valuable ally. He knows that figures have meaning to the businessman, and the businessman respects his judgment—when it's supported by statistics. The support of scientific research has often helped put a new sales idea across to an over-cautious advertiser; and likewise when an idea is blamed for the ineffectiveness of a campaign, research is the creative man's friend by disclosing the real weakness is price, or distribution, or even the product itself. Just as the word "creative" has a significance peculiar to the advertising vocabulary, the connotation of "scientific" is also rather freely applied. Like the Chinese symbols we spoke of earlier, these words have many meanings for advertising that aren't quite like the dictionary definitions. We know what they mean and use them most conveniently.

Advertising, consciously or otherwise, is continually adapting its creative ideas from the field of fine arts. These adaptations are useful, however, only when the general public understands them. Knowing when they safely service the end-purpose of all advertising—the stimulation of sales—is a matter of judgment and investigation. Constant testing, using many techniques of inquiry, is employed to guard against getting too far ahead of the public's experience. Advertising cannot assume the prerogative of improving the public's cultural progress. The purpose of advertising is to make sales. Any diversion from that aim unfairly places the advertiser's investment in jeopardy. Better let the products advertised accelerate the progress of culture. Captains of industry willingly and generously contribute to civic and cultural welfare organizations devoted to that purpose. Naturally they suspect that art-trained creative people in advertising are inclined to promote their products and the culture of the consumer simultaneously. That's one reason they favor testing devices that are objective.

Testing Devices

Ever read a speech into a recorder? The playback might lack spark, but you don't worry too much. You know when you're giving your talk to the audience their reactions will guide you. You'll feel the kind of impression you're making. If the audience doesn't seem to be getting your meaning, you take steps to make the point clear right then and there. You sense when your ideas are getting across. You feel the *rapport*; if you don't, you get to work on it fast or you suffer the agony of doubt. You revise your script, call on your intuition, charm, talent, personality, sense of humor and experience—everything you've got—and you finally win your audience! You make your point; you successfully communicate and sell your idea. Advertising is also the communication of ideas. To find out what the consumer will think about these ideas, copy tests are made. To learn the size of the audience, market studies are made. To find out how to reach them, media studies are made.

However, advertising can't do what you did when you made your speech. Sure, you knew the kind of people you'd be talking to, how many and where the meeting would take place. Advertising has that information too. But you talked directly to your audience. Advertisers must find out by various testing devices how the audience will react to safeguard their invest-

a.

b.

A. 1921   B. 1926   C. 1948

c.

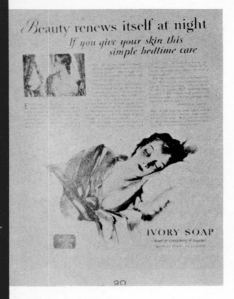

a.

b.

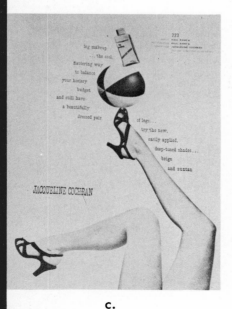

c.

ment. So, segments of the audience are interviewed. The results of those tests tell how well the audience understood the message, what the potential response would be, and if the ad would pay off. Naturally this pre-testing seems a logical precaution.

More probing and less guessing is all to the good. Business likes to work that way, with facts. And no business-like art director would deny the benefits of sound pre-testing or even post-testing aids. But facts in relation to *human emotions* refuse to resolve into a reliable formula. There's the rub!

Readership figures, listening habits and sales data can appear to be irrefutable as mass information, but can also lead to wrong numbers in the person-to-person communication that advertising really is.

Mass Research

A while ago we were talking about making a speech. Isn't this true? You face your audience and focus your attention on one person in that whole group of people? Good speakers pick out just the kind of friendly face that they like, for obvious reasons. In addressing yourself to a congenial person, your ideas travel a direct line of communication. You feel inspired, relaxed, friendly, and confident. You know by focusing your attention and power of conviction on one, you're likely to reach with equal directness the entire audience. Now let's see how mass research works. The audience is looked over, then noted as individually as the technique used permits, and the sum of these notations is subjected to statistical analysis. The result is a choice that represents the measured typical person in that audience. Unfortunately for you, statistics say he's the man you must direct your message to, even if he's not the man to inspire you with confidence! You don't feel relaxed; you're cold; you're dull; you're not congenial; you're a flop to the statistically chosen individual and to the whole audience.

The show is a flop! You couldn't put yourself across. You were stymied by that guy you had to keep your eye on. You had the brake on. You lacked that human touch because the computor was your coach. Your talent and your personality bowed to the galvanometer, or the survey, or the poll in the readership study, or the eye camera, or the motivation interview, or the phychological depth report and other measuring devices for computing what goes on in the human mind.

Creative Idea Communication

Intellectual curiosity is a prerequisite for anyone doing creative work, and the creative art director has his full share. He welcomes light on any shadowy sub-

Photographs/H. M. Mason Jr.

ject. If surveys, polls and readership studies can be useful, he'll be grateful for their help. He's aware that the more tools he knows how to use, the broader his scope of imagination and the greater his creative skill in visual selling. But when science routs his intuition and regiments his creative activities, advertising doesn't get its money's worth. Production-line methods are fine for the production of standardized products and, likewise, the production-line approach to advertising will produce a standardized type of advertising. What an opportunity to be outstanding is thereby made available to the advertiser who cuts loose with a fresh creative approach!

Experienced advertisers agree that advertising is more art than science. And the art, we're convinced, is one of idea communication. Creativeness is essential to the production of ideas. Creative ideas are the product of talent, experience and knowledge. The object of science is to *substantiate that knowledge or disprove it.* No sincere creative worker can refuse to acknowledge a valid ally. When science can be added constructively to his kit of creative tools, the creative art director receives it with enthusiasm.

The restless spirit of creative admen makes them impatient. Their articulation voices their dissatisfaction over anything that gets in their way toward more effective visual salesmanship. Despite the fears and figures of the impatient, advertising is improving creatively. The tremendous increase recently in advertising volume makes it difficult to see immediately the changes that are for the better. Take a look at the parade of positive progress in the direction of art. Some reproductions appear here. See the whole show in the library of *Art Directors Annuals.* Then stop and think about this *Picture Era* we're living in. Does science implement it? It certainly does. Does science fight creativeness? Only when you let the vs. run away with your imagination.

EDITORIAL NOTE

There is, of course, no substitute for the creative mind in producing great visual concepts.

Creativeness that searches out the strongest appeal and presents it unencumbered by superficial devices, cannot be endangered by the intelligent use of modern research.

Such creativeness by its directness, integration with copy, and good taste will leave a lasting and productive impact on the reader.

Research today not only studies immediate reactions, but also determines the impact a few days after the ad appeared.

Through intense market studies and depth interviews with actual prospects the motivation factors for buying are predetermined.

The creative team of copy and art can then direct their arrows much closer to the bull's-eye.

Today many art directors make use of the valuable assistance of research and find little conflict with creative thinking.

Walter Grotz

a.

b.

c.

A. 1936   B. 1932   C. 1953

The Media Battle of the Century

by William Strosahl

Creative Director, Wm. Esty Company, Inc.

THE future of advertising art directors and artists will be controlled by the selection of media by the agencies and clients. How much of the art director's work will be concerned with magazine and newspaper ads and how many hours will be spent planning TV ads (commercials) depends entirely on the media structure. Here are a few cogent facts.

The space buying (TV or print) of the next 10 years will be controlled by the very same yardstick as in the past 50 years. Stated simply, the determining factors are: what medium for my product advertising creates the biggest audience at the lowest cost per thousand consumers and *produces the most effective sales results?*

TV is, and will continue to be, a major media investment when you consider that from 30-50% of national advertisers' budgets are allocated to TV. Of all national advertisers, 95% are TV prospects . . . and 90% of these have been on television either in programming or through spot commercials. The majority is still using TV, consistently or periodically.

This is a lot of television, you'll agree, when you consider that about 500 commercials arrive in the living room *per week*. Multiply that by 40 million living rooms, or the number of sets in operation in 1955-56,

and you'll see that TV has an impact that agency, client or art director cannot ignore . . . especially when research reveals that approximately four hours per day, per house, is spent in front of the glass screen.

To these consumers, television is real and alive—person-to-person selling is easier because they are more susceptible. Dad comes home from a hard day's work, flops in a chair—Mom finishes the dishes and sits in

17

the other chair and they both say "Entertain me". They don't even have to turn a page. Commercial influence is at its peak.

Adjustments in Media Planning

Now, let's not get carried away with the magic of television. The great cost of these programs, the availability of good time franchises, the budget limitations of other than top spenders, all are contributing to an adjustment in media planning for the future.

Multiple sponsorship is already an accepted and workable plan. Hour long programs with five or six different products, half-hours with alternate sponsors have opened up greater coverage for big advertisers and have permitted smaller sponsors to afford TV. In addition, many advertisers are continuing to use print to its fullest advantage. This linking of TV and print and billboard advertising is the healthiest thing that could happen to an art director.

The Chicago Tribune, in a recent attack on TV commercials, implied that the sponsors were not getting a fair break for their money. Through a series of phone interviews "with people at the time they were actually viewing programs", the *Tribune* findings alleged "more than half the audience was unable to identify the sponsor of the program."

It happens on magazine and newspaper ads too. However, the battle of the media can only result in one thing—better advertising for all media. Even now, print ads are better than 20 years ago . . . better looking, simpler and more appetizing. In a way, television is responsible for a greater acceptance of good photography. Both consumer and client are becoming more picture-minded—the photo or illustration in print ads is gaining more importance, spacewise, in each ad, and the illustration is working harder to stop the reader and strengthen the message of the copywriter. Today's art director is not content just to make a layout. The headline and picture must perform the same service in print as the voice and picture do in TV. This is a tougher chore but a real challenge to artist and AD.

Many of us remember when radio first became a competent selling medium . . . the days when print campaign budgets were cut in half to allow sponsors to get the benefits of the then new and effective medium of radio. Radio was the fair-haired boy—the panacea of sales doldrums. Then came years of appraising the various media until a happy balance was made. The best medium or combination (magazine, newspaper and radio) was determined for each product and everybody was happy. Television is still being appraised— its effectiveness for each product is under close scrutiny by our clients and, while it outshines any other

179

1
One little
two little
three little
hum hum

2
Four little
five little
six little
hum hum

3
Seven little
eight little
nine little
hum hum

4
Ten little
hum hum hum

5
SOUND:
WHISTLES TUNE

6
SNIP

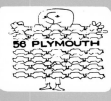
7
31 big beautiful body styles in the '56 Plymouth

8
Come in
and browse

medium for face-to-face selling, it will eventually take its rightful place in advertising appropriations.

The Color TV Potential

How soon this will be depends on the electronic boys. Now they have color TV. Every day color is nearer and the potential is staggering. Video tape is rapidly being perfected and who knows—next step, three dimension?

Color TV at an estimated 25% increase in cost over black-and-white will open new fields beyond belief in the next 10 years. Established artists will have to adapt their skills to the new art and new artisans will develop. From storyboard to set dressing, color TV is more demanding and more detailed than anything the art director has ever attempted. But who is better fitted to handle the problems of this bright, complex story-telling in pictures than the art director?*

Color sense, taste, advertising know-how and the artistry of putting ideas into motion will be the sole responsibility of the art director. These are not learned in a day and the agency that does not avail itself of these skills is remiss in its responsibility to its clients.

New Vistas Through Video Tape

Video tape, another scientific miracle, will open up new fields for the art director or TV art director. When this is perfected the agency can record a storyboard on tape, with sound, and play it for the client an hour later. TV tape is a magnetic recording, similar to ordinary tape recording, of both *pictures and sound* and in monochrome or *full color*. Experimental equipment, at present, is priced too high for ordinary use and runs to high footage (30,000 feet in a half-hour show). However, engineers predict simplification, and soon. The tape can be erased and reused. Imagine shooting a commercial at 10 o'clock in the morning—editing the footage for two hours and putting it on the air at noon. Newspapers will have a hard time competing with that kind of newsiness.

The ten year goal of the nation's advertising forces is a 33% increase in the standard of living. At a recent ANA convention, it was claimed that more effective marketing efforts by American advertisers could raise the average income to $7,000 per year and create new markets for increased production. If this worthwhile goal is reached it will mean greater advertising expenditures, greater employment, more things and more time to enjoy them for all America. The picture looks good.

As to what form the advertising will take — who knows? In the past, TV users had the advantage of novelty, periodical ads had the advantage of long established campaigns. Now the media battle of the century is here. May the best ads win.

18

* See Elwood Whitney's comments, page 28, and those of Paul Smith, page 116, in this connection—Ed.

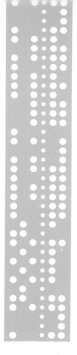

Professional Practice
Under a Code of Ethics

General Chairman, Joint Committee; Secretary-Treasurer, N.S.A.D.

THE Special Committee on Ethics and Relationships with Artists appointed by the Art Directors Club solicits your co-operation and advice in the preparation of a code of ethics and professional practice for the buying and selling of art work. This club consists of art directors of advertising agencies, art services, magazines and other businesses, and free lance illustrators, designers and craftsmen whose work comprehends in part or parallels that of an art director.

"Among the objects of the club is the promotion of the best interests of art, applied art and advertising by collective public participation in art affairs. In furtherance of this object the club believes that the time has come to set up a code of ethics, such as those recognized in architecture, medicine, law and engineering."

Thus, in 1921—within a year of its founding—the Art Directors Club of New York announced the beginning of its formulation of a code to serve as a guide to professional practice in art directing. And in 1920 also, another organization had been formed by a second group with somewhat different yet related interests—the Free-Lance Artists Guild (subsequently shortened to the Artists Guild). It too set up certain standards of practice in its By-Laws which, it was hoped, would aid in effecting better understanding of the problems of buying, selling and representation of the graphic arts.

Even earlier, however—1901, in fact—still another organization had come into being in New York for the original purpose of establishing rights for the artist and illustrator. This was the Society of Illustrators which, too endeavoured to formulate standards of ethics.

These three organizations, in spite of a certain degree of interlocking membership and related interests, continued to work individually toward a common goal. Not until 1945, however, were they to agree on joint action, or workable machinery to achieve practical results. At that time a committee of nine was formed, three members from each of the three organizations, and named The Joint Ethics Committee. Almost immediately this Committee was plunged into problems which, ever since, it has helped to mediate and settle.

One significant achievement was the writing of a Code of Fair Practice—a composite of the previous codes of the three contributing organizations, and conforming in pattern to the code of the American Association of Advertising Agencies. In 1952, the Code was adopted by the membership of the National Society of Art Directors, thus gaining recognition throughout the U.S.A. and Canada.

The operation and scope of The Joint Ethics Committee are outlined in a handsome booklet, reproduced here together with The Code of Fair Practice.

Code

OF FAIR PRACTICE

CODE OF FAIR PRACTICE *as formulated in New York City by the Joint Ethics Committee of the Society of Illustrators, Art Directors Club, Artists Guild, and adopted by the National Society of Art Directors.*

I Introduction

In 1945 a group of artists and art directors in the City of New York, concerned with the growing abuses, misunderstandings, and disregard of uniform standards of conduct in their field, met to consider possibilities for improvement. They reached the conclusion that any effort, to be successful, must start with the most widespread backing, and further that it must be a continuing, not a temporary, activity. On their recommendation three leading New York art organizations together established and financed a committee known as the Joint Ethics Committee. This is published in response to the many requests for information about operations and scope of the Committee.

II Personnel

The Joint Ethics Committee is composed of three members each from the Society of Illustrators, The Art Directors Club and the Artists Guild, appointed by the directing bodies of each of these organizations, but serving jointly in furtherance of the purposes for which the Committee was founded.

Members of the Joint Ethics Committee are selected with great care by their respective organizations. Their selection is based upon their experience in the profession, their proven mature thinking and temperament, and their reputation for impartiality.

III Code of Fair Practice

The Code of Fair Practice, as established by the Joint Ethics Committee and endorsed by the National Society of Art Directors was conceived with the idea of equity, not alone for the artist but for the art representative and the buyers of art.

The Committee zealously upholds the ethical standards set forth in the Code and invites with equal readiness any and all reports of violations on the parts of artists, art representatives or buyers of art.

IV Action

The Committee meets one or more times a month to read and act upon complaints, requests for guidance, and reports of Code violations. The proceedings and records of the Committee are held in strict confidence. In the interest of the profession typical cases are published periodically without identification of the parties involved. However, in the case of flagrant violation, the governing bodies of the parent organizations may be fully informed. All communications to the Committee must be made in writing. When a complaint justifies action, a copy of the complaining letter is sent, with the plaintiff's permission, to the alleged offender. In the exchange of correspondence which follows, matters are frequently settled by a mere clarification of the issues. Further action by the Committee becomes unnecessary, and in many instances both sides resume friendly and profitable relationships. When, however, a continued exchange of correspondence indicates that a ready adjustment of difference is improbable, the Committee may suggest mediation or offer its facilities for arbitration.

V Mediation

Both parties meet informally under the auspices of a panel of mediators composed of three members of the Committee. If the dispute requires guidance in a field not represented in the committee's membership, a specially qualified mediator with the required experience may be included. The names of members of the panel are submitted to both parties for acceptance.

The conduct of a panel of mediators is friendly and informal. The function of the panel members is to guide; not to render any verdict. The panel's purpose is to direct the discussion along such lines and in such a manner as to bring about a meeting of minds on the questions involved. If mediation fails, or seems unlikely to bring about satisfactory settlement, arbitration may be suggested.

VI Arbitration

A panel of five arbitrators is appointed. One or more is selected from the Committee, and the remainder are chosen by virtue of their particular experience and understanding of the problems presented by the dispute. Names of the panel members are submitted to both parties for their approval. Both parties involved sign an agreement and take oath to abide by the decision of the panel. The panel itself is sworn in and the proceedings are held in compliance with the Arbitration Law of the State of New York. After both sides are heard, the panel deliberates in private and renders its decision, opinion and award. These are duly formulated by the Committee's counsel for service on the parties and, if the losing side should balk, for entry of judgment according to law.

So far, every award has been fully honored. The decisions and opinions of this Committee are rapidly becoming precedent for guidance in similar situations. The Committee's Code has been cited as legal precedent.

VII Committee Scope

The Committee acts upon matters which can be defined by them as involving a violation of the Code or a need for its enforcement.

Upon occasion, the Committee has been asked to aid in settling questions not specifically covered by the Code of Fair Practice. The Committee gladly renders such aid, providing it does not exceed the limitations of its authority.

VIII Committee Limitations

The Committee offers no legal advice on contracts, copyrights, bill collecting or similar matters. But its judgments and decisions as to what is fair and ethical in any given situation, are backed by the support of the entire profession represented by the Committee.

The Committee's influence is derived from widespread moral support, and while it has neither judicial nor police powers, and cannot punish offenders, nor summon alleged violators to its presence, still, its growing prestige and dignity of operation have made it a highly respected tribunal to which few have ever failed to respond when invited to settle their differences.

IX Committee Maintenance

No fees or expenses are charged to anyone requiring the services of the Committee. The Committee's facilities are not limited to members of its supporting groups. They are freely offered to any individual, business, or professional organization.

The operating expenses of the Committee are defrayed by the three organizations represented. The time and services of the members and legal counsel are voluntarily contributed without any form of personal gain.

Relations Between Artist and Art Director

1 Dealings between an artist or his agent and an agency or publication should be conducted only through an authorized art director or art buyer.

2 Orders to an artist or agent should be in writing and should include the price, delivery date and a summarized description of the work. In the case of publications, the acceptance of a manuscript by the artist constitutes an order.

3 All changes and additions not due to the fault of the artist or agent should be billed to the purchaser as an additional and separate charge.

4 There should be no charge for revisions made necessary by errors on the part of the artist or his agent.

5 Alterations to artwork should not be made without consulting the artist. Where alterations or revisions are necessary and time permits and where the artist has maintained his usual standard of quality, he should be given the opportunity of making such changes.

6 The artist should notify the buyer of an anticipated delay in delivery. Should the artist fail to keep his contract through unreasonable delay in delivery, or non-conformance with agreed specifications, it should be considered a breach of contract by the artist and should release the buyer from responsibility.

7 Work stopped by a buyer after it has been started should be delivered immediately and billed on the basis of the time and effort expended and expenses incurred.

8 An artist should not be asked to work on speculation. However, work originating with the artist may be marketed on its merit. Such work remains the property of the artist unless paid for.

9 Art contests except for educational or philanthropic purposes are not approved because of their speculative character.

10 There should be no secret rebates, discounts, gifts or bonuses to buyers by the artist or his agent.

11 If the purchase price of artwork is based specifically on limited use and later this material is used more extensively than originally planned, the artist is to receive adequate additional remuneration.

12 If comprehensives or other preliminary work are subsequently published as finished art, the price should be increased to the satisfaction of artist and buyer.

13 If preliminary drawings or comprehensives are bought from an artist with the intention or possibility that another artist will be assigned to do the finished work, this should be made clear at the time of placing the order.

14 The right of an artist to place his signature upon artwork is subject to agreement between artist and buyer.

15 There should be no plagiarism of any creative artwork.

16 If an artist is specifically requested to produce any artwork during unreasonable working hours, fair additional remuneration should be allowed.

Relations Between Artist and Representative

17 An artist entering into an agreement with an agent or studio for exclusive representation should not accept an order from, nor permit his work to be shown by any other agent or studio. Any agreement which is not intended to be exclusive should set forth in writing the exact restrictions agreed upon between the two parties.

18 All illustrative artwork or reproductions submitted as samples to a buyer by artists' agents or art studio representatives should bear the name of the artist or artists responsible for the creation.

19 No agent or studio should continue to show the work of an artist as samples after the termination of their association.

20 After termination of an association between artist and agent, the agent should be entitled to a commission on work already under contract for a period of time not exceeding six months.

21 Original artwork furnished to an agent or submitted to a prospective purchaser shall remain the property of the artist and should be returned to him in good condition.

22 Interpretation of this code shall be in the hands of the Joint Ethics Committee and is subject to changes and additions at the discretion of of the parent organizations.

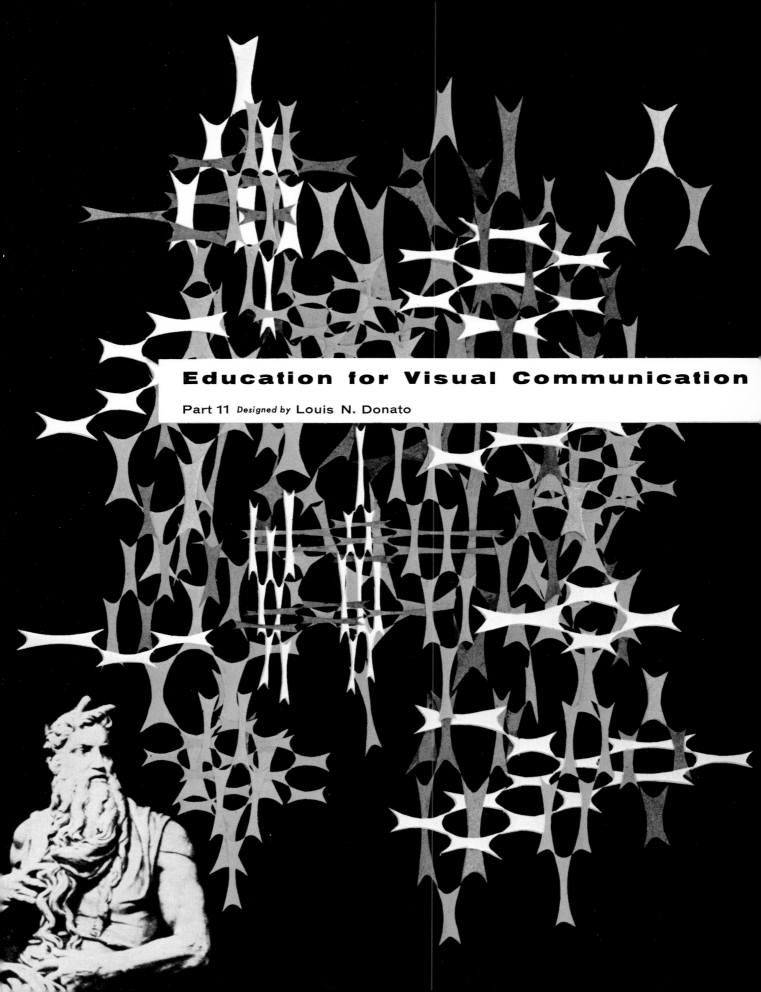

Education for Visual Communication

Part 11 *Designed by* Louis N. Donato

Art Training
For Industry

by Dr. James C. Boudreau

Dean Emeritus, The Art School, Pratt Institute

The art director is concerned with art education, and with collateral training programs in the field of visual communication, in these four ways:

1 — As applied to his job of creating advertisements or other forms of visual communication.

2 — As concerned with his responsibilities in the buying of art for reproduction.

3 — As related to his problem of selecting suitable artists for employment on his staff.

4 — As his own self-expression in the creative arts is affected thereby.

How educators and art directors are meeting—and solving—these problems in the light of today's needs is set forth in some detail in this section of our book. Here are outlined the objectives, and the actual programs, of representative institutions concerned with education in the visual arts. And there is a brief description of a stimulating cooperative training program initiated by the Art Directors Club of New York. For all concerned with careers in art directing or related fields, there is also a concise, practical summary on "finding the right job."

In all of these areas, moreover, the Art Directors Club has under constant review the relationship of the professional AD, not only to the broad field of art education but to the student or novice as well—the art director of the future.

The Editorial Committee

A QUARTER of a century ago the graduating student was apt to leave art school undecided as to whether his future lay in the field of illustration, easel painting, or commercial design. Today he is apt to emerge from the not-so-cloistered area of a similar institution prepared to serve, and serve well, some particular field of commerce chosen by him in his early years at school.

To supply a "product" capable of filling the demands of commerce and industry, our country's leading art institutions have turned to industry itself in the search for experienced personnel to aid in the setting up of its programs of study. Skilled practitioners from the very areas in which students will eventually serve now participate actively on governing boards, on the lecture platforms and, most important, in the classrooms. Thus the schools keep in close contact with the ever-expanding needs of commerce and industry and their leaders use this opportunity to guide the thinking of future designers into channels that they hope will eventually prove to be mutually advantageous.

The art schools that are furnishing industry with capable art graduates are stressing the value of a curriculum founded on practicality and vision. A student trained to furnish a forthright and practical answer to an art problem is of value but he is of limited use in today's world unless he has also developed vision; the horizons are ever widening and in this modern world of commerce the prizes of achievement are great but these vast potentialities of modern industry demand the services of the artist with vision as well as the practical artisan. This special blending of student talents is the major task that faces the country's art schools and upon their ability to achieve this amalgam of the dreamer and the practical artist rests the creative future of modern business.

As in every other aspect of our busy and exciting mid-twentieth century life, vital art education presents a continuously changing program that synchronizes with the best contemporary professional practices. The most challenging of these vitalizing adjustments are here set forth.

The Foundation Course

In most schools the art student's choice of a specific program of study is made only after a year of orientation and thorough grounding in basic drawing and design. During the first year he will also be exposed to guided experimentation as a means of stimulating new interests in the world about him; he will explore the creative possibilities of his surroundings and, with the spiralling of his interests, be better able to choose the path to his future course of study. It is in this

186

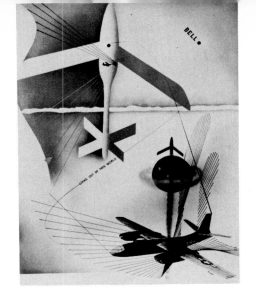

preliminary period that he will also find the inspiration for original and creative thinking that should later prove of much value to industry.

These programs are truly foundational in intent and in content. A double obligation is assumed—first, that organized sequential experiences be presented so that the student develops both a design concept and a presentational facility; second, that this introductory period be exploratory in nature. Near the end of this phase of his art education, the student is then in a position to make a more valid selection of his major field of study on the basis of accumulated experiences that set forth the pattern of his special personal interests.

Structural Representation

The intention of presentational facility implies much more than skill in manipulating tools and materials with appropriate techniques. The typical studio drawing class of the past, irrespective of the subject matter under consideration, too often connoted a "mental holiday." Today the approach to representation centers about vital materials typically expressive of our commercial and industrial era—quantity manufactured and distributed items. Most such items, because of their technological genesis, are inherently designed and produced upon a structural basis. Therefore, emphasis is placed upon their synthetic significance rather than their superficial exterior experience. In other words, objects are graphically presented on the scientific structural basis from the inside out. Ideal teachers for this structural representational approach are artists who have had the advantages of both an engineering and an art background. With the expansion of industrial design in our American economy, such qualified teachers are increasingly available.*

While great stress is now being placed upon structural understanding of manufactured products, the same approach has vitalized the study of the figure and of nature. In both these areas a highly functional organization is evident and in the case of the figure its manipulative mechanism is truly wonderful. It involves almost all of the basic principles of engineering.

Design

Because of the growing inter-dependency of commerce, industry and education the curriculums of our art schools are focused more sharply upon the area of design. This is a natural direction for the school's program to take since it is industry's insatiable appetite for designers that will absorb most of the "product" of the schools.

The typical American Drawing School of the past is fading away. In its place is arising the American

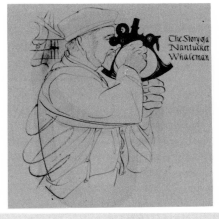

---

* See Donald Deskey's analysis of the industrial designer's functions, page 158—Ed.

School of Design. Increasing emphasis upon the significance of both two and three dimensional design is evident throughout the country. Never has such a great variety of materials been incorporated in developing a design concept through controlled manipulative experiences. Clay, cardboard, sheet metal, plaster, wood, stone constitute some of the basic materials ever present in a well balanced design course.

Color, a very important aspect of the total design experience, is now being organized and presented through a varied and successful series of problems that are most clarifying and useful.

The conscious importance of design in our art educational philosophy is objectively evident in the inclusion of the word in our professional vocabulary. Recently thirty American independent art schools and art divisions of colleges and universities organized for the purpose of developing a closer relationship for examining and improving their educational practices. Significantly, the organization is called the "National Association of Schools of Design." The typical curriculums offered in these institutions also express the prevalance of the term; for example, Advertising Design, Pictorial Design, Industrial Design, Textile Design, and Interior Design.

The Four Year Degree Program

Until rather recently most art schools were narrowly technical in the various courses they offered. This strictly vocational emphasis was fostered partly because young artists have had a strong desire for a delimited program that confined itself to the design and execution of art work but especially because economic pressure in the past had required a minimum of time to be devoted to reaching an employable level. Both of these conditions have changed favorably. Those responsible for this practical vocational emphasis have generally been conscious of the fact that they were offering a training and not an education. Students have often been reminded of its limitations.

There are many who would emphasize the encouragement of a broader sociologic interest in art through the study of science and the humanities. Changing circumstances following World War II have favored an expansion and enrichment of these two and three year studio and laboratory courses to four year programs leading to appropriate undergraduate degrees. While the swing to degree curriculums has not been realized in all art schools, the trend is definite and expanding.

Included among the changing circumstances that have fostered these expanded art educational services may be cited the following: first, and most important, the need to help all students prepare themselves to satisfy their full obligation to our democratic society. No longer may we rest content with qualifying our students to make a living; we must actively aid in their need to make a life—a participating, democratic life. Second, there is a growing conscious desire among art school students for a general education as well as an art training. Third, faculties and administrative staffs are aware of their enlarging responsibilities and wholeheartedly advocate adjusting to them. Fourth, commerce and industry are urging that artists who intend to qualify for employment henceforth be educated as well as trained. They seek young blood that can think and act beyond the limited horizon of art service only. This is especially true for potential junior executives. Fifth, practicing artists in various fields of endeavor are pressing for full legal professional status. National organizations such as the Art Directors Clubs, the Society of Illustrators, the American Institute of Decorators, the American Designers Institute and the Society of Industrial Designers have been studying the problem for several years. A basic requirement for such a legal professional status will be a college degree that substantiates an integrated program of general education and technical training.

Since the market was satisfied with the level of art attainment that the technical course graduates brought to their first employment, those schools that have lengthened and enriched their offerings have devoted the additional year of study to subjects in the area of general education. In no case has this been an academic year required before entering art study nor has it been a fourth year devoted solely to liberal arts. Rather, and appropriately so, these broadening experiences have been integrated with the technical courses throughout the four year program.

While the areas of possible exploration in general education appear to be limitless, nevertheless there is a tendency toward agreement in the major areas now incorporated in the recently expanded art education programs. As in other institutions of higher learning, "Written and Oral English" invariably appears as an integral part of the Freshman program. Further study in English includes a wide selection from our literary heritage with a tendency to designate these experiences under the generic title "Great Books."

Because the central intent of the program enrichment was to qualify graduates not only to become self-supporting members of society but even more important to be society-supporting members, a major part of the general disciplines naturally are drawn from the Social Studies. History of Art, which appeared quite often in the shorter technical programs, is now a basic subject in the degree offerings and in many institutions has enjoyed an expansion in time devoted to it. Special attention is directed to a recognition of controls that are ever present in all design problems together with the successful solutions great creative artists have evolved. The artist, as a vital member of his contemporary culture, is studied with the intention of awakening in the students an awareness of their own potentialities in the American and world scene today.

Under the title of Social Institutions, an opportunity is available for an introductory knowledge of the origins and development of various types of social organizations. Beginning with the anthropological background it considers the development of personality in society and the main principles of collective behavior. Another Social Study area often present in the four year art curriculum presents the adjustment of the individual to his associates in his family, professional and community relationships. It is appropriately called "Human Relations."

European and American History are popular social disciplines. Even more prevalent is the study of present-day national and international society with emphasis on major American economic and political trends, the challenge of competing politico-economic systems together with problems of world organization under the course designation "Contemporary Civilization."

The tremendous influence of science and its major application, technology, upon our present and even more on our future, strongly advises the inclusion of a study area that stresses the "Impact of Science" rather than the typical laboratory courses. Such an investigation develops an understanding of the nature of science, its historical development, its conditioning by social environment together with its influence on social change. Many art schools are giving an important place to this vital subject in their expanded services.

The above cited areas of educational investigation appear often in the General Education program of forward looking art schools. Variety and flexibility, however, mark the selection. This freedom should continue for there is no one best program. Modern languages and Mathematics are sometimes included in place of other subjects already mentioned.

The importance of art for commerce and industry is receiving more and more attention in the art divisions of our colleges and universities. Several have instituted new majors in Advertising Design and Industrial Design, thus broadening their former programs.

Graduate Study in Art

As a natural sequence of growth some art schools that recently expanded to the four year degree programs are now offering graduate study leading to appropriate advanced degrees in several areas. In the foreseeable future we can expect graduate art programs in advertising and publishing that will have as their central thesis the special qualifications and preparation for art direction. With the active participation of the local Art Director's Club this could constitute a major educational contribution in the development of junior art executives.*

The Many-Faceted Designer

Our country is known throughout the world for its overwhelmingly high degree of specialization in most fields of endeavor. This is evident in art education today. Fortunately, serious thought is being given to the possibility of a broader base of school experiences that will preserve a major area of special art service and yet permit exploration in other art areas. The intention points to the gradual reestablishment of the many-faceted designer, so well exemplified in the Renaissance artist. Already we see such a person emerging in the successful industrial designer who, through his varied services, tends toward the former universal artist.

Enriched Course Content

It is recognized that most of the statements and thoughts expressed so far in this presentation of today's art education are general and therefore apply to all aspects of programs that develop young artists. They have been set forth in some detail since they have a profound influence on the student who intends to find his place in advertising and publishing. Comparable adjustments to changing needs are evident within his selected curriculum. Some areas of study are being enriched, others are new.

Packaging design has grown tremendously in market significance within the last few years. Alert schools now offer well developed study in this important advertising medium. An interesting application of basic three dimensional design may be found in many art programs under the title of Display, including problems that range from small counter displays to large convention booths and retail store areas.

Typography, a central element in advertising and publishing design, while receiving increased attention in educational programs of art for commerce, has not found its rightful place in either time or emphasis to date. This is an area that invites careful exploration.

Television, the new advertising medium, that appears to offer an unlimited challenge to the art designer, has come upon the scene within recent years. Its growth has been phenomenal; its future expansion is unpredictable yet assuredly tremendous. With this new facility the artist must meet the challenge of combining the audio-visual arts employing both time and space. Many schools are expanding their services to include an insight into this youngest of design challenges.

* It will be interesting to refer to the program described by Bernard Brussel-Smith, in this connection, page 198—Ed.

"Ability To Think...
Power To Act"
...Professional
Objectives
in Art Education

The reproductions shown reflect creative solutions to problems by Cooper Union Art School students.

by Dana P. Vaughan
Dean, Cooper Union Art School

EDUCATIONAL institutions are set up for certain objectives, which may be intangible, indirect or very specific and positive. Generalizing, it might be said that professional education has broader and deeper aims while the more tangible or specific aims are, in their extremes, related to a vocational level. The demands of advertising and publishing are very complex in relationship to an educational institution's objective, particularly in considering them as only part of a larger professional area, the visual arts. Therefore, to train for the larger field of the visual arts and at the same time prepare a student for a particular demand is not an easy task. In the final analysis a graduate must function in a specific professional area. The professional outlets in the advertising and publishing fields, where the distinction between a paste-up man, layout man, art director, free-lancer, between technician and designer are not always clearly definable, leave scant grounds upon which to build educational objectives.

Defining Professional Objectives

Training for professions, such as engineering, law, medicine, architecture has one great advantage over training for the visual arts in that the former are clear cut in their professional levels and demands. Therefore educational objectives may be more efficiently defined when professional outlets are reasonably clear and generally understood. An architect is not expected to be a capable carpenter, nor is carpentry a requirement for entree into the profession of architect. A policeman is not expected to be a lawyer because he is also involved with the law. An engineer may not be a good mechanic, nor is becoming a mechanic confused with becoming an engineer.

There are demands in the advertising and publishing fields that can very justly require a technically trained person to do the purely technical jobs; and it is quite possible that a person with sufficient basic aesthetic sensitivity and intelligence can develop from a technical job to a professional position in these fields. However it is unrealistic to set up an institution for higher education whether it be a college, university or independent school—all inferring higher education—and devote time to the purely mechanical and technical side of a fragment of a profession. Carpentry would probably be an advantage to any architect, down-to-earth nuts and bolts and simple mechanics could be an advantage to an engineer, but within the scope of higher education there is a very definite limitation as to how much skill can be developed at the sacrifice of intellectual and aesthetic development. At the secondary school level the problem is quite different, but here again, a clear understanding should be made of what is vocational training—training for a specific job—or education for its own sake as a base for later education in the higher levels of a profession. From current information it would appear that too often high schools do not keep a clear distinction between broad and specific education, and in many cases profess to train for careers in the professions. There are doubtless as many approaches or methods for teaching art in general, or advertising and publishing in particular, as there are schools professing to do so.

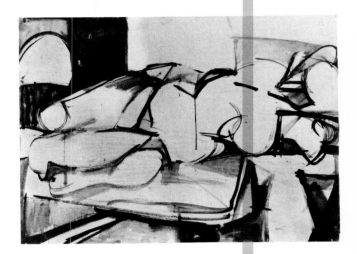

The important point is that any educational institution itself must know what it aims toward and must create an environment conducive to the fulfillment of its stated objectives. By so doing faculty and students may have a reasonable understanding of what they are driving for and will usually respond accordingly. The professional demands are obviously important to the clear and high-level formation of objectives in educational institutions offering training for this area. It is interesting to note that the powerful regional accrediting boards, so essential to the high standards of higher education, make this point their chief requirement—a clear statement of purpose and evidence of adequate implementation of this purpose.

Here is an indication of how one institution works toward this solution. Though it may not be identical to other institutions of higher education in the area of the are professions, it is possible that it may be typical.

How One Institution Operates

The institution states its purpose or objective, "this school aims to serve that segment of the public whose innate capacities for intellectual, aesthetic, and technical growth make possible the development of highest efficiency in the art professions. The school believes it can best prepare its selected students by creating an environment conducive to the development of aesthetic sensitivity, the ability to think, and the power to act."

Every student enters the school without commitment to the special phase of the art profession he may finally

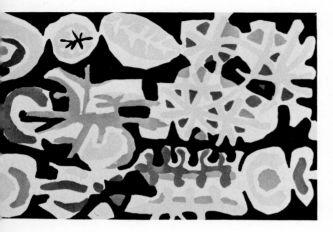

pursue. All are required to take a foundation course consisting of architecture, calligraphy, drawing, two- and three-dimensional design, English, history of art and sculpture. After this first year one of two directions is taken—architecture or fine and graphic arts. In architecture the requirements are concentrated on the area related to this highly organized and specialized profession. Students selecting the fine and graphic arts are required to take painting, calligraphy, and two-dimensional design. Electives may be taken in advertising design, graphic techniques, photography and typography, and sculpture. All fine and graphic arts students take six hours of painting each week, no more and no less. The interdependence of all of these subjects on total development is considered basic and essential to the rounding out of students' capacities and potentials.

"Aibility to Think . . . Power to Act"

The active interplay of the humanities—literature, music and art—is of natural concern to an art student. "The ability to think" is given major emphasis. One of the essential factors in developing this ability to think is the selection of a faculty whose mental and philosophical approach to life appears to be as keen as their professional competence. The environment referred to earlier as essential to aesthetic development is equally true of intellectual development, which is fostered by the traditionally academic studies—English, history of art, elements of aesthetics, history of architecture, studies in cultural values, contemporary thought, oral

English, cultural traditions. These courses help to broaden the students' understanding and interest in the humanities, of which art and architecture are part and parcel. As language is the universal means of communication both for expressing oneself orally, in writing and for enrichment received through reading, we consider this another essential part of their development.

"The power to act" is another way of expressing the capacity to synthesize feeling, knowledge and skill where, in the experimental atmosphere of school, students are encouraged to develop these three attributes into workable relationship. As a result, when they go on into outside experiences they will have the confidence and the capacity to function in the highest brackets of the art professions with the training to meet the wide range in art careers, yet with sufficient specialization to make a toehold without being limited by their first adjustment to the immediate requirements of a specific specialty.

For higher education, one must assume that students are admitted according to their abilities and in this respect students are screened for their intellectual capacities, aesthetic sensitivity and potential learning capabilities. Such screening, of course, is not infallible. Human personalities are dynamic, not static. This school attempts to select a faculty whose professional performance indicates a high degree of capacity successfully carried through and in addition a wide, deep understanding of human relationships and a broad concept of the relationship of their specialty to the larger body of knowledge and culture. These two areas

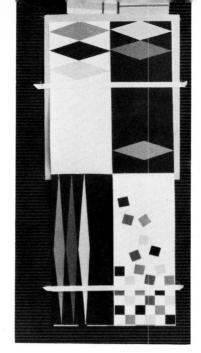

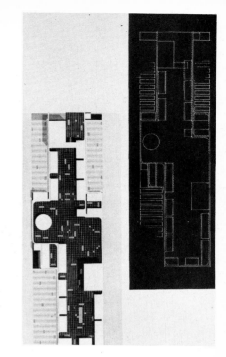

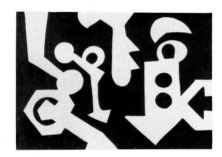

of selection within the limited control of administration and the limits of human judgment leave the curriculum as another element through which education proceeds. Again, in higher education, the breadth and depth of a curriculum is essential and this is doubly important because an art department or art school is by its very nature already dealing with a specialized area of education.

The school does not ignore the bridge from the ivory tower to the solid earth; such specific subject matter as typography, photography, advertising design, and other related subjects are part of the curriculum. But they are also taught by highly professional people, with the emphasis upon the aesthetic elements and the higher aspects of the subject. Projects are undertaken at various times to give experiences as close to reality as is consistent with sound policy and worthwhile values. It is in the area of advertising and publishing that such projects are most advantageous and effective.

The school does not in any way compromise. If it does not feel that students can achieve the higher levels through the curriculum which it requires, it does not carry such students on. There are other schools and other situations where this student may succeed. There is a theory that a genius may break a school or a school may break a genius. But school is not the only door to success, particularly in this field of the advertising and publishing professions. It is, however, a field that is constantly requiring a higher level of performance, aesthetically and intellectually and education must be geared to achieve that requirement.

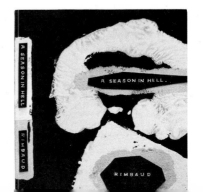

The Home Study Art School

by Albert Dorne

President, The Famous Artists Schools, Westport, Connecticut

EVERY year an impressive number of Americans enroll in home-study courses. They want to learn how to draw or paint, they feel their English needs improvement, or they wish to become photographers, draftsmen or cartoonists. Americans are dedicated to the principle of self-improvement, and annually seven hundred thousand of them give inspiring proof of this dedication by starting home-study courses.

It would be hard to find a subject that isn't offered by one or another of our correspondence schools. Through the varied courses of study they teach, large numbers of people are enabled to fill in the gaps in their education. Even larger numbers get the basic training they need to begin a career. Many of these people go on to become highly successful in their chosen professions — a good percentage of them, it should be noted, in the field of visual communication, where art direction plays such a vital role.

Why a Home-Study School?

Why do so many of our fellow citizens go to the correspondence schools for increase of knowledge and to advance themselves in the useful arts and sciences? The reason is simply that most of these seven hundred thousand cannot obtain the training they need from any school but a correspondence school. They are people with special problems:

They work for a living, and cannot attend school at regular hours.

They cannot meet the academic requirements of the residence schools, colleges, universities or technical and professional institutes giving the courses they want.

They have dependents to support, and so cannot take off the time or afford the money for full-time residence study.

They live in areas where there are no residence schools teaching the things they want to learn or they want advanced training to supplement their previous training and experience.

For one or more of these compelling reasons, the ambitious person turns to the correspondence school for help. And, if he is self-disciplined as a student, if he is dedicated to learning and possessed of a fair share of intelligence and ability, the school can help him greatly. True, it cannot provide him with the association and stimulation of fellow students, and he may miss a personal relationship with his instructors. But the home-study school can give him a complete course of study and individualized training which, in many fields, including the graphic arts, will equip him to make a useful, creative contribution.

There are many excellent residence schools, and I have the highest regard for them. Their distinguished administrators and teachers have trained countless successful artists and art directors in whose achievements they may take justifiable pride. Home study, however, is not a competitor of residence teaching. Both work in the same area, but with people in different situations. Each was created to satisfy the same need, but through different means. I have no intention of comparing these two dissimilar kinds of teaching.

Still, I do feel that we can fairly judge home-study schools on the same basis as any other educational

19

institution. We can assess them in terms of their objectives, their educational programs, personnel, equipment, organization, and student body — and the extent to which their programs achieve the aims they are intended to. The fact that a home-study school makes use of the United States Mails is only incidental and has nothing whatever to do with either the merit of the school's service or the quality of its teaching.

Just how does the home-study school work? What unique devices has the modern correspondence school developed to teach its students — particularly art students? I can best explain these things as I see them daily at the school with which I am associated. This school is the first and only school teaching art that has attempted standards of teaching by mail comparable to those of the finest residence schools.

Personalized Instruction

Art lends itself to visual teaching, and so it is ideally suited for home study. Is it not logical to assume that the art of making pictures should be taught with pictures? The textbooks covering the three-year Commercial Art training program in the Famous Artists Course contain more than 7,000 pictures — 5,000 of which were especially drawn to illustrate some 200,000 words of text. The artistic stature and practical experience of the contributors to the texts are well known. In most other home-study courses, as a matter of fact, the textbook material is contributed by outstanding authorities in their respective fields.

Serious people want to study seriously and the home-study course is planned to help them do this. In the Career Course in Commercial Art and Illustration there are twenty-four sections. Each one is designed to cover thoroughly a single fundamental aspect of the program as a whole. For example: Form — Composition and Design — Human Form — Figure Drawing — Layout and Lettering — Today's Men and Women — Style — Textures — Line — Halftone and Color — Commercial and Editorial Illustration — Advanced Techniques — and finally, Workshop Methods and Studio Procedures. These subjects are carefully explained step-by-step with words and pictures. Detailed instructions for practice are provided, and there are drawing assignments for each section to test the student's comprehension of the subject and his growing skill. The student sends these assignments to the school for criticism.

The home-study school is well aware of the handicaps under which many students normally labor. It knows that in any particular month the student may have little or no time to give to his studies, but that he may be able to make up for this the following month. The school also knows that different students learn at different rates. Accordingly, the student in the Commercial Art training program receives all the textbooks and lessons of his course when he enrolls so that he may forge ahead at his own pace. He is allowed fully three years to complete his training. If the student needs it, he may have an extra year.

A basic concept of the instruction program is the way it is personalized. Upon enrollment, each student must fill out a comprehensive biographical questionnaire of his complete background, education, previous training and aspirations; to this he attaches a photograph of himself. His instructors consult this material constantly. The nature and principle of home-study teaching requires, in every case, working with the student as an individual, on his own terms.

With this questionnaire as a basis, the school pro-

ceeds to develop a complete file and record of the student's progress throughout his training. Into this file goes a duplicate of each instructor's letter of criticism and advice to the student, so that subsequent instructors are always up-to-date on the student's rate of progress and potential — not only as an artist but as a personality. Each new assignment drawing the student sends in is studied by the instructor in the light of this important dossier of the student's past work, his strong and weak points, and his personal history.

The same instructor does not grade each assignment of an individual student throughout the entire course — nor does any instructor work on the same lesson, year in and year out. All the lessons that arrive at the school each day are distributed among the entire staff with little regard to which instructor receives which lesson, other than his qualification to teach the special subject of that lesson. This arrangement serves a double purpose. For the student, it provides an opportunity to profit from the teaching of not just one, but of many instructors, each with his own artistic back-

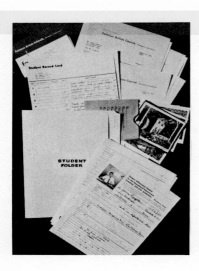

ground and insights. For the instructor, it provides variety and breadth of scope — a living, changing experience instead of treadmill teaching.

Criticism Through Visual Techniques

Visual teaching methods are not only the heart of the art textbooks — they are also a basic tool in criticizing the assignment drawings the student submits. The instructor makes an overlay sketch of each drawing of the student's assignment. On this overlay he corrects the student's mistakes, and points out where and how the drawing could be improved. To explain this visual criticism, he writes a lengthy personal letter discussing the lesson in greater detail and commenting on aesthetic values. (This letter is returned to the student with his drawings and the overlays.) Further along in the course, the instructor often prepares his criticism in full color, doing over all or part of the student's picture. He also adds several diagrammatic pictures to drive home important points in picture making.

The Guiding Faculty, who wrote the textbooks of the Commercial Course and the Painting Course and developed the training techniques of the school, do none of the actual criticizing and teaching directly to the student. They do, however, supervise the instruction, develop revisions and improvements for the courses, and work with the teaching staffs.

There is a staff of approximately forty-five artist-instructors, all "working artists" who (in the case of Commercial Course and Cartoon Course teachers) derive a large part of their total incomes from free-lance illustration or (if they are Painting Course instructors) are recognized professional fine arts painters outside the school. It is a basic concept of the school that the instructors must be successful practicing artists themselves in order to teach effectively.

Although a complete and detailed dossier on a student's personality, background, and progress is maintained and developed throughout his enrollment period, there are limitations in dealing with the education of his personality. The home-study student represents every conceivable age bracket, walk of life, and intellectual level. Because of this, it is difficult to establish a norm on which to base an academic program directed toward the character and personality development of an individual. He may, however, go out into the world as a well-equipped artist, with regular, workmanlike habits and high standards of craftsmanship which the school has helped him to develop.

Rounded Training — Employment Opportunities

Home-study students reside in virtually every town and hamlet and in cities of every size. The majority live outside metropolitan areas. A commercial artist, to earn a living and, in fact, to function best anywhere — except in the larger cities — must be trained and equipped to operate often as a one-man art service.

He may be called upon to undertake many of the responsibilities of the art director — to do the layout, the comprehensive, the figure drawings, the product pictures, and frequently the lettering. In addition, he often functions as a one-man production department.

Since there is so little opportunity in the small community to specialize, an important service of the home-study school is to give the student the all-around artistic training he needs for these jobs. In essence, an important aspect of the program is the principle of equipping people to earn their living as artists in their own communities, through sound training and practical artistic philosophies.

The Famous Artists Schools has developed its own unique method of bringing the work of its promising students to the attention of art buyers throughout the country. It edits and publishes its own magazine — the *Famous Artists Magazine* — entirely in the interests of its students. A regular feature of each issue presents examples of work done by outstanding students, selected from different sections of the country. Over 8,000 art buyers and art directors receive this publication. As a result, scores of students whose work has been published have made worthwhile and profitable connections both locally and nationally.

In addition to using the magazine as a vehicle for developing employment opportunities, the school keeps on file a special folder containing samples of art work, a detailed questionnaire, pertinent facts regarding job requirements, experience, and background on each of those students who are properly equipped to supply merchandisable art work. With this comprehensive information on hand, the school services inquiries from prospective employers.

The teaching of the fundamental architecture and language of art as they are universally recognized is one of the stated aims of the school. Since it is conducted by the most highly successful practitioners, the school also places strong emphasis on the objective use, in the area of commerce and communication, of the things it teaches. Students of the school are employed in the art departments of most of the large advertising agencies of this country; they work as artists for department stores, studios, designers, newspapers, magazines, book publishers, television, and in every conceivable phase of the graphic arts. They are earning good livings, are launched on fine careers, and are achieving growth in human values through their work. In the final analysis, it is they who offer the ultimate validation for the home-study art school. For the end consideration of any school or philosophy of learning must be the developed potentials and the fulfilled objectives of its students. The extent to which this goal is achieved is the yardstick of a school's merit — whether it teaches through correspondence or otherwise.

"How We Solve Our Problems"...
A Unique and Exciting Program
For Future ADs.

by Bernard Brussel-Smith

EIGHT years ago the Art Directors Club of New York planned and put into effect an educational program designed to help prepare for the professional field a select group of future art directors. Led by some devoted and selfless members, the Education and Scholarship Committee, and supported by all accredited art schools, this program aimed to extend the regular art school curriculum by exposing the student to all phases of the work of the art director, by presenting to him the real problems ahead of him, and by introducing him to some of the top people in the field.

From the very beginning the highest standards were set and have been maintained in the preparation and presentation of these scholarship programs. Carefully planned, they have been broad in their coverage of material, varied in approach and type of speakers, stimulating in the problems submitted.

The program consists of a series of forum-lectures, exhibitions, demonstrations, given over a period of six or seven weeks. Every phase of art directing is involved. Every type of art directorship is examined, whether it be magazine, agency, television, outdoor advertising, individual manufacturer, specialized agency (medical, public relations, etc.). All allied parts of immediate concern to art direction, such as illustration, type, photoengraving, electrotyping, media, mechanicals, photography, are explored, as are organizational set-ups within the agencies themselves. The art directing problems run the gamut from traditional through the *avant garde*. Market research, joint ethics, type setting are all exposed for consideration by the art student.

Each session takes up two or three phases specifically relevant to the art director's work. As always, the very best men available in the field are called upon to share their experience with talks, slides, movies and demonstrations. The caliber of the men participating has always been of the highest. To name them would be to call the role of our finest.

The students attending are the most outstanding of each current crop from the major art schools in and around the metropolitan area of New York. Also participating for the past three years are students fom the Rhode Island School of Design, Philadelphia Museum School of Art and the Newark School of Art. Attendance has never lagged and even art school instructors have engaged actively in the forums.

Simulated On-the-Job Problems

In order to foster a more intimate relationship between art director and student, two committee members are assigned to liaison work with the small group from each school. The student cannot help but absorb a great deal of what practical art direction is. As a culmination of the series he is given an opportunity to solve an ad problem as it would be presented to him in the field. The copy is always prepared by a professional copy writer. Similarly the product is expertly designed by a member of the Club. From here on each student is strictly on his own, except that the liaison members of the committee are available for advice on interpretation of the rules.

What is unique about this project is that great efforts are made to simulate an actual on-the-job problem. Upon completion of the ad project, each student keys his work with a symbol so that his name does not appear on the finished problem. The jury of awards is made up of the entire committee and awards are made on best work received from each school. At the final scholarship session a rotating panel of committee members discusses the awards. The students are all welcome participants in this discussion.

The enthusiasm of the students through these many years has been a source of great satisfaction both to the Art Directors Club and to the art schools. The committee itself has attracted a small army of members to its very stimulating and beneficial work. It is heartening to note that so many of today's busy AD's take the time and effort to help those of tomorrow.

Finding The Right Job... How to Fit Your Talents Into Business

by Dorothy Chapple

Former Assistant Editor, Art Direction and Rush Magazines

THE commercial art profession offers a wide scope of potential employment to the art school graduate. Due to the marked degree of specialization he has an opportunity eventually to find an area for the recognition of his specific talents.

Yet the very nature of this specialization may thwart him in the beginning. Rarely will the novice start out as an artist (though there are a few brilliant exceptions). Instead, he will very likely wield paste-pot and scissors, cut mats and run errands for the first several months. He must be willing to serve, with grace, a long apprenticeship and work gradually into positions that utilize his full potential. His adaptability, his demonstrated interest and competence are as important as his portfolio—perhaps even more important.

The accompanying chart suggests the most likely sources of employment and for free-lance art work. But it should be noted that rarely do specialists offer the beginning artist a position, though he may certainly consult them—even if only for an opinion on the work he has done. Such organizations as direct mail firms, publicity people, lettering houses will occasionally offer apprenticeship jobs. The artist will, however, be better prepared for specializing after sound practical experience in an art studio or agency.

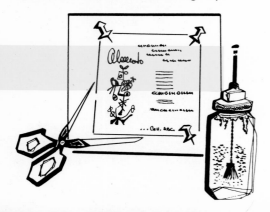

The Portfolio

Here are some suggestions on compiling a portfolio:
1. Half dozen pieces representing the artist's specialty.
2. A few layouts—roughs, comprehensives and finished.
3. Spot drawings in ink and wash.
4. Actual reproductions of work done, if any.
5. Include no more than a dozen pieces altogether—all neatly matted and organized for presentation.

The Organized Search

Here are some suggestions for finding a job:
1. The art school counseling and placement service.
2. Classified newspaper ads.
3. Employment agencies specializing in placing artists.
4. Classified telephone directories—for lists of art studios and other sources.
5. Directories of advertising agencies and advertisers such as McKittrick's and Standard Advertising Register. *Art Direction* magazine carries extensive advertising of art and photographic studios and services; its Buyer's Guide issue each February includes further classified lists.

Opportunities for Women

As in much of the business world, women may have a difficult time in the commercial art profession. They are often considered undependable and lacking in a serious approach to their work. Moreover, studios and agencies may hesitate to ask women to run errands or do heavy work—which is often required during the apprenticeship.

The picture for women has, however, improved over the years. There are now women in top positions in all areas of the field, but they are proportionally few. With patience, a good portfolio and an adaptable, interested attitude, a woman will probably get a start. She would do well, nevertheless, to gear her thinking to the fact that the odds are against her, though certainly less so than ten years ago.

A Mature Perspective

The beginning artist must be aware of his potential and his limitations. His search for work should be organized according to his interests and abilities, and his attitude should be that of the creative business man willing to start from the bottom in an organization. The shortcuts happen in exceptional cases, but these are indeed rare.

Above all, the young artist should keep abreast of the trends in advertising and editorial art and design. He must strive continually to develop his creativity.

SOURCES OF EMPLOYMENT

Employment opportunities	Types of jobs	Function of art department
Agencies	AD; studio manager; illustrators and cartoonists; directors; comp renderers; letterers; retouchers; diagram and chart artists; mechanicals; pasteups; mat cutters and file clerks	Conceive ideas, design ads, make layouts; type specification; prepare finished art ready for reproduction. Most illustration and photography is bought from art studios and free-lancers.
Studios	AD; studio manager, illustrators and cartoonists; photographers; layout artists; letterers; retouchers; comp renderers; pasteups; errand boys	Provide various styles of illustration and/or photography to agencies and other advertising and editorial art buyers. Most studios have a complete pasteup and layout service where type and production knowledge is essential.
Publications (magazines, newspapers and book publishing firms)	AD; asst. AD; layout artists; some illustrators (spots, etc.) promotion piece designers and illustrators; letterers	Editorial and advertising layout, type specification; occasional illustration—though most is bought from studios and free-lancers. Preparation of promotion pieces. Production knowledge essential.
Manufacturers	AD; asst. AD; layout artists; product and package designers; illustrators; diagram and chart artists	Art department makes ad layouts, designs brochures, direct mail, annual reports, house organs. Use editorial layout and illustration artists. Product and package design.
Retail stores	AD; layout artists; illustrators, esp. fashion and product; display designers; show card letterers	Design of ads (chiefly newspaper), point-of-purchase displays, interior and window display design.
Printers	Layout artists and illustrators	Provide design, type and production service for direct mail brochures, ads, displays, posters, etc.

Opportunities for the free lancer

agencies
publications
manufacturers
record album producers
greeting card publishers
direct mail firms
designers of brochures, booklets, etc.
book publishers
display houses
printers
poster producers
TV art departments
textile designers
package designers and producers
package designers, producers
stage set designing
cartooning
spots

Specialty organizations

letterers
direct mail
publicity
package design
display design
poster design
TV art departments
motion pictures
record album producers
greeting card publishers
product design
industrial design
architectural design
textile design
costume styling
stage set design
libraries
schools
government operations
pharmaceutical houses
research firms

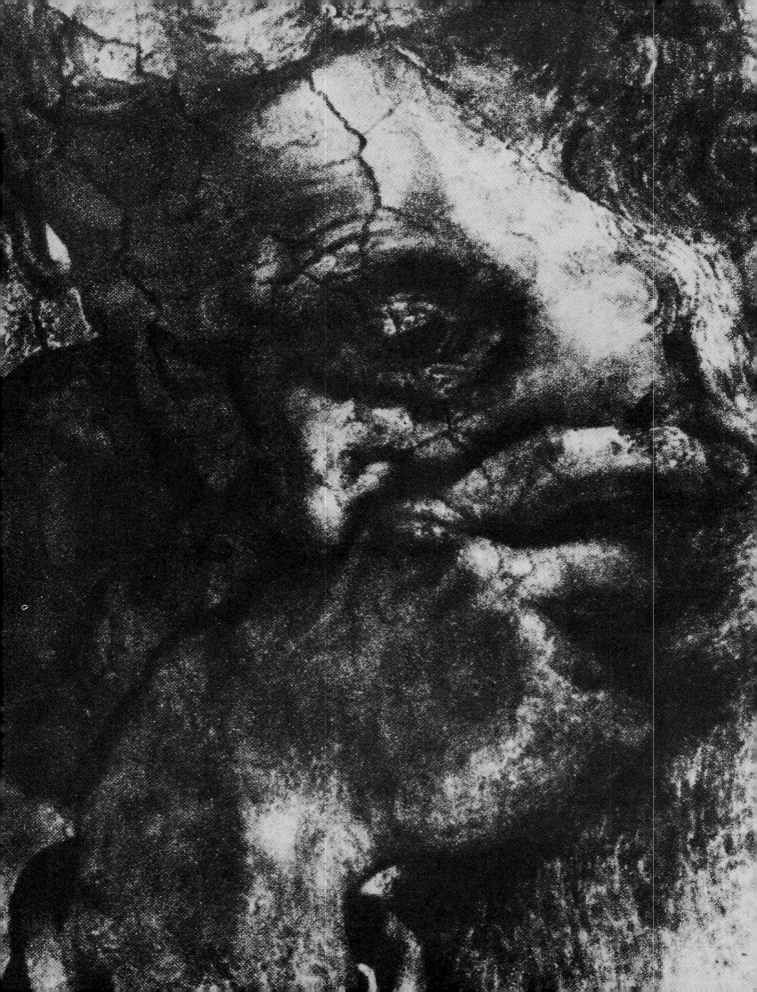

The Profession:
Its Growth and
Development

Part 12 *Designed by* Salvatore J. Taibbi

After 35 Years . . . What Next?

by Frank Baker

Senior Art Director, McCann-Erickson, Inc.

THE profession of art directing, which is the business of talking to people through the medium of their eyes, has come a long way in the last thirty-five years. This is a good time to ask ourselves "what next?" It seems to me that the history of the Art Directors Club of New York is the history of our profession, so if we take a look at that, we can see where we have been. I think this will also give us ideas where we are going.

To my mind the history of the Club can be divided into three parts. The first two are behind us, and we have just entered the third stage.* Originally, the Club was started thirty-five years ago by a group of young men who banded together because they had a common need. They met in the Roof Tree Inn (on West 29th Street now the Olde Garden Restaurant) to search for the answers to this puzzling new profession into which they had been thrust. The advertising business had reached a point in its development where it needed men to plan the visual presentations of its advertisements. This was the start of art directing. These fledgling art directors came from varied backgrounds, but if you can generalize, you might say that most of them developed out of the illustration field. Indeed, this was a natural sequence. Although they had many problems, there was one which was common to all. They found that a great many artists would not work for ad-

* See Peirce Johnson's fascinating "history" of the Club, page 208—Ed.

vertising, since they considered this a commercialization of their talents and therefore not a desirable use of their abilities. This is a hard thing for us to to believe today. Nevertheless, it was true.

The First Phase

The solving of this problem is, to my mind, part one in the history of our Club. The method devised to accomplish this was an ingenious one. The men felt that if it were possible to show all artists that the standard for art in advertising was truly high, and that many very fine pieces of art appeared before a vast audience through this medium of advertising, that the artist might then "break down" a bit. The artist, too, could have a hand in the battle for the use of better art in advertising, but only if he were a part of it . . . certainly not viewing it from afar. The device that was hit upon to accomplish this objective was the "First Annual Exhibition of Advertising Art." The Exhibits were later printed as a book, just as the current Exhibitions are today. The success of this project is well known—and there is scarcely an artist or photographer in the world today who is not available to the advertising and editorial businesses.

It was this purpose and its accomplishment that motivated our Club into becoming what it is today. A club, like all organizations, must have a goal—a reason for being—or it dries up and is nothing. The idea worked.

Part Two

The Exhibition and its accompanying *Annual* were an excellent device. The original objective long since accomplished, it has grown and grown until it is now a thing by itself. It has led the way for art in advertising throughout the world. All of our careers have been affected by it—much more than we probably realize. It has set a high standard of excellence. As we have been influenced, our advertising and editorial pages reflect this and, in turn, the taste and desires of the readers themselves. The Club has grown and flourished with this as its motivation.

But now as we come to part three, what has happened? Let's face it, the Exhibition has lost some of its momentum. It is no longer unique. Because of our success most of the member clubs of the National Society of Art Directors now have their own local shows and some even print annuals. Actually this is good for all of us, but at the same time we·are no longer alone in the exhibition-annual "business." Moreover, there have been vast developments in the total area of communication which affect all of us today and will continue increasingly to affect us tomorrow.

For some time we have needed a new objective. Something that we can all get behind and push. An idea to which we can hitch our star. I think we have it. I have long contended that the true responsibility of our Club to its members is to set a background for the profession, which favorably reflects on the individual art director. We cannot put talent in a member's hand nor brains in his head, but we can and must project the profession of art directing into the minds of all people associated with it, particularly the man who writes our salary checks.

The Third Stage Begins

I believe that the "First Annual Conference on Visual Communication," sponsored by the Art Directors Club of New York, and the successive Conferences will do just that. Not as a gimmick but as tangible evidence for all to see that the art director has come of age, and finally understands his true position and destiny in the application of art directing talent to the business of influencing people's ideas and buying habits. That's a long sentence, but it says it. This is not an abstract idea. Many individual art directors have enjoyed wonderfully successful careers because they understood their true function in business. As a group, however, I don't think it is so true. In fact, I think we appear actually to resist the facts of life—of what our real function in the commercial world is. *A visual presentation is nothing if it does not talk to other people.*

Unfortunately our Exhibition confirms to many—if they think about it at all—that the art director is not really reaching for the same goal as the advertiser or editor.

This is an awkward thought to leave uncorrected. We can do, and are doing, something about changing this misconception without destroying the stimulating quality of our Exhibition. In a sense, you might say that the Exhibition has been off on a side road while the advertising and editorial businesses have been barreling along the highway at a tangent, with the gap getting wider all the time. We must close this gap and get back on the main road. This is what the Conferences on Visual Communication will do. These conferences will confirm that the art director is just as curious as anyone about how you climb inside a person's head to influence his thinking. This is a logical endeavor of the Art Directors Club of New York to sponsor. After all, the world is increasingly becoming a "how-things-look" world.

You know if *we* don't find these things out, someone else will, and we will be relegated to the back room with a pencil in our hand and no more. This will not happen.

So you might say we are entering part three in the development of the profession of art directing. This is the period when the art director truly fulfills his destiny by understanding and confirming his value to the commercial world. It is at this point that growth starts. At any rate, this is how one art director sees it on December 4, 1955 as he flies over the Rockies to California on a photographic assignment. These pictures are going to *sell* our client's product. Happy Seventy!

It Started With The Art Directors Club of New York

...The Future Is In Our Past

by Peirce Johnson (deceased)

Founding Member and Past President, Art Directors Club of New York

A STUDY of art directing is incomplete without reference to the organization which first pointed out its professional nature and which, if it did not actually coin the title of art director, quickly gave the title currency. This organization is the *Art Directors Club of New York,* founded in 1920.

That a group from New York City, rather than some place else in the nation, should have taken the lead in such matters and, in addition, should have defined the duties and responsibilities of this lively new profession much as they exist today, is not surprising. For New York in 1920 was not only the acknowledged art center of the country; it was the headquarters of the rapidly growing advertising industry. And art-trained and sales-minded people, with ideas and outlook surprisingly alike,

were flocking here from all sections of the country—material for a cause or a crusade.

Yet art directing, strictly speaking, does not date from these pioneers. Its ancestral roots go back further—to the opening decade of the century. In that period two noteworthy influences were to affect it.

One of these was a series of yearly exhibitions of advertising art held at the National Arts Club in New York. The initial exhibition had opened in 1908. Earnest Elmo Calkins, president of Calkins and Holden, later to be regarded as one of advertising's "immortals", was the originator of the idea and organizer of the show. Here for the first time, were brought together top-flight artists and business leaders, and the exhibition demonstrated—to the surprise of some—that real illustrative art was being used profitably in advertising. Artists of the caliber of Maxfield Parrish, Jules Guerin, Walter Dorwin Teague, Edward Penfield, Adolph Treidler and the Leyendeckers were represented. Firms such as Pierce-Arrow, Procter and Gamble, Wanamaker cooperated—to cite a few.

It was a "daring experiment". Supposed commercial success was not enough; exhibits had to comply with the recognized rules of art—were chosen solely for artistic merit and fitness. Yet the experiment worked. Business executives, artists and idea men from the agencies thronged the galleries on Gramercy Park. They returned to offices and studios conceding that originality, taste and a high order of craftsmanship might indeed have commercial value. . . A second exhibition followed a year later; and a third show, in 1910, was distinguished by its selection of posters by Hohlwein, Bernhardt, Steinlen—masters of that art.

The second significant development which prepared the way for the pioneers of 1920 was the well-publicized and well-attended Armory Show of 1913, also in New York. Remembered chiefly for Marcel DuChamps' "Nude Descending Staircase" (subject of derisive, if good-humored, comment), it was America's introduction to Modern Art and the first show to exert a pronounced influence on the public. Art directors-in-the-embryo noted this influence. It offered hope for experimentation in their own vocation.

"A Blend of Art and the Selling Urge"

This vocation had been taking shape now since shortly after the turn of the century. It had required a curious blend of art-consciousness and the selling urge, liberally sprinkled with idealism. For the latter ingredient World War I must be given some credit. America's entrance into the struggle had seemed to almost every one both necessary and inevitable. There was then little of the cynicism that characterized subsequent world upheavals. Enthusiasm ran high in advertising offices, as it did in most businesses. Art and production men by the scores were eager to enlist. They were soon in training camps, busy camouflaging ships, patrolling sea lanes, directing traffic in battle areas with M.P. bands on their arms, fighting it out in the trenches.

Most—not all!—came back from that War to jobs held open to them. It had been a grim and costly adventure. But it had been worth what it cost, they guessed, for had not a great end been gained? War, they were told, was to be outlawed for all time. And the idealism it had generated might now find a peace-time outlet. One New York City man who believed very strongly in this latter possibility was Louis C. Pedlar.

Louis Pedlar had once worked for the Calkins and Holden advertising agency and was now conducting his own art service. He was in daily contact with agency personnel—art buyers, art department managers, experienced layout artists. He knew that the artist in these men often

made them stubborn individualists. But the pattern of their lives was similar, their interests often identical and they had common business problems. He was convinced that were they brought together—in an organization where they could meet regularly, discuss their problems, and pool ideas and knowledge—industry and art alike would be the gainers. He disclosed the plan to some of these business friends who happily welcomed his suggestions and agreed to attend an exploratory luncheon, which Pedlar volunteered to arrange.

Very early in 1920 the meeting took place in the pleasantly comfortable atmosphere of the Roof Tree Inn on 29th Street, a tea room characteristic of the era. Over unfinished wooden tables, lighted by candles in pewter holders, a representative group met and laid plans for a permanent organization. It was to be called the Art Directors Club, and membership was to consist of two groups: (a) salaried people, for the most part, who were engaged in the direction and production of illustration and design for agencies, publications, and art services, and (b) a second group made up of those who operated chiefly as individuals, such as typographers and free-lance artists.

The roster of the earliest or charter members reads like a Who's Who in the advertising, illustrative and graphic arts fields. Among the first names to appear were those of Richard Walsh who became the Club's first president, Stanford Briggs, Fred Farrar, Guy Gaylor Clark, advertising personalities. There were type experts Everett Currier, William Kittredge, Benjamin Sherbrow. There were Cushman Parker and Louis Fancher, artists. A total of 53 members appeared in the Club's files for June 1920, representing the cream of the two membership classifications.

These practical idealists—"wistful adventurers", Heyworth Campbell later termed them—set to work at once on the mechanics of the organization Louis Pedlar had brought into being. They arranged for weekly meetings, encouraged others in the advertising and allied fields to join them; and elected a slate of officers which in addition to Richard Walsh, leader, was made up of two vice-presidents, Thomas Booth and Guy Clark; a secretary, Egbert G. Jacobson; and a treasurer, William Schaefer—all advertising agency men. The

Louis C. Pedlar

Club was to be financed by dues, and it may be mentioned that by August of its first year Treasurer Schaefer was able to show a balance of over $800.00, not including a government tax of $2.50 per member collected. A good record, it seems, for a body of men whose primary concern was production, not finance.

While such details were in the making, and before, President Walsh, gifted in the use of words since his Harvard days, became by common consent the *voice* of the Club. He had the ability, greater than most of his confreres, to express in simple concise phraseology what the vocational trends were and what the Club stood for. His judgment, moreover, was so sound that today the Club's underlying philosophy and its objectives are essentially those Richard Walsh charted in the year One of the Club's existence.

Definition of an "Art Director' — 1920

Walsh explained an art director as "one who counsels in the buying, selling and creation of art work, and whose services have been accepted by any reputable organization." Of the art director's work he thought it might be "the creation of an esthetic effect through the workmanship of another, but to which the art director adds something of his own." Art directing he defined as "the highly specialized vocation of advising commerce in the use of art, and interpreting to art the requirements of commerce." It was a vocation, he believed, which had made rapid strides and *had become a recognized profession.*

As Richard Walsh and his associates saw it, this society of professional people should do more than promote the material interests of its members. Like the professions of Law and Medicine, it ought to serve the industry of which it was part and make some contribution to the betterment of daily living.

These convictions were reflected in the Constitution and By-Laws of the Club which Egbert Jacobson, its secretary, and some teammates drafted in the spring and summer months. Among the stated objectives was one to dignify and improve the work of artists and art directors by direction and guidance. Another pledged collective public participation in art affairs "to promote the best interests of art, applied art and advertising." Thus, while other purposes were mentioned, such as maintaining a club room for members, en-

couraging study courses, sketch classes and the like, clearly the Club's main purpose was not self interest but "to improve conditions in the field."

It was a democratic document, this Constitution, which anticipated that no clique, however beneficent, should gain control or remain in power contrary to the wishes of the majority. Elections were to be held yearly. The Executive Board was required to appoint two independent nominating committees, with a provision that any five club members might submit still another slate, if filed within a reasonable time. Ballots distributed to members were to be mailed back in sealed envelopes. The Club's work was to be carried on by many committees whose chairmen, though appointed by the Executive Board, were free to select their own subordinates. Even here, any seven members of the Club might constitute themselves a *special* committee, subject to the Executive Board's authorization.

The Constitution was argued over in successive open meetings of the Club and finally adopted. But committee activity had not waited on final authorization. Particularly was this true of the Ethics Committee (described in some detail in the preceding section of this book). Ethics as a primary interest of the Club had been discussed in June 1920; organization came soon after. Nathaniel Pousette-Dart, as its chairman, presented a circular at a meeting at Mouquin's Restaurant which read in part: "The art director must exercise judicial functions between clients and artists with complete impartiality; he must command respect and confidence."

The First Exhibition of Advetrising Art

Along with the Ethics Committee came the Art, or as it was afterward to be called, the Exhibition Committee which worked through the heat of the summer on plans for the Club's *First Annual Exhibition of Advertising Paintings and Drawings.* Ralph Shultz, as chairman, had seven men helping him. In November they sent invitations to submit proofs of advertising illustrations which had appeared in magazines, newspapers, booklets or as posters, to a list of likely exhibitors. Thousands of such proofs came in. From them exactly 292 pieces of finished art were chosen. And the basis of selection? Artistic merit. Purpose of show? "To encourage the knowledge and use of better illustration and design, particularly in advertising."

One way of encouraging meritorious work was, of course, the awarding of prizes to outstanding examples. Paul Manship, nationally known sculptor who had designed some notable war medals and was then living in New York, was commissioned to design a medal for the exhibition to be cast in silver. For the face of the medal its creator chose to depict Pegasus, the mythological winged horse, at the kick of whose hoof gushed forth the spring at which the nine muses found inspiration, beast and rider symbolizing the arts, as they also symbolized poetry. The reverse of the medal featured an artist with palette.

Three of the coveted Manship medals were awarded at the opening of the exhibition at the galleries of the National Arts Club on March 2, 1921: one to Frederick R. Gruger, veteran illustrator, the others to René Clarke, protegé of Earnest Elmo Calkins at Calkins and Holden, and to Emerston Heitland, an up-and-coming young artist with a fine flair for color. Seldom had New York art circles noted so impressive a jury. There served on it in addition to Richard Walsh, its chairman, Robert Henri, Charles Dana Gibson, E. H. Blashfield, Arthur Wesley Dow and Joseph Pennell. A quintet, certainly, of notables.

The Club's First "Annual"

The show which these men judged was a success, in quality of work, in attendance and—it may be added—financially; for it had the support of numerous advertising agencies, publishing houses, and art and graphic art concerns. As to merit the student of today, fortunately, need take no eye witness's word for it. The record exists in the Club's first *Annual* published late in 1921—118 pages of reproductions of art and complete advertisements. There he may discover a spottiness, perhaps, some work which lacks inspiration, some work which is dated—as much by manner of painting as by costume or accessories. But he will also find posterized drawings by Penfield, Teague and René Clarke; architectural sketches by Jules Guerin and Hugh Ferriss; etchings by Pennell and Earl Horter; and illustrations by Cornwall, Raleigh and Preston which would receive equal recognition today. Club members Treidler and Oberhardt, artists, and Lejaren Hiller, photographer, it should be mentioned, were in this illustrious company.

While the Art and Exhibition Committee, expanded to twenty-six persons and headed now by Frederick Suhr, was busying itself with the innumerable details of staging the exhibition just described, the Club was well occupied otherwise. In April 1921 it had made the first move to incorporate and on August 13th filed its papers at Albany. It conducted a letterhead competition among its members which produced the modification of the Albrecht Dürer monogram, since used extensively as the Club's trade mark. It approved a Placement Service for Individuals and Firms (man seeking job or vice versa) and decided to act as a clearing house for the project, using the services of the Club's secretary. It inaugurated a series of sketch classes for Club members. It adopted the policy of inviting outside speakers to its weekly luncheons at Brown's Chop House, entertaining such celebrities as Frederick Goudy, type designer; Fred Cooper, artist; Bruce Barton, writer; Robert Benchley, dramatics editor of *Life*; and President O'Shaughnessy of the American Association of Advertising Agencies—the "4-A's".

President Richard Walsh undertook to sum up the achievements of the Club's first year in his annual report and to re-state its aims. In the report he said: "We thought we might help to improve the look and feel of common objects . . . (to that end) we wanted the Club not to rest with advertising alone, but to broaden and take in art directors and designers from such other fields as textiles, furniture, ceramics, architecture . . . stage, motion pictures . . . even automobile factories." Again he reminded his fellow Club members that they were creating a profession, and should live up to their professional standing and must insist on an observance of ethics.

Walsh, shortly before the opening of the First Annual Exhibition, turned over the gavel to a successor and Heyworth Campbell, who had been one of the Roof Tree Inn "adventurers," became the Club's second president. To assist him the Club had elected Joseph Hawley Chapin and Stanford Briggs vice-presidents, and James Ethridge and Ralph Shultz respectively, secretary and treasurer. In addition, there was an Executive Committee of four members. The Campbell administration was—and is—memorable for two things: corralling distinguished speakers for weekly luncheon meetings—many at colorful Brown's Chop House, others at the Hotel Martinique—

and the decision to affiliate with the newly organized Art Center on 56th Street.

The new president was singularly qualified for the first accomplishment. A man of charm and engaging manner, with a host of personal friends, Heyworth Campbell was art editor of *Vogue* Magazine and a member of the Dutch Treat Club, composed of outstanding personalities in the newspaper and publications field and in the world of art and letters. He could, because of these contacts, lend help to his Program Committee. And note these names of 1921 speakers: Dave Wark Griffith, producer of "Birth of a Nation"; Don Marquis and Heywood Broun, columnists; Christopher Morley, author of a score of best sellers; Lee Simonson, theatrical designer; Frank Harris, British writer; Joseph Schildkraut, star of "Lilliom"; Albert Sterner, painter; and among other celebrities, Fiorello LaGuardia, New York's "Little Flower", then President of the Board of Aldermen. An amazing list, truly, to honor a struggling young organization by their presence!

The Art Center

Joining forces with the Art Center had been a project under discussion about the time this new administration took office. It offered interesting possibilities. To begin with it offered a headquarters and a home to a society which had neither. It was installed in a converted brown-stone on dignified 56th Street. Its ground floor was suitable for exhibitions, with extra gallery space on the floor above where luncheon meetings might also be held. There was office space on the top floor. But more important, than any of these advantages, perhaps, was its *raison d'etre*.

Mrs. Ripley Hitchcock, a public-spirited New Yorker whose dream the Art Center had been, had envisioned the project as one wherein a group of independently-operated societies devoted to the applied arts and the handicrafts might have a common headquarters and might collaborate to advance the cause of Art in Industry. This art included all forms of reproductive illustration, whether for books or for advertising. The Center called for educational efforts of all kinds and the holding of exhibitions. Already, when the Art Directors Club was apprehended, several societies were committed to the plan, including such kindred organizations as the Society of Illustrators and the American Institute of Graphic Arts.

The Art Center idea found much support, therefore, among members of the Art Directors Club. The Executive and House Committees unanimously recommended that funds be given the latter to obtain quarters in the Art Center building. By May 1921 final action to affiliate had been taken. And shortly thereafter Club members were cooperating in the sale of Art Center bonds in denominations of $10., $100. and $1000. whose proceeds, it was hoped, would put on its feet the parent organization which, in the interest of the constituent organizations, had been incorporated as a holding company for real estate.

In October the Art Directors Club participated in the first exhibition staged by the seven combined societies at the Art Center, its contribution being a personal showing of the function of an art director in producing a magazine advertisement—from his initial rough sketch and dummy layout to the finished magazine proof. Simultaneously occurred the dedication ceremonies of the Art Center Building, presided over by Mrs. Hitchcock and Charles Dana Gibson, vice-president.

As this recital suggests, in the crucial second year of the Club's existence a lot had happened. Its prestige had been built up. It had found a habitation. And much of the credit went, as it properly should, to Heyworth Campbell. Yet, in a sense, Heyworth Campbell's contribution to the Club went deeper than any of these things indicate. If Louis Pedlar brought the Club into being and Richard Walsh formulated its philosophy and became its spokesman, Heyworth Campbell, by his own extraordinary capacity for friendship made the Club, not just another successful trade organization, but an association of friends—which, it may be said, it has since remained.

A grateful Club, on March 31st, 1922, when his year of office had ended, gave Heyworth Campbell a testimonial dinner at the Coffee House Club on 45th Street—and thereby established a custom of honoring retiring presidents. It was a formal yet relaxed affair, concluding with a one-act farce "Oh, Mamselle", presented by Frederick Suhr and its author, Joseph Chapin, the Club's new president.

Joseph Hawley Chapin was then art editor of *Scribner's* Magazine. As impressive in appearance as he was capable,

Chapin was in the tradition of a line of distinguished magazine art editors which followed the famed "Drake of the *Century*". He had, like his predecessor, a wide acquaintance with important figures in art circles.

The more showy of the 1922 meetings were monthly affairs held on Tuesday evenings, in an Art Center gallery or at the Martinique Hotel. At the regular weekly meetings, which continued, programs were utilitarian. Prominent speakers discussed such down-to-earth subjects as layouts and visuals, the responsibility of the art director, magazine make-up, engravings and roto-gravure—even office systems.

Meanwhile Club activities encompassed such things as Gordon Aymar's design of a Club bookplate, Stanword Briggs' appointment to represent the Club at the American Federation of Arts Convention in Washington and teaching help given to the Society of Illustrators' School for Disabled Soldiers.

The Second Annual Exhibition

President Chapin and his Executive Board, which included Frederick Suhr and Walter Whitehead, vice-presidents, worked hard to make the second exhibition of the various Art Center societies a success. All six of the Art Center galleries and its club room were filled by exhibits from the seven constituent organizations. A gala reception and private view on October 11, 1922 commemorated the founding, just one year before, of the Art Center, now a flourishing institution with 3,000 members. But the Art Directors Club did some crowing independently. They were making history. This was their *2nd Annual Exhibition of Advertising Art*. It would be recorded permanently in a published *Annual*.

And in December the Club elected its first Honorary Members. They were Louis Pedlar, Richard Walsh and Earnest Elmo Calkins. Three months later in April, 1923, it honored Joseph Chapin, but this time with a Retirement Dinner at the Coffee House as his term of office reached its end. In tribute the Club presented Chapin with a book of original water colors, drawings, etchings and verse contributed by Club members.

When Frederick Suhr took office as Chapin's successor the Club had found its stride and was a smoothly functioning organization. Suhr was determined that it should take no backward step. His vigorous

—and often salty—"pep talks" were calculated to remove any complacency among fellow art directors; and he kept committee members on their toes. With Suhr's encouragement Nathaniel Pousette-Dart, convinced from the inception of the Club that art education should be one of its prime purposes, went ahead with plans for "Talks to Young Art Students." The Ethics Committee of which P-D was chairman printed its first memorable Standards of Practice. The Membership Committee enrolled some score of desirable new members. The Exhibition Committee proposed a Poster Contest (advertising the forthcoming 3rd Annual Exhibition) open to students at art schools.

AD Clubs Start in Other Cities

Suhr and his vice-presidents, Henry Quinan, able art editor of the *Woman's Home Companion*, and Gordon C. Aymar were intrigued by the idea of forming chapters of the New York Club in other cities, where the advertising industry had taken hold. Representing the New York organization, and accompanied by Heyworth Campbell, Suhr went to Chicago and addressed a meeting of 200 art directors, artists and guests to inaugurate a Chicago Art Directors Club, sponsored by Walter Whitehead and Gerald Page-Wood. Suhr's talk was enthusiastically received . . . Philadelphia was soon to follow, staging its own Art Director's Club exhibition.

The 3rd Annual Exhibition of Advertising Art opened at the Art Center in April 1923—almost a year and a half after its preceding exhibition. Club members Byron Musser and William Oberhardt were responsible for the hanging. Gordon Aymar, chairman, in reviewing the exhibit for the *Annual* which recorded it, saw a perceptible improvement in the pictures and in the larger number available. "In posters", he wrote, "we are still behind Germany in design, and behind England in beauty."

In April 1924, Nathaniel Pousette-Dart took over the helm as president, with Morris Ayleshire and Louis Fancher (one of the Club's charter members) seconds in command. "P-D", as the Club's fifth president was affectionately known throughout the profession, was a Utopian (in the better sense of that word) whose twin enthusiasms were art directing and part-time fine arts painting. In both pursuits his work had shown a high degree of creativeness. And he had, his friends knew, an especial concern with organization and planning.

Expanding Activities

So it was not surprising that, soon after taking office, P-D should submit a carefully worked out program of Club activities which included such innovations as a movement to further promote better design in household furnishings—from stoves to lighting fixtures—and the formation of an "Adventurers' Club" as one of the activities of the Educational Committee. Stuart Campbell was appointed Chairman of the last named. The "Adventurers" held their first dinner meeting at the Hotel Fairfax on 56th Street, then went to Adolph Treidler's studio, a block away, to draw from a model and afterward to conduct a discussion on subjects of general interest in the arts field.

Plans matured for the "Talks to Young Art Students", which the Club had now aproved. They were to deal with such subjects as layout, designing, lettering, color, posters, package designs, window display and the processes concerned, and were to be given by successful practitioners in the various fields. It was intended that "they should bridge the gap between academic art school education of today and the more or less exacting requirements of the professional activity of commercial art." They were designed "for the mutual benefit of artist and art director." . . . Heyworth Campbell was made chairman of the series of Talks which opened in January 1925 with a talk by Ben Nash. (See Bernard Brussel-Smith's article, page 200—Ed.)

In October 1924 there was staged another of the exhibitions of the combined Art Center societies, filling all the galleries of the Center. The Art Directors Club's contribution this time was a "Playtime" Show open to Club members which P-D hoped would be the first of a series to be held annually. Sketches, water colors, wood carvings were included, among them two by the Club's president.

During these busy months the routine affairs of the Club proceeded smothly. There were big turnouts at the weekly meetings. Adolfo Best-Maugard, once Art Director of Mexico; Earnest Haskell, etcher; Burton Emmett, agency head; Joseph Stella, whom Augustus John was quoted as saying was the "only good painter in America!" were some of the speakers. Club membership increased by 30%, enlisting such members as René Clarke, Emil Bistran, Charles Coiner and

"Hal" Halpert, all widely known for their contributions to art and to advertising. Additional Club committees were appointed —nine such were active.

As usual the big event of the Club year was the *Annual Exhibition of Advertising Art — the Club's 4th —* occupying the Art Center's main galleries on two floors. Preparations under Gordon Aymar, again as chairman, and Willard Fairchild as vice-chairman, had been under way since fall; the Exhibition opened in April 1925 and drew favorable comment. The eight-man Jury of Awards, under Gordon Aymar, set a precedent. With the single exception of Charles Dana Gibson, all were former officers of the Club, members or art directors.

Balloting for Club officers at its annual election had proceeded during the course of the Exhibition. At the conclusion of both a new administration was ready to take over. To its retiring President the Club gave a profusely illustrated volume on the painter Ingres, suitably inscribed. The book, and the banquet at Keen's Chop House, where the presentation took place, were tangible evidences of the regard all had for Nathaniel Pousette-Dart who had a fighting faith in the things the Club stood for, and who had served it unselfishly and well.

Walter Whitehead was now president. Club members Johnson and Oberhardt were his V.P.'s. The latter was winning fame for his portraits of celebrities, in the crayon medium—he had already limned Gibson, J. Thompson Willing and many others, and was starting on his series of A.D. Club presidents. In his portrait of Whitehead, at the end of the year, he would capture the essence of this man, luckily endowed with all the qualities that go to make a leader. At one of the meetings at which Whitehead presided, someone asked him how much authority an art director should have. "Only so much", was the reply, "as he is able to seize ("grab off" was probably the term used) through his own ability!" The remark was characteristic.

The Fight to Preserve the Art Center

And the 1925-26 period was one in which the Club would profit from an authoritative and able spokesman, for important decisions had to be made. There was, for example, the question of the Art Center's financial health. The value of its services to the community and to the nation was unquestioned. But gallery rentals, membership fees, and generous but irregular contributions were not enough to sustain it. An Endowment Fund Campaign was proposed by the Art Center's governing Board.

The Fund, totaling $750,000, was to be divided into three parts: a Men's Special Gifts Committee, and "Members of the Constituent Societies," each of the three groups being assigned a quota of $250,000. An individual quota of $125. was suggested for every member of each of the Constituent Societies. "Give it—or *get* it" was the slogan.

Whitehead laid the plan before the Club; support for it was promptly voted and a Club committee was soon soliciting subscriptions. The Drive got under way officially on February 24, 1926 with a dinner at the Hotel Commodore, attended by 300 men and women, and was well sponsored. A former Ambassador to France was its honorary chairman, the president of one of the greatest department stores in the country was active on the committee, as were two leading bankers.

Meanwhile, another of the Art Director's Club Playtime Shows had been held at the Art Center in October 1925 in conjunction with exhibitions of the other Constituent Societies. Whitehead, who had gained a reputation professionally by his poster work, was represented on the walls as were Gordon Aymar, Charles Coiner and "P-D". There were the new names, too, of Vaughan Flannery and Lurelle Guild. And there had been another—the second—series of Educational Lectures, excellently attended, at which such subjects as "Use of Decoration," handled by Walter Dorwin Teague; "Use of Color", Royal Bailey Farnum; and "What Business Asks of the Artist" attracted so much attention that they were subsequently reproduced in part in the printed *5th Annual.*

The Fifth Annual Exhibition of Advertising Art, was held at the Art Center in May 1926, and in the character of the exhibits there seemed for the first time to be a change of direction—a trend—observable, if ever so slight a one. Literalism still ruled. But perhaps it was just a stepping-up of taste; perhaps the committee of selection, headed by Willard Fairchild and including such names as Edward Molyneux, René Clarke and Henry Quinan was unusually selective. The printed record of the show, whatever the reason, is fresh and pleasant to thumb through, even at this late date . . . The jury which awarded eight medals included C. D. Gibson, whom the Club could never delight enough to honor, Robert Henri, the painter and four others more directly connected with advertising.

"Lengthened Shadows of Individual Men"

In this sketch of the beginnings of the Art Directors Club, if undue stress seems to have been placed on presiding officers and their separate administrations, there is an explanation. Important institutions, some one has said, are but the lengthened shadows of individual men. Equally far-seeing, highly competent persons were to guide the destinies of the Club in the years to come. But it seems certain that the half dozen or so men who were its first officers determined, by what they were no less than by what they did, the Club's abiding spirit and personality.

So it may be both convenient for the reader and fair to all concerned to *group* together the next half dozen administrations, and to high-light events at the expense of personalities. The administrations which immediately followed that of Walter Whitehead were, in their order, those of Peirce Johnson, 1926-27; Arthur Munn, 1927-28; Vaughn Flannery, 1928-29; Stuart Campbell, 1929-30; Guy Gaylor Clark, 1930-31; and the two administrations of Edward Molyneux, from the spring of 1931 to spring of 1933.

The 6th Annual of Advertising Art opened on May 4, 1927. Edward F. Molyneux managed this Show, with Stuart Campbell serving as vice-chairman. It was a Show not unlike its predecessors but critics thought it more "daring", and there seemed to be an increase of so-called "modern" illustrations. There were three art directors on the Jury of Awards and three outsiders, among the latter Harvey Dunn, illustrator and inspiring teacher of a younger generation of magazine and advertising artists.

Faith in the aims of the Art Center, which itself was having hard sledding during most of this period, continued undiminished for the most part. Club members regarded it as a sort of United Nations in the art world. They wondered now and then if they had sacrificed too much independence of action by joining. They "griped" about the food served in the Art

DINNER
IN HONOR OF
HEYWORTH CAMPBELL
AT THE COFFEE HOUSE, 54 WEST 45TH STREET
FRIDAY EVENING, MARCH 31ST
AT 6:30 O'CLOCK

Center's dining room for the Club's weekly lunches—and experimented with strange restaurants, chop houses and hotels, never too successfully. Yet they felt that here was a combinaiton of forces committed to one of their own primary objectives — democratizing art.

The many competitions which their sister societies or the Art Center itself were conducting were examples of this democratizing process—for improved package designs; for better household furnishings, ceramics, textiles; and of especial interest, perhaps, to art directors, the several successive competitions for Wayside Refreshment Stands, initiated by Mrs. John D. Rockefeller, Jr. for the Art Center and judged by outstanding architects. Club members were enthusiastic about contests such as this, which could produce demonstrable results within a single season—could substitute for the stark disorder and ugliness of the average roadside stand or filling station simple structures of attractive design, in settings of trees, flowers and shrubbery.

All of these contests were recorded in the monthly Art Center Bulletin which each Art Director's Club member received —a slick paper periodical, generously illustrated with cuts, both tone and line. Space in it was shared by the different societies. The Art Directors Club columns were usually devoted to descriptions of its committee activities, to the review of an event such as the Annual Exhibition, and to chit-chat about members.

There were 209 names on the Club's membership list now, and new applications were coming in. Stuart Campbell cautioned about the caliber of men proposed: "The future of the Club depends on this". And P-D, in the same vein, asserted: "No one should belong who would use the club for selling personal or organization services". Fortunately, the self interest which occasionally had wrecked other organizations was never a serious problem for the A.D.C.

"An Unmistakable Advance in Taste"

A lengthy review of the Club's 7th Annual Exhibition, in May 1928, got first space in the Art Center Bulletin. The reviewer, noting the drift away from photographic realism, saw in the exhibition "an unmistakable advance in taste". Roy S. Durstine, in a Foreword in the printed Annual which came out late in the year, wrote: "You will detect certain exhilarating trends of design . . . that the ideal of making good pictures in advertising is brightened by the increased number of good pictures which the public insists on liking, and which the advertiser insists on buying." Credit for this Show, and for the Annual went to Chairman Stuart Campbell.

Held also at the Art Center while the 8th Annual was on display was the first of the series of lectures on Art and Advertising. Vaughn Flannery, Art Directors Club president; Paul Theo Frankl, interior decoration trail-blazer; Myron Perley, prominent art director; John B. Watson, founder of the school of "Behaviorism" in psychology, were speakers. A change in the composition of audiences was observable—a drive to enroll young advertising agency employees, along with artists and art students, was producing results.

About this time art for newspaper reproduction came in for a good deal of study. Some of the agency art directors felt that one or two of the big metropolitan dailies were cutting their requirements too fine, stippling areas of drawings intended to be black to an innocuous gray. A committee, headed by Maurice Collette, was appointed to take this "censorship of cuts" up with the New York Times. If, as happened, the argument ended in a draw it is likely that the Club got some valuable tips to pass on to artists.

A poster designed by Merritt Cutler, and circulated among business firms and local schools and colleges, heralded the 8th Annual Exhibition of Advertising Art, May 4-31, 1929, at the Art Center. Nine Club members selected the pictures to be hung. In accepting or rejecting a submitted proof, committee members had been pressed to ask themselves such questions as: Does it arouse enthusiasm in me? Has it originality of conception? Does it indicate an approach or style peculiar to its creator? Has it taste? Does it illustrate superlatively well? Recognizing woman's influence on advertising, the Committee invited two distinguished women to serve on the Jury of Awards with four male jurors—Mrs. Charles Dana Gibson and Mrs. Helen Appleton Read.

Recognition of art directing as a profession got a boost from Edward L. Bernays, public relations counsel, who addressed the Club at a luncheon. "Art directors are a powerful force for art in industry", Bernays said, "They must educate the trades as to their importance . . . regard themselves and their counsel as lawyer and engineer regards his counsel to client . . . must learn to sell themselves as a group . . . must make themselves an established body of authority. Their society should have all the dignity of an Academy".

Luncheon talks did not consist exclusively of sage advice. Curator of Mammals Raymond L. Dittmars, of the Bronx Zoo, brought a box of favorite snakes, poisonous and otherwise, to adorn a witty speech. The renowned circus clown—friend of Mark Twain and Thomas A. Edison—Bob Sherwood, enlivened another meeting; Count Felix von Luckner, "sea devil", still another; Col. Eduard Steichen talked on photography before an audience which packed the hall.

Of minor importance, perhaps, yet indicative of the concerns of Club members, was a decision to revise the Club's Constitution once again; a Chapter for Detroit was discussed; the Executive Committee planned help for teachers of art in New York City's High Schools, consulting with Forest Grant, the Schools' Director of Art. In May 1930 Club members were polled on a proposal to extend the presidency to a term of two years.

Help For Future AD's

And in the same year a questionnaire, addressed to "Directors of all Art Schools", was prepared by the Educational Committee, headed by Nathaniel Pousette-Dart. This Questionnaire had as its special purpose help for the young art student—the coming commercial artist on whom the art directors would have to rely—to find the best possible course of instruction and the most suitable school to prepare him for an industry-serving career. To this end sixty questions were asked dealing with schools, instructors, methods of training and other closely allied subjects. Printed as a four-page circular, the Questionnaire was distributed to school heads from coast to coast, and brought a gratifying percentage of returns and invaluable data. Though the Club (wisely, perhaps) did not follow up by printing a list of recommended schools, there can be little doubt that this Questionnaire had a stimulating effect on art instruction in many American localities.

The 9th Annual Exhibition of Advertising Art, at the Art Center, was held in

May 1930. "Doors were open to all producers and designers of advertising art, and material poured in from every source", reported George Welp, chairman, though the entry fee for exhibits had been raised to $10.00 each. On the Jury of Awards were Mrs. Harry Payne Whitney, art patron; Eugene Speicher, painter; Frank Crownin-shield, editor; and Margaret Bruening, critic. The majority of prize-winning pictures in the show, it was learned later, were those for which New York Club members were responsible. Of the quality of the show, Henry Eckhardt, advertising agency executive, had this to say: "Illustrations have a freshness equalled by no previous Annual . . . citadel of realism has succumbed to the decorative dramatic trend . . . little of five years ago is left." George Welp and Edwin Georgi, who had managed the big show just mentioned, managed another one in the fall. They hung a selection of the "Fifty Best Proofs of the Year", featuring examples of the art director's own planning and direction, and open to contestants in the U.S.A.

P-D proposed a Speakers Bureau for the Club. For some time requests for speakers along art and production lines had been coming in, from teachers' associations, clubs and similar non-commercial bodies. To meet the situation the Educational Committee called for volunteer talent, and soon had a sizeable list of names to draw upon, with available dates noted. It was made clear to responsible inquiries that talks by any of these authorities would be given gratis, as one of the community service activities of the Club.

The Club's records reveal these 1930 items: Ethics Committee Standards of Practice revised by four ex-presidents of the Club, one of whom was the newly appointed committee chairman. The second series of the Questionnaire on Art Education went out to art school heads. The second series of talks on Art and Advertising, initiated the preceding year, had as its theme, "Styling". It dealt with Modern Merchandise, the Advertising Campaign, the Advertising Page, the Advertising Illustrations, Sales Promotion Media, each subject handled by an expert. At Grand Central Palace, again the Club exhibited "50 Outstanding Advertisements". Regular weekly meetings of the Club held in the day time were "informal and infrequent".

Monthly meetings at night drew crowds. A favorite was "A Night with Currier and Ives", at which one of the original lithographers of these historic color prints was present and spoke.

These, it is remembered, were depression years, The unemployment situation was affecting all forms of art, and was bound to limit somewhat the 10th *Exhibition of Advertising Art.* At the Art Center, where it was held April 18th to May 18, 1931, it was remarked that "the exhibit . . . was smaller, reflecting the retrenchments of hard times." Yet Edwin Georgi and his vice-chairman, Elwood Whitney, came in for praise. A commentator saw in the pictures they had chosen "tangible evidence that the artist is approaching his problems more sympathetically — giving more inspirational quality to advertising art." Eugene Speicher served again on the Jury of Awards, and with him Dr. Mehemed Femy Agha and Harry Wickey. John Atherton, artist, made the poster for the show . . . This exhibition, it should be mentioned, like the preceding one—the 9th—was shipped to the mid-west, to be exhibited in Detroit, thus establishing the practice of Traveling Exhibitions which has since continued.

Problems of the "Depression Years"

Not only were advertising appropriations reduced and less art bought in the business depression of the Thirties, but in the offices of many of the substantial advertising agencies a condition of aesthetic insensitiveness seemingly prevailed. Art directors were cautioned by their superiors to forget any fancy ideas they might have that art work should live up to any long standing rules. Its sole job, while the emergency lasted, they said, was the one of immediate hard-fisted selling.

The attitude was understandable and not wholly without excuse. But there followed a plague of badly designed and completely uninspired advertisements in magazines and newspapers which must have dismayed even the staunchest advocate of the hard-fisted school. Here and there in advertising circles voices were raised in protest. Heyworth Campbell echoed the opinions of many of his fellow Club members in an article he wrote for *Printer's Ink Monthly*, entitled "Going Buckeye". It undertook to explain the then current tendencies and was an eloquent plea for a more intelligent use of art and the display on the printed page

of better manners.

And René Clarke, witnessing the same phenomena, contributed a remarkable three-page essay to the Advertising Arts section of *Advertising and Selling*, January 1932 issue, which has become a classic in the literature of art in advertising. Headed "Challenge", René Clarke wrote: "Bring Me Idealism" . . . "Bring Me Courage" . . . "Bring Me Imagination". *"The Quality of Leadership"*, he wrote, *"is tested by adversity. Because we have adversity, do you renounce your leadership and hoard your visions against that time when someone else has made a market for your talent?"* "It was a piece of writing to bolster sagging spirits and to restore faith.

The Club, of course, had more than its state of heart and morale to consider. Dues were dropping off. There were resignations. But the Molyneux administration, which bore the brunt of the blow, took speedy action for unemployment relief and seemed to carry on its major projects with increased vigor. The 3rd Art and Advertising series of talks, opening late in 1931 at the Roosevelt House on 20th Street, with Abbott Kimball as chairman, and discussing such topics as the "Challenge of the Camera" "was profitable . . . "one of the best attended".

Elwood Whitney was another Club member who refused to let the depression wear him down. The 11th *Annual Exhibition of Advertising Art* which he managed, with the assistance of Jack Tarleton and a small committee of capable men, was equally a success, and showed no compromise with quality. One lone "agency art director", it is true, quoted by a Marketing Service publication, found fault. "The Committee has gone 'arty'," this individual said, of the show which ran from April 23rd to May 14, 1932 at the Art Center. "It has favored anemic-mannered compositions in today's advertisements, which must sell goods". Yet Edward Alden Jewell, the *New Yorw Times* critic, found in it "much that is highly competent".

Troubles of the Art Center

The depression had gone harder with the Art Center than with some of the constituent societies. Its income had come from membership dues, from leases of quarters to the various societies, from the sales of its bonds, and (at times of recurring crises, to tide it over) from the gifts of generous friends who were interested in its work. This support had now diminished, but it had never been sufficient to meet the demands put upon it; and its troubles had antedated the hard times of the Thirties. A drastic change was inevitable and the depression was merely a *coup de grâce*.

The economic engineer called in to investigate the condition, financial and otherwise, of the Art Center had presented a 136-page report in 1931 recommending a complete reorganization, which the Center's Board of Directors had approved. Shortly thereafter, what had been the Art Center became the National Alliance of Art in Industry, the original name being retained only by a holding company, or landlord, which now took title to the land, building and furnishings at the 56th Street headquarters.

The working or "activities" organization, according to plan, would operate on a wider scale than before. Its nucleus would be the seven original societies, with manufacturers, business men and artists serving on its governing board and supervising such things as industrial art exhibitions.

Club members had watched these changes with mixed emotions. They had believed in the Art Center's aims, which indeed paralleled their own. And they had been influenced, unconsciously perhaps, by gracious surroundings which counteracted tendencies to Bohemianism, often the charm of, but also a liability to purely art societies. Yet there was a growing feeling that the work of the Club was sufficiently important to be carried on independently of other organizations.

President Edward Molyneux presented the situation, its pros and cons, in a report he read to the Club in 1932. The Club, he said in effect, feels apart . . . it is afraid that in so great an organization with so varied a membership it might lose its identity . . . have its activities submerged. Acknowledging moral obligations to the old Art Center, Molyneux concluded: "The Art Directors Club feels it is time to end half-hearted affiliations for the good of both parties and to strike out for itself and begin a new and more vigorous independent life".

The die had been cast. In February 1932 the Club proposed to hold its weekly meetings at the Architectural League on 40th Street. It issued its own monthly News Bulletin, in place of the defunct Art Center Bulletin. It relinquished its club room at the Art Center building, and purchased new rooms at the Architectural League. By December it was installed in its new quarters. For a time relations with the National Alliance contained, but the Club had begun its "more vigorous independent life".

This new life began auspiciously. The Club had weathered the worst of the depression with its own finances in order. "The economic picture improves," Wm. L. Chenery, editor of *Collier's*, was writing of the national situation, "communities, industries, here and there are winning back to health."

A Pattern Has Been Set

In this historical sketch of the beginnings of the Art Directors Club of New York, the intention has been to trace some of the steps by which art directing developed into a profession. The gradual accumulation of specialized knowledge and experience, the increasing importance of the individual art director, in his own estimation, in the eyes of his employer, in the social scheme, — a final general acceptance of his professional status — all these, the reader may discover, seem to have been mirrored in the events and personages of the Club's earliest years.

The sketch should afford also, to anyone interested in this new profession, a glimpse into the mental make-up of art directors, past and present. It should show what distinctive qualities or what temperament a representative art director is likely to possess, what his chief interests are, what is apt to stir his enthusiasms. What makes him *click*, in short, in New York City or elsewhere.

The Club year 1932-1933 is as appropriate a date as any for bringing the narrative to a close. By then the Club was entirely on its own. It was installed in quarters that were to be permanent. It had demonstrated its stamina in withstanding the worst of the depression. But more important than all else, in its attitudes and its methods, in its easy adaptation to such startling changes as television had occasioned, it had set a *pattern* that would continue with little or no alteration over the succeeding years.

The years ahead, notwithstanding, were eventful and exciting. Their story is told in part in the Club's printed *Annuals*. There, for example, the student of advertising art will note that two of the nation's great department stores, Altman's and Macy's, turned over their galleries to the Club for annual exhibitions (the latter store registering an attendance of 13,000 over a three weeks periods). He will find that twice—in 1942 and 1947—the Metropolitan Museum of Art was host to Art Directors' exhibitions. And that the Club's 1949 show was housed in the Museum of Modern Art.

In the *Annuals* the student may observe the impact of World War II, climaxed by the hanging in the 1945 show of the famous Rosenthal picture of Marines raising the flag atop Iwo Jima. The Club's response to war, it must be recorded, had been immediate. With Pearl Harbor fresh in mind, Vaughn Flannery, newly appointed Director of Graphic Arts for the U.S. Government, was telling eager Club members, in a lecture at the Metropolitan Museum, how they might help in the war effort, put their talent and ingenuity to work, contribute illustrative ideas, layouts and art work . . . For the increasing number of Club members in the armed forces, the Club declared a moratorium on dues for the duration. For those thrown out of jobs by the economic dislocation, it offered the free use of its rooms for interviewing or for free-lance work, and free telephone and secretarial help.

Innovations of the more recent years include the inauguration of Reader Research Classes in 1950, which is discussed elsewhere in this book, and the highly successful experiment of staging exhibits of paintings by the children of Club members under the inspired title: "Future Art Directors Exhibit." Also there was the formation in 1942 of an Advisory Board for the Club, wholly made up of ex-presidents plus the active president. Created by a vote of the Executive Committee and of the entire membership of the Club, and originally expected to replace the Ethics Committee, the Advisory Board had turned over to it by President William Adriance the revived proposal for a national association of Art Directors Clubs, with the request for a review and recommendations. The outcome of this study, as everyone knows, is the present National Society of Art Directors.

As this volume went to press the Club

offered dramatic proof of vision and vitality. Its first annual Visual Communications Conference June 4-8, 1956, exploring visual sales ideas and forecasting developments in the process of communicating with people through their eyes, coincided with the showing of the *35th Anniversary Exhibition of Advertising and Editorial Art*. Conceived during the regime of President Frank Baker, well-timed and conducted by William McK. Spierer, chairman, and his committee associates, the project was the most ambitious yet undertaken by the Club in the educational field.

Thus the influence of the Club continues to expand—across the nation—throughout the world. Keeping alive great traditions.

Oberhardt

by WALTER H. GEOGHEGAN
Calkins & Holden, Inc.; Past President Art Directors Club of New York

IS THERE anyone who wouldn't want the privilege of sitting for "Obie", who has painted and drawn from life so many national celebrities? And in our own collection of heads of the Presidents of the Art Directors Club, has he not made each man speak for himself? Note, as Ernest W. Watson once wrote in *American Artist*, "the pensive, contemplative expression of 'P-D' and Molinyeux; the geniality of Geoghegan; the alert, questioning eye of Peirce Johnson; the satisfied assurance of Chapin; Hawkins' satiric humor; Whitehead's cool, judgelike countenance; the classic profile of Aymar, as well as Irwin's look of bubbling enthusiasm; and Heyworth Campbell's alert appearance . . ."

It was Nathaniel Pousette-Dart, I think, who first suggested that "Obie" perpetuate the likenesses of the Presidents; the suggestion was accepted enthusiastically and conscientiously. I have not been the first nor the last to admit that the thought of being drawn by "Obie" is one of the incentives of becoming President of the Art Directors Club. And "Obie" has been drawing them "free of charge" since 1920. He is still at it!

217

Walsh H. Campbell Chapin Suhr Pousette-Dart

Whitehead Johnson Munn Flannery S. Campbell

Clark Molyneux Aymar Agha Platt

Uptegrove Geoghegan Loh Stone Adriance

Irwin Hawkins Smith Rondell O'Brien

Tillotson Jamison Archer Baker Buckley

The Advisory Board:

The Thread That Binds

by John Jamison

Chairman, Advisory Board, Art Directors Club of New York

THE development and growth of any organization depends on people, their experience, devotion and objectives.

The Executive Board of the Art Directors Club of New York had people with these qualifications in mind when in 1942, under the presidency of William Adriance, it created the Advisory Board consisting of the current president and all past presidents.

With such a reservoir of active interest the Advisory Board was in an excellent position to carry out its duties. These duties were clearly defined: To advise the Executive Board in all matters concerning the operation of the club, and to assist in long term projects and the development of ideas and plans that might be brought to their attention.

The first meeting was held in June, 1942 and Edward Molyneux, president 1931-32, was elected chairman. The agenda covered a variety of subjects that the Executive Board had under discussion. Among them was a dream of a National Society of Art Directors that William Adriance and Nathaniel Pousette-Dart had proposed many years before. This concept of a national organization that would embrace fellow art directors clubs from all over the nation presented a great challenge. It could only have been realized with the support of a strong united club such as the Art Directors Club of New York, and the devoted efforts of a few far-sighted men who could see the great advantages to the profession of art direction of bringing together representatives of art director clubs from our major cities. (See page 220 for the story of NSAD.)

The NSAD

The Advisory Board was amazed at the reception of the idea. City after city requested information and offered help. In organizing the Society they realized that this was one of the greatest steps in the history of their field. At this writing 23 clubs —representing the centers of advertisng, editorial art and design in the United States and Canada—are members of the National Society. This dream of the Advisory Board has at last been realized.

Following the formation of the NSAD came the adoption of its official publication —*Art Director and Studio News*. This magazine, published monthly, has recently been renamed *Art Direction* and is the only publication in the world devoted solely to the profession of art direction and design. It brought to the individual art director an opportunity to communicate with his colleagues, to better understand the problems that each faced and to share new developments. The two men who did so much to finalize this effort were Gordon Aymar and Arthur Hawkins, both past presidents and members of the Advisory Board.

Code of Ethics

In 1920 the Club had recognized the need of a uniform standard of conduct in the profession and established the first Ethics Committee. In 1921 this committee composed a code of ethics that was to become the basis of all future standards. With the end of World War II the field of art direction expanded tremendously, and with it grew also the inevitable instances of mis-

21

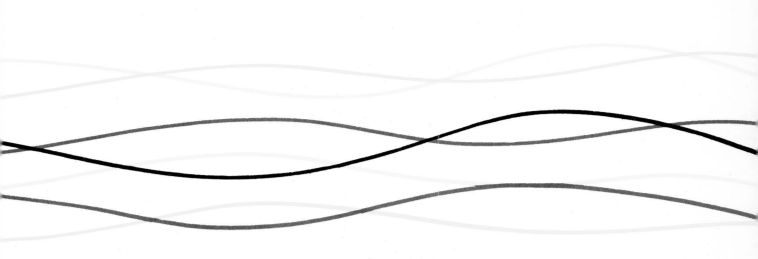

understandings between the various branches of our industry. The complexities of modern business created problems that could only be solved by men who, through their experience and judgment, were capable of drawing up procedures to be used as a yardstick in settling disputes that otherwise would have ended in a court of law. The Joint Ethics Committee of the three leading art organizations—the Society of Illustrators, the Art Directors Club of New York and the Artists Guild—formulated the Code of Fair Practice, which is now the accepted "bible" of the industry. (See page 182). The effectiveness of the Code is a tribute to the many hours of discussion and review that the members of these organizations, and the Advisory Board, devoted to this purpose. Its national acceptance is a result of the insistance of the Board that every member of the National Society agree to abide by its principles.

In 1954 the Executive Board recommended that the Club sponsor a conference in conjunction with the Annual Exhibition and the Awards Luncheon. The Advisory Board was consulted and assisted in the early planning. The suggestion was made that such a Conference should be conducted on a high level and include speakers representing every phase of our field. Its purpose would be to stress the importance of the art director's role in the communication of ideas. In 1956 the First Visual Communications Conference came into being and its success far exceeded the hopes of those whose efforts made it possible.

Advisory Board at Work

A list of the accomplishments of the Advisory Board would be a long one for its activities cover every area of club life. It acts as the official "watch dog" of the Annual Exhibition of Advertising and Editorial Art and Design, and directs the Awards Luncheon. No major project would be attempted without first consulting the members of the Board, and matters such as scholarships to students, revisions of the Constitution and decisions regarding policy are generally referred to them.

Some of the many projects that the Board has discussed over the years are: methods of classification and judging of the Annual Exhibition; assistance to needy members; membership application forms; educational work in conjunction with art schools; status of the National Society; research studies; operation of Awards Luncheon; Constitutional revision; housing; official publication of the National Society. These and many other subjects have received intelligent and thoughtful study; the results speak well for the mature judgment of the men of the Advisory Board.

Those in the club who originally conceived the idea for this Board were convinced that no group would have a better over-all picture of the Club's needs, purposes or possibilities than its ex-presidents, who were attached to the club by a deep sense of loyalty and who could be counted on to serve completely free from ulterior motives. The Board is ever aware of that trust.

The men of the Adisory Board are proud to have been leaders of an organization that represents the finest standards of their profession and to them the honor of membership is the reward of service.

Richard J. Walsh
Heyworth Campbell (deceased)
Joseph Chapin (deceased)
Fred Suhr (deceased)
Nathaniel Pousette-Dart
Walter Whitehead (deceased)
Peirce Johnson (deceased)
Arthur Munn (deceased)
Vaughn Flannery (deceased)
Stuart Campbell
Guy Gayler Clark
Edward F. Molyneux
Gordon C. Aymar
Mehemed Fehmy Agha
Joseph Platt
Deane Uptegrove
Walter B. Geoghegan
Lester Jay Loh
Loren B. Stone
William A. Adriance
William A. Irwin
Arthur Hawkins, Jr.
Paul Smith
Lester Rondell
Harry O'Brien
Roy W. Tillotson
John Jamison
Julian Archer
Frank Baker
William H. Buckley

The National Society of Art Directors

by Arthur Hawkins,
Secretary-Treasurer, N.S.A.D. 1945-1952

and Cecil Baumgarten,
Secretary-Treasurer, N.S.A.D. 1952 —

IN THE spring of 1945, the legal machinery necessary to establish the National Society of Art Directors was ready and waiting for the go-ahead signal. It came when six men, convening in a gallery at Rockefeller Center, wrote their names on a legal document. These six were: William A. Irwin, president of the New York Art Directors Club (1943-45); William Oberhardt; Lester Jay Loh; Earnest Elmo Calkins; Rene Clarke; and Dr. M. F. Agha. The document was the charter of the National Society of Art Directors, granted by the State of New York.

It sounds simple, but actually almost twenty years of false starts, delayed action, periodic apathy and legal blocks had been encountered before an unanimously acceptable national organization could be blueprinted.

False Starts

One of the false starts occurred back in 1930 when a plan was presented to change the name of the New York Art Directors Club to the Art Directors Club of America. National headquarters were to be established in New York City and non-resident memberships were to be built up from among the art directors of other American cities. This movement fell through. It was held, and not without logic, that the New York club with its exclusively local activities was not justified in assuming a national title. Furthermore, no satisfactory method could be devised for passing on the qualifications of prospective members outside of New York, nor could a satisfactory method be conceived for keeping such widely scattered members interested enough to remain together once they had been accepted.

The disappointment resulting from this failure to set up a national organization stymied further activities for a number of years. It was not until thirteen years later, in 1943, that a really active effort was made to revive the project. By then new interest had developed to such a point that the New York club asked its Advisory Board to tackle the problem as a specific project. (See page 218). After considerable deliberation it was decided to scrap the idea of an organization of art directors and to substitute one grounded on the various art directors *clubs* which had come into existence in the intervening years. The growing membership and broadening activities of clubs in Philadelphia, Chicago, Los Angeles and Boston indicated that the project was ripe for discussion—and action.

It was further proposed that all these groups change their names uniformly from "clubs" to some title less social-sounding, such as "association", "society" or "institute". The local clubs would then be known as, say the "Art-Directors Society of Philadelphia'," and the national federation as the 'Art Directors Society of America".

A letter making these proposals to the out-of-town clubs received an enthusiastic reply from each. A committee was then set up under William A. Adriance to work out organizational details, and liaison vice

Signing the charter for the National Society
of Art Directors, May 1945. Left to right
(standing): Rene Clark, Dr. M. F. Agha,
William Oberhardt, Lester Loh; (seated):
Earnest Elmo Calkins, William Irwin. Society
then comprised 5 clubs — Boston, Chicago,
Los Angeles, New York, Philadelphia. There
are now 26 clubs throughout the U.S.A. and Canada.

National Society of Art Directors. From top,
left to right: Past presidents Guy Fry
(Philadelphia), Charles Gerhart (Cincinnati),
Wallace Elton (New York); Janet K. Brewster,
secretary-treasurer; Cecil Baumgarten
(New York), past secretary-treasurer; Gordon
Aymar (New York), past president; Arthur
Hawkins (New York), past secretary-treasurer;
Roy W. Tillotson (New York), president.

chairmen were appointed to provide personal contact with these original five widely separated clubs. Lawyer John T. McGovern worked to solve the legal details.

All through the winter of 1944-45, the work went on. In the spring a charter was drawn up, approved by all five clubs and by the Supreme Court of New York State, and literally signed, sealed and delivered. Another year was to be spent in devising, revising and ratifying an acceptable Constitution and By-laws. Then, in the spring of 1946, after representatives had been elected and officers had been chosen, the National Society of Art Directors was in business. A twenty-year dream was, at long last, a reality!

How the NSAD Works

The representatives—two are elected by each local club, regardless of size—govern the Society's affairs. From among them officers are chosen according to a planned rotation by club seniority. An exception is observed in case of secretary-treasurer who must be, according to the Charter, a New York resident. Officers and representatives serve for two years. An annual spring meeting transacts the important business and future plans, while interim affairs are managed by mail.

The National Society aims for a membership of at least two-thirds bona fide art directors. This is by no means a discriminatory procedure against the free-lance and

allied craftsmen, but an attempt to keep the dominating power within the hands of the art directors for whose interests, aims and problems the National Society was founded.

Though developments are slow, due to the wide dispersal of member clubs and to the fact that representatives work in their spare time, the National Society has grown rapidly nonetheless. In the past eleven years the Society has expanded from its original five clubs to twenty-three clubs through the United States and Canada. The advice and guidance of the National Society of Art Directors is now being sought by groups in no less than five other cities in this country who do not have Art Directors Clubs but who are anxious to organize and become a part of the national organization.

In 1947 an Annual Award was established to recognize the accomplishments of outstanding art directors. In 1948 the Award, a brass T-Square with ebony head, was

made by President Gordon Aymar to Paul Sherriff for his "distinguished art direction of the film *Henry V.*" The ceremony took place in the auditorium of the Museum of Modern Art following a dinner attended by the officers and representatives of the National Society, the British Consul, and officers of the J. Arthur Rank Company. Since that date, the award has become an annual event with nominees selected by all the clubs in the Society and all members privileged to ballot for the popular choice.

In 1949 the NSAD made an alliance with the publishers of *Studio News* to fulfill the need for a national publication. The move proved to be a wise one; the magazine became known as *Art Director and Studio News* and more recently, *Art Direction*. It has, from the date of our affiliation, become the national organ of the NSAD, a union that has been proved mutually beneficial. While published under private ownership, it is under the editorial guidance of a special committee selected from the Advisory Board of the NSAD, and the association is one of complete understanding and singleness of purpose.

Of perhaps greatest importance is the Code of Fair Practice, reproduced on pages 182-184 of this book. The Code has been adopted by every member club of the NSAD and agreement to abide by it is a prerequisite for any club seeking membership in the Society.

The Future

The Society's future plans are manifold. In progress is the establishment of a Speakers' Bureau to aid the out-of-town clubs in securing outstanding guests for their local meetings. A well-organized Traveling Slide Show is maintained for the purpose of displaying the best in advertising art, selected in the various exhibitions throughout the country. A National Exhibition of Art Directors' Fine Art is now being planned and it is the hope of the Society that this will become an annual event. to publicize further the art director's personal expression of talent and good taste. Expanding the NSAD's scope to international and overseas dimensions is another project currently under consideration.

Just as the first Art Directors Club, organized in New York in 1920, grew of its own impetus to its present substantial proportions it is not inconceivable that the National Society may in time girdle the world. This would fulfill a dream of the Society's founding fathers—an effort to unify the professional objectives of the art director, to carry on the spirit and aims of NSAD.

Working "Tools" . . . Reference

Part 13 Designed by Gregory Bruno

The Language of Art Directing

Including Some Terms From
Advertising -- Printing --
Publishing -- Television

OBVIOUSLY, it would be quite impossible to list and define all the technical terms—the jargon—used or encountered by the art director in his daily work. Moreover as this book makes abundantly clear, the professional interests of today's art director are very wide indeed; and they embrace many other fields whose special terminology, too, is extensive.

So the brief dictionary included here has been confined merely to some of the terms with which art directors are familiar. It is hoped that these concise definitions may be helpful to the novice or to others concerned with the activities and problems of visual communication.

We are indebted to H. Victor Grohmann, president of Needham and Grohmann, Inc., for permission to use certain definitions from his book, *Advertising Terminology*. Adaptations of a number of terms and additional definitions included here were compiled by Henry Mitchell Havemeyer, president of Hoyt Howard, Inc.

A

ACCOUNT

Generic term for advertiser. An advertising agency expression.

ACCOUNT EXECUTIVE

Member of an advertising agency staff who directs and services a client's advertising. Acts as principal contact between agency and advertiser.

ADVERTISING AGENCY

An organization which plans and executes advertising campaigns for its clients. The agency is not legally an "agent" but contracts with media in its own name, as an independent contractor.

AGATE LINE

A unit by which advertising space is sold, measuring 5½ points deep by one column wide. There are 14 agate lines to the inch.

AIR BRUSH

A type of sprayer operating on compressed air capable of producing a very fine spray which gives subtle gradations of tone. Used principally in the retouching of photographs and for smooth backgrounds in posters, etc.

ANIMATE

To arrange and photograph on motion picture film static drawings or objects, so that when the film is projected, it produces the illusion of movement.

ANNUAL REPORT

A booklet or brochure printed for stockholders of a relatively large corporation to summarize its financial condition and other important phases of the year's operation.

ANSCO COLOR

Color photography film material manufactured by Ansco. Also the transparency (after exposing and processing).

ART

General term for art work, comprising any hand drawn elements of an advertisement. This classification would include illustration, spot drawings diagrams, lettering, decoration, etc.

ART BUYER

The person in an advertising agency who looks at samples, keeps a file of artists and photographers and arranges for the purchase of such art material.

ART DIRECTOR

The person responsible by visual means, for delivering the reader (or TV viewer), *in a favorable mood*, to the selling message. In essence this is what our book is endeavoring to convey. See Copywriter.

ART EDITOR

The person responsible, by visual means, for delivering the reader, *in a favorable mood*, to the story or article.

ART REPRESENTATIVE

A salesman or agent for a studio, a group, or an individual artist or photographer.

AUTHOR'S ALTERATIONS

Changes from the original copy made after type has been set. Commonly called "A.A.'s".

B

BALOP

Abreviation of Balopticon. A projection machine or mechanism used in television to project objects, photographs, still pictures.

BEN DAY PROCESS

Method of obtaining a gray tone in a line cut by "screening" or breaking up the surface into a pattern of lines or dots without resorting to halftone work.

BILLBOARD

See Outdoor Advertising.

BILLING

Gross advertising expenditures; an agency expression.

BLEED PAGE

An ad which is not confined to the editorial margins of the publication, but printed to the very edge of the page.

22

BLIND EMBOSSING

A stamping process where the surface of the paper or other material is raised, or lowered. Requires a special type of engraving and is often used to show display copy, trade marks, etc., on covers of brochures, annual reports. etc.

BLOW-UP

An enlarged reproduction of photographs, artwork or other advertising matter for display purposes.

BLUEPRINT

See Van Dyke.

BOLD FACE

A characteristic of type face which gives the overall effect or blackness, heaviness, boldness.

BOOKLET

An advertising medium in small book form. Usually made of paper and folded or bound by saddle wire stitching.

BOURGES (pronounced "burgess")

Trade name for a series of colored transparent sheets used as overlays on layouts or finished art. Color may be removed where desired.

BROADSIDE

A promotion piece consisting of one large sheet of paper, generally printed on one side only.

BROCHURE

An elaborate type of booklet usually bound with a special cover.

BULLET

A heavy dot, available in various sizes, used to draw attention to phrases in the text.

BULL PEN

The section of an agency art department or of a studio where comprehensive layouts and other art work are rendered from the art director's visual or rough.

BURNISHING

Process by which an engraver can darken areas on a halftone plate.

C

CALLIGRAPHY

Lettering or type style derived from writing with a broad tipped pen.

CAMERA LUCIDA ("LUCY")

A device consisting of a partly silvered prism and supplementary lenses, by which a picture may be reduced or enlarged to any desired size.

CAMPAIGN

A series of advertisements using a definite theme or appeal planned to accomplish a specific task. May be local or national in scope and may last from a few weeks to several years.

CAPS

Abbreviation for capital letters.

CAPTION

Text matter describing an illustration. Also called "title," or "legend."

CARBRO

A photographic print in color. See Dye Transfer Print.

CAR CARD

A small card generally with poster-like design placed in busses, street cars and subways.

CARDBOARD ENGINEER

A specialist in the mechanics of producing display and packaging material.

CARTOUCHE

An ornamental frame-like design.

CENTER SPREAD

An advertisement appearing on the two facing center pages of a publication, printed as a single sheet.

CHROMALITE

Trade name for a process, using special chemicals, whereby wash drawings in black-and-white are prepared for the engraver so that the white areas automatically do not have any screen (i.e. an automatic drop-out). Similar to Kemart.

CLIENT ADVERTISER

An agency expression.

CLOSING DATE

The day when all copy and plates must arrive at the publication if advertisement is to appear in a particular issue. Also known as "dead-line." Closing dates are specified in advance by the publisher.

COLOR-AID

Trade name for a series of colored papers, used chiefly on comprehensive layouts.

COLOR OVERLAY

A transparent paper overlay on a black-and-white drawing on which colors are indicated as a guide for reproduction.

COLOR TONING

A method for coloring a black-and-white photograph by the use of bleaches and dyes. Obsolescent; see Flexichrome.

COLUMN

One of two or more sections of type composition separated by a rule or a blank space; i.e., newspaper column. Also a regular feature article written by a special editor or columnist.

COMBINATION PLATE

A single engraving in which both line and half-tone reproduction are combined.

COMPOSITION

Setting type according to a layout or other specifications and assembling it with cuts, ready for a complete proof.

COMPREHENSIVE

See Layout.

CONSUMER ADVERTISING

Advertising placed in publications, radio, television, billboards or other media reaching the general public.

CONTINUITY

A series of pictures in panels with the copy in balloons, similar to newspaper comics.

COPY

The text or reading matter, including headlines, sub-heads and captions. Also used in referring to completed artwork for the engraver.

COPY PRINT

A photographic print (usually glossy) from a negative obtained by photographing the original artwork or photograph.

COPYWRITER

The person responsible for phrasing the selling message. See Art Director.

CROPPING

Trimming off a portion of an illustration, photograph or other art work.

CUT

An engraving or electrotype. Usually refers to a single illustration or design. See Plate. Note that this is also a camera term used in TV.

D

DIE CUT

A sheet of paper cut to any shape other than rectangular; a cut-out of any shape in a promotion piece.

DIORAMA

Miniature setting used to give illusion of large locations which are impossible to construct in TV studios; also used in displays.

DIRECT ADVERTISING

Advertising material reproduced in quantity and distributed directly to prospects, either by mail, house-to-house delivery, bag stuffers, etc.

DIRECT-MAIL ADVERTISING

Letters, folders, reprints or other material sent through the mails direct to prospective purchasers.

DISPLAY

Material used, usually in retail outlets, to influence the sale of a product or service, i.e., window display, floor display, etc.

DISSOLVE

A television control technique by which a picture on the air is gradually faded out as a picture from another camera is simultaneously brought into full view. In a "lap" (overlap) dissolve, one picture appears to be wiped off, leaving another in its place.

DROP-OUT HALFTONE

A printing plate in which the halftone screen is dropped out in the very light areas. See also Silhouette.

DUMMY

Name used to designate layout for a book, booklet or folder, usually folded or bound to represent the finished product.

DUOTONE

Halftone engraving in two colors.

DYE TRANSFER PRINT

A photographic print in color.

E

EKTACHROME

Color photography film material manufactured by the Eastman Kodak Company. Also the transparency (after exposing and processing).

ELECTRONIC FLASH

High speed light source used in commercial photography as a substitute for flash bulbs. Eliminates necessity of changing flash bulbs after each shot.

ELECTROTYPE

Duplicate engraving made by taking an impression of the original. Always SS.

ENGRAVING

Plate used in letterpress printing. Made from art work or photograph in either line or halftone.

ETCHING

Process by which an engraver can lighten halftone areas on a plate.

EXPOSURE

Photograph.

F

FADE-IN, FADE-OUT

A television control technique by which a scene is gradually brought into view or is gradually dimmed from view.

FILM STRIP

Still or animated drawings or photos reproduced on movie film for projection with or without sound effects.

FINISHED ART

Art work which is complete and ready for reproduction.

FLASH

Source of light used in commercial photography to stop action. This term includes use of electronic flash as well as flash bulbs.

FLEXICHROME

Trade name for a method for hand coloring a black-and-white photograph, similar to color toning.

FLIP CARDS

Drawings on individual cards in either black-and-white or color to be "flipped over" for TV commercials.

FLUSH

Type matter lined up and set even with the edge of a page ·or block of printed matter; i.e., "set flush right."

FOLIO

Page number in a book or booklet.

FONT

A complete assortment of letters, numbers, punctuation marks, etc., of any one size and style of type.

FORMAT

The size, shape and style of a book, brochure, house organ or other printed work.

FREE LANCE

An artist or writer who takes individual assignments from different advertisers or advertising agencies but is not in their full time employ.

FRISKET

A very thin paper applied over a photograph or art work in which areas are cut away, the remaining areas acting as a mask, for retouching, etc.

G

GALLEY

A shallow tray in which type is placed for assembling or storage. Proofs of type that has been set in a single deep column without regard to pagination.

GLASSINE

Type proof printed on glassine paper (a thin, translucent stock) used to facilitate checking against the layout. Sometimes used to prove engravings in a second color to check register.

GLOSSY PRINT

A photograph or photostat which has been finished with a high gloss on the surface, making detail within the art more definite.

GRAVURE

The process of printing from plates where the ink is transferred to the paper from shallow depressions in the plate's surface; intaglio.

GUTTER

The line where two facing pages of a book or booklet meet. In certain types of binding the gutter may be invisible to the reader.

H

HALFTONE

An engraving which prints shades or tones. A screen is used to break up the design into small dots of varying size.

HEADING

A group of words which, used as a title or caption, is given importance in an advertisement by reason of size, position and content.

HIGH KEY (photograph)

Tones in a picture which all lie toward the lighter end of the scale. Also applies to degree and contrast of lighting on an image, TV set, etc.

HOUSE ORGAN

A publication prepared periodically by a business organization and issued to its employees or to clients and prospects.

I

IMPRINTING

Reprinting a finished printed piece to insert additional copy.

INTERTYPE

See Linotype.

ITALIC

A variation of a roman type face slanting to the right.

22

J

JUSTIFY

To line up.

K

KEMART

Trade name for a process, using special chemicals, whereby wash drawings in black-and-white are prepared for the engraver so that white areas automatically do not have any screen (i.e., an automatic drop-out). Similar to Chromalite.

KEYING AN ADVERTISEMENT

Inserting in the address or coupon a different code for each medium used, so that inquiries can be traced and media effectiveness compared.

KEYLINE

Lines drawn on a mechanical to indicate position, size, and shape of elements.

KODACHROME

Color photography film material manufactured by the Eastman Kodak Company. Also the transparency (after exposing and processing). Obsolescent. See Ektachrome and Ansocolor.

L

LAYOUT

The form in which the elements of an advertisement are combined:

1. Rough (Visual)—Preliminary sketch to show idea only. See Thumbnail.
2. Semi "Comp."—A more well-defined sketch of the idea giving a close resemblance of art and type style.
3. Comprehensive Layout ("Comp.")— a layout worked to a more finished state showing as nearly as possible how the completed advertisement will look.

LEAD

Strip of metal used to increase spacing between lines of type. (Pronounced "led").

LEADER

A line of periods or bullets used to lead the eye from one group of words to another.

LETTERING

The hand drawing of letters for reproduction as differentiated from mechanical means such as type process lettering.

LETTERPRESS

Direct printing from raised surfaces consisting of type, line plates and halftone engravings.

LETTERSPACING

Spacing between letters in type or lettering.

LINE

A typographic measure of depth of space. Usually refers to agate lines, of which there are 14 lines to the inch.

LINAGE

The amount of newspaper advertising space in terms of agate lines.

LINE CUT

Engraving for letterpress on zinc or copper (for delicate work), from artwork in black-and-white (no grays).

LINOTYPE

Method of setting type by keyboard (similar to that of a typewriter) resulting in a type metal casting of each entire line. Same as Intertype.

LITHOGRAPHY

The process of reproducing type matter and illustrations from a greasy material applied to a planographic surface of stone or zinc or other metal. See Offset Lithography.

LOGOTYPE

The distinctive design of the name of an advertiser or product used repeatedly in advertising and promotion.

LOWER CASE

Small letters as opposed to Capital Letters.

LOW KEY (Photograph)

Photograph which is predominantly dark in color.

LUDLOW

Method for casting larger (display) sizes of type in metal.

M

MARGIN

Unprinted area adjacent to the edges of a printed page.

MASKING OUT

Blocking out certain areas of a drawing that are not desired for reproduction.

MAT

Lightweight mold of an advertisement or engraving made of papier-mâché. It is used as an economical substitute for an electro and mailed to a newspaper to be cast into a stereotype. Also a cardboard frame for layout or finished art.

MATTE PRINT

Print of a photograph or photostat with a dull surface. (Pronounced "mat")

MATTE SURFACE

A dull-surfaced paper or photograph.

MEASURE

Width (a typographic term).

MECHANICAL

An accurate assembly of the various parts of an advertisement or printed piece indicating size, position and placement of elements preparatory to reproduction.

MEDIA

The vehicle (newspaper, magazine, poster, radio, TV, direct mail, etc.) which transmits the sales message to its market.

MONOTYPE

Method of setting type by keyboard (similar to that of a typewriter), resulting in a metal casting of each letter. Cf Linotype.

MONTAGE

(Short for photo-montage). Groups of photographs or drawings blended together to produce the effect of a single illustration. In television, usually three or more images transmitted simultaneously by means of dissolve technique.

MORTISE

A hole cut in an engraving to accommodate changes of material.

MULTILITH

Trade name for small offset press.

N

NEGATIVE

Developed film from which photo prints and engravings are made. Also the first print made by a photostat machine from original copy.

O

OFFSET LITHOGRAPHY

A printing process in which the impression is transferred from the printing plate to a rubber "blanket" and then onto the paper. (See also Lithography.)

OUTDOOR ADVERTISING

Display-type advertising (billboards, posters, signs, etc.) placed out-of-doors, along highways and railroads, or on walls and roofs of buildings, usually in larger cities.

P

PAGINATION

The organization of book or booklet material into pages.

PAN

Abbreviation of "panorama"—to move the TV camera from side to side or up and down. Also abbreviation of "panchromatic" film, any black-and-white film uniformly sensitive to all colors.

PASTE-UP

A general term often use interchangeably with mechanical.

PHOTO ENGRAVING

The making of relief printing plates from artwork, proofs, photos, etc., by a photo-chemical process.

PHOTO-GELATIN

Reproduction process using continuous tone (no halftone screen); economical for relatively short printing runs. Same as Colotype.

PHOTOSTAT

Photographic reproduction made by rapid, inexpensive process. Also called a "stat."

PICA

A typographer's and a printer's term to denote measure of width and sometimes depth. There are 6 picas to the inch.

POINT

A measure for size of type and type rules. There are 72 points to the inch.

POSTER

A sign affixed to a wall or board.

PRESENTATION

An accumulation of facts, figures, and ideas, both graphic and written, usually used in presenting and selling an advertising campaign to a client.

PRINTON

Relatively inexpensive kind of color print identifiable by its plastic base.

PROCESS LETTERING

Method of producing, in photo print form, display lettering from alphabets prepared for this purpose.

PROGRESSIVE PROOFS "PROGS."

Proofs of color plates showing each color separately, then in combination with one another. Used as a guide to the pressman.

PROOF

A sheet of paper imprinted from type or plates for correction, approval or for use in reproducing the type.

R

RATE HOLDER

Small ad inserted in a publication to obtain a frequency of insertion that permits a lower overall cost for the space used.

REGISTER

Term used in printing to devote proper positioning of two or more colors on the printed surface.

REP

Representative (salesman) for media, studio, artist, or photographer.

RESEARCH

Means of measuring quantitatively (and to some extent qualitatively) the markets reached by advertising.

RESCALE

To redesign and proportion an advertisement to fit a larger or smaller space.

RETOUCHING

Work done on a photograph to improve its reproductive qualities or change its content before reproduction.

ROMAN TYPE

The regular style of type used in book and newspaper composition as distinquished from italic.

ROTOGRAVURE

The process of making intaglio impressions on a rotary press. See Gravure.

ROUGH

(See Layout)

RULE

A line, commonly used as a border or to separate elements. Thickness may be hairline or in various point sizes.

S

SANS SERIF

Type of lettering or type face which has no cross strokes at top or bottom of the letter.

SCREEN

The number of rows of dots per inch in halftone engravings. Varies from coarse, 55 lines of screen in newspapers, to more than 133-screen on coated paper and 150-300 screen for offset or gravure work.

SERIF

The short cross-line at the ends of the main strokes of some styles of type faces.

SHOT

Photograph.

SILHOUETTE

The outline form of an object. Also used as a verb meaning to block out the background of a photograph.

SILK SCREEN

Process of printing in which colors are printed one at a time through separate silk screens prepared so that ink passes only through that area which is to be printed. Main difference between this and other methods is that neither raised or gravure principles are used. It is similar to a stencil technique.

SLIDE

Art work or titles on film mounted for projection.

SLOGAN

A sentence or phrase which through repeated usage becomes identified with the advertiser's product or service.

SLUG

A relatively small piece of metal prepared for letterpress printing. May be a line of type or signature or trade mark.

SPECTACULAR

Out of the ordinary form of outdoor display which attracts the eye through its size, illumination or motion. Examples: Display signs in the Times Square area in New York City.

SS

Same size.

STARCH REPORT

Research statistics on an advertisement; compiled by the Daniel Starch organization.

STEREO

Stereotype. Metal casting from a mat.

STOCK

Paper for printing.

STOP MOTION

A production technique in TV films similar to animation, but more simplified and generally less expensive.

STORY BOARD

A series of drawings showing the sequence of a TV film, announcement or program. One drawing is used for each change of scene, and both pictures and script are included. (See also Film Strip.)

STROBE

Stroboscopic lights; multiple electronic flash illuminating a moving subject several times against a dark background, for exposure on a single piece of film.

STUFFER

Envelope stuffer. Small printed sheet or folder, light in weight, that is included in periodic mailing such as a monthly bill from a department store.

SUB-HEAD

A secondary title or heading. A caption inserted in text to break up lengthy columns of type. Same as Side Head.

SUPERIMPOSITION

In television, picking up the image (lettering or artwork, for example) from one camera and electronically blending it so that appears on the image projected from another camera.

SURPRINTING

Superimposing one negative on another in making engravings.

SWATCH

A sample of paper or fabric used as a guide for matching color or texture.

T

TEASER CAMPAIGN

A series of advertisements, usually in small space, designed to arouse curiosity and create interest before an important announcement is made.

TELEVISION GRAY SCALE

Resolution of colors in artwork, scenery, costumes, and performers' faces into corresponding gray values in black-and-white TV. Has a shorter contrast range than other photographic media.

TELOP

Method of projecting an opaque card or slide used for TV titles, etc.

229

TEST CAMPAIGN

Testing an advertising idea on a local or regional basis before proceeding with a large-scale campaign.

THUMBNAIL

A miniature layout, usually very rough.

TIGHT

A TV camera shot that is restricted in area and that includes only essential information. Also, artwork which is ultrarealistically or finically rendered.

TINT BLOCK

A printing plate used to produce color areas.

TITLES

Announcements or credits of a TV program produced on film, cards, or slides.

TRADE-MARK

Any mark or design affixed to a product which identifies its source and distinguishes it from others.

TRADE NAME

A name identifying a business. Also, a brand name of a product or service.

TRADE AD

An ad planned for insertion in an industrial or trade publication.

TRANSPARENCY

Photograph in color on film. See Anscocolor, Ektachrome, Kodachrome.

TYPOGRAPHY

The art of setting and arranging type for printing or reproduction.

U

UPPER CASE

Capital letters, as opposed to small or lower case letters.

V

VAN DYKE

Contact print from an offset negative used for securing approval before making the plate. Color of print is brown; similar to a blueprint, except for color.

VARITYPE

Trade name for words typed in a special typewriter which has a number of interchangeable "type faces". Inexpensive substitute for type proofs.

VELOX

A photographic print of artwork screened into halftone dots for use as line copy.

VIGNETTE

A technique used to fade out gradually the edge of an illustration or photograph to pure white without leaving a line of separation.

VISUAL

A preliminary rough sketch showing variety of ways in which various elements in an advertisement can be arranged. (See Layout.)

W

WIDOW

Very short final line of a paragraph.

WIPE

Transition between scenes in television, where one scene replaces another in geometric fashion, i.e., expanding circle, a fan, a roll, etc.

WORD SPACING

Space between words in type or lettering.

Design/Phil Hays

The Art Director's Working Library

THIS outline was prepared by a research committee for this book under the chairmanship of Marc Brody, Decca Records, Inc. and Alfred B. Stenzel, Johnstone & Cushing.

As this book amply demonstrates, the art director's professional activities and interests are so widespread—his personal background and training so varied—that it is difficult indeed to do more than generalize about his working library.

Yet books and periodicals, bulletins, reports and the like are, in reality, essential "tools"—for they can be of untold value in helping the AD to keep abreast of trends, of new techniques and fresh ideas in all fields of special concern to him. It should be recalled, moreover, that the cost of such professional periodicals and books is generally recognized as a deductible expense for income tax purposes.

The following outline is not intended to be definitive or all-inclusive. Rather, it is presented primarily as a brief check-list which, in itself, may serve as an "idea-starter" for building or maintaining a working library.

Periodicals

In addition to the numerous and varied "general" magazines — and those devoted particularly to the fields of fashion, home service, and so on—to which the AD will want to give more or less regular attention, there are many specialized or technical periodicals aimed primarily at certain "functional" interests. Included among the latter are:

Art Direction, official publication of the National Society of Art Directors, is a "must" for all AD's. *Art in Advertising,* too, offers thought-provoking material of special interest. *American Artist* regularly includes sections on illustration and commercial art. And the "fine arts" magazines, such as *Art News* and *Arts,* can also be sources of inspiration.

For design ideas and current techniques from all over the world, the creative AD will want to follow one or more of the international periodicals (usually bi-monthly), including: *Graphis* (Switzerland); *Gebrauchsgraphik* (Germany); *Publimondial* (France).

Advertising in all its branches is represented by such magazines as: *Advertising Age; Advertising Agency; Advertising Requirements* (particularly for production, promotion, merchandising); *Industrial Marketing; Printers' Ink; Tide; Western Advertising.*

Graphic arts, printing and production periodicals include these: *American Printer; Graphic Arts Monthly; Inland Printer; Print; Productionwise; Rush; Western Printer and Lithographer.*

Photography is another field in which many art directors should keep abreast, and this includes magazines such as: *Industrial Photography; Modern Photography; U. S. Camera.* There are a number of top-grade foreign periodicals as well.

Package and product design are represented by periodicals such as: *Industrial Design; Modern Packaging; Package Parade.*

A few of the magazines in the fields of display, architecture and related design are: *Arts and Architecture; Display World; Interiors; Interior Design; Signs of the Times.*

Television has its own specialized periodicals too, including: *Broadcasting-Telecasting; Sponsor; Television.*

As has been mentioned above, this brief summary is merely intended to be suggestive. Many of the specialized periodicals will normally be available to art directors in agencies, publishing offices and other businesses through company library or other subscriptions. Others may be consulted in the public libraries (particularly in the larger cities). Moreover, most libraries have comprehensive indexes of periodical literature, cross-referenced by subject, which can be referred to for specific information. Such indexes often include also references to bulletins and other periodical reports.

Annuals

The art director can build a permanent file of ideas and inspiration, of techniques and trends, around the Annuals that are regularly published on advertising and editorial art and design, on the graphic arts, and in other fields of related interest. Such annual publications include:

KEY CHART FOR THE ART DIRECTORS CLUB LIBRARY

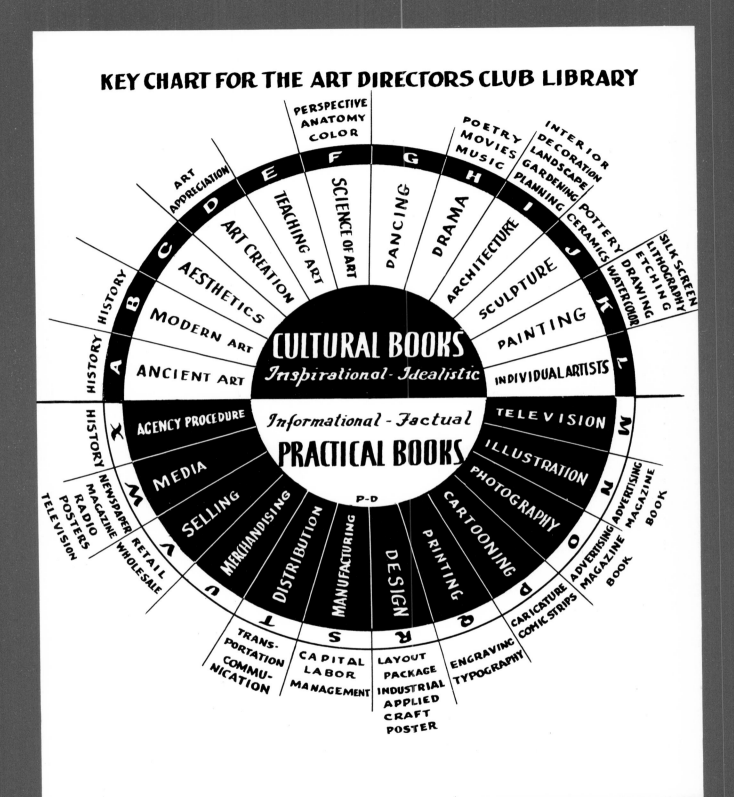

Annual of Advertising and Editorial Art and Design of the Art Directors Club of New York. Publication, in the fall of 1956, of its 35th edition marks this as the oldest continuous American national publication in its field. A "must" for all AD's, naturally.

Canadian Art Directors Annual (Toronto) reproduces the best current advertising and editorial art in Canada.

Decorative Art (England) includes international industrial and decorative design.

Graphis Annual of International Advertising Art (Switzerland) reproduces the cream of current visual art in practically all media from all over the world.

Idea (Germany) is devoted to international industrial design; includes some packaging.

International Poster Annual (Switzerland)—published every 18 months—is devoted exclusively to outstanding poster art and design from some 25 countries.

Modern Publicity (England) covers British and European advertising and graphic arts.

Outdoor Advertising Annual (Chicago) shows the best American outdoor posters and billboard advertising.

Penrose Annual: International Review of the Graphic Arts (England) includes examples of almost very kind of printing process, with lavish color work; full of design ideas.

Publicité (France)—published about every two years—includes handsome examples of French and other European advertising art and design.

U. S. Camera Annual (New York) provides a wealth of photographic ideas.

Western Advertising Art (San Francisco) annual issue of *Western Advertising*, includes the outstanding advertising and editorial art from the West Coast states.

Books

Long ago someone observed: "Of the making of books, there is no end." While nowadays there are practical limitations to to this, it is nonetheless true that a multi-tude of books are published each year—many of them informative, practical and useful for the art director. In addition, of course, there is the great mass of existing literature—the books previously published —available from book stores or other dealers, from the publishers themselves, or (even though "out of print") at libraries of all sorts.

So how to suggest a selection for a "working library' from such a vast storehouse of knowledge? To list *all* suitable books would be an impossibility. Even to exclude all except those of recent vintage would require more space than is available here. Moreover, such method would also exclude many standard works that still convey sound information and stimulating ideas—"classics" such as Chenault's *Advertising Layout*; Dalgin's *Advertising Production*; Dwiggins' *Layout in Advertising*; Jacobson's *Basic Color*; Longyear's *Type and Lettering*; Mayer's *Artists' Handbook of Materials and Techniques*; Nesbitt's *Lettering from A to Z*; Ogg's *An Alphabet Source Book*; Rand's *Thoughts on Design*; and many more.

It was decided, therefore, not to include specific book titles here but to suggest instead the *subject areas* in which the AD's working library could logically be classified. These subjects, in turn, indicate something of the varied fields with which the profession is necessarily concerned in greater or lesser degree—a clue to the "practicality and the idealism" mentioned in our Foreword, and emphasized many times throughout this book. In everyday terms, such classification may suggest to the AD how to make his own selections of books and periodicals, or how he may be guided in his search for information in a public library or elsewhere.

The accompanying chart was selected as depicting graphically these subject areas —classified, as will be noted, in two main groupings: the cultural and the practical. It was originally prepared as a key to the library of the Art Directors Club of New York by Nathaniel Pousette-Dart. In itself, it is worthy of study and reflection.

Who's Who Among Our Contributors

233

JULIAN M. ARCHER*

Studied at Nat'l. Sch. Fine & Applied Art, Washington, was 4 years as staff artist and AD of Washington *Herald*. After association with Daniel Starch, Barton & Gould, Rickard & Co., joined Fuller & Smith & Ross 14 years ago. Now v.p. and dir. of art. past pres. ADC-NY.

MERLE ARMITAGE*

A many-sided career includes civil engineer, theatre set des., concert mgr. and impressario. Wrote 36 of the 92 books he designed. Has designed mags. and newspapers and was AD for *Look* for 6 years, of which he is now consultant. Now AD and ed. board mem. *Western Family* mag.

FRANK BAKER*

Studied at Pennsylvania Museum Sch., Phila. Started advertising career at Gimbel Bros. then to N. W. Ayer & Son. Became AD of Ayer London and San Francisco offices. After one year with Otto Kleppner, New York, and two years with J. Walter Thompson, joined McCann-Erickson, Inc. where he is now senior AD. Past pres. ADC-NY.

CECIL BAUMGARTEN*

Consultant AD, sec'y-treas. of NSAD and general chairman of The Joint Ethics Committee, he has been a member of ADC-NY since 1932. Numerous awards from ADC-NY and DMAA. Mem. SOI.

LESTER BEALL*

Born in Kansas City, graduated from Univ. of Chicago. Has always worked independently, first in Chicago and now at his unique Dumbarton Farm, Brookfield Center Conn. Has been exhibited in museums here and abroad, and reviewed in U.S. and foreign publications. Principal fields: packaging, periodical and product styling, advertising design, development of integrated corporate design programs.

WILLIAM BERNBACH

Pres. Doyle, Dane, Bernbach, founded 7 years ago with Ohrbach's as first account. Believes advertising is fundamentally not a science but an art. Considers himself and everyone on his creative staff as an ad-builder rather than as a copywriter or AD. Believes an ad is just words and pictures until some great ideas bring it to life.

DR. JAMES C. BOUDREAU*

Art educator, author, painter, lithographer, he was dean of the Art School, Pratt Inst. from 1928 until retirement in 1956. Studied at Columbia, Pittsburgh, Alfred Univ. and in Europe. Taught art at Carnegie Inst. and Penn State Coll. Mem. leading educational art ass'ns., Royal Soc. of Arts (London), SOI.

WILLIAM P. BROCKMEIER*

Graduate of N.Y.-Phoenix Sch. of Des. he has been associated with ad agencies and department stores. Now AD for Eastman Chemical Products, subsidiary of Eastman Kodak. Has won numerous design awards.

MARC BRODY*

Native New Yorker, studied at Mechanics Inst., N.Y.U. Art Stud. Lea., in France and Austria. Has illustrated children's books, designed textiles and stage sets, record album covers, book jackets. Now AD, Decca Records, Inc. Mem. SOI.

BERNARD BRUSSEL-SMITH*

"Wood engraving" and "Brussel-Smith" are usually quoted simultaneously. An assoc. of Nat'l Academy, he teaches at Cooper Union, Brooklyn and Phila. Museums. But he still cannot say "no" to two agencies he continues to serve as consulting AD, and also serves as chr. Ed. Com. ADC-NY.

C. EDWARD CERULLO*

Art ed., *True* mag., he was educated at Art Stud. Lea., Nat'l Acad. of Des., Beaux Arts. Has illustrated for leading fiction mags. and ad agencies. As AD he designed more than 20 mags. in a variety of fields. Has won many awards from AIGA and ADC-NY, Chicago, Los Angeles, San Francisco. Mem. SOI, Westport Artists, Dutch Treat Club.

DOROTHY S. CHAPPLE

Arkansas born, Vanderbilt Univ. graduate, and former asistant ed. of *Art Direction* and *Rush* magazines, she is now a freelance writer.

MAHLON A. CLINE*

A graduate of Pratt Inst. where he is now dir. of Evening Art Sch., he is an AD, des. and typog. consultant for leading firms. Owns a private print shop where he experiments with type, paper, color in limited editions. Currently treas. ADC-NY. Mem. Type Dir. Club, Salmagundi, AIGA.

CHARLES T. COINER*

Studied at Chicago Acad. of Fine Arts, joined A. W. Ayer & Son, Philadelphia, as layout des. in 1924, became AD in 1929 and v.p. in charge of art in 1939. Has always aimed to prove top-quality art is necessary to top-quality visual advertising. In 1949 he received the first Annual Award of NASD. He writes regularly for numerous advertising art mags.

GARDNER COWLES

Iowa born, graduate of Harvard Univ., he holds numerous honorary degress. Entered publishing as city ed. of Des Moines *Register-Tribune* of which he is now pres. Founded *Look* mag. in 1936; ed. since its founding. Domestic dir. Office War Information in World War II. Dir. of many national firms, and educational and charitable organizations.

RALPH DADDIO*

New York City born, attended Art Stud. Lea. and New Sch. Former AD Franklin Simon, Bonwit Teller, *Seventeen* mag., adv. dir. G. Fox, Hartford and John Wanamaker. Now adv. and sales prom. dir. Kresge's-Newark, Inc.

DONALD DESKEY*

Founder, senior partner, Donald Deskey Assoc., he has been leader in industrial design for over 25 years. Minnesota born, studied at Univ. of California, Chicago Art Inst. Art Stud. Lea. and in Paris. Has won many exhibition awards and was prominent in designs at Chicago and New York World's Fairs. Fellow Soc. Ind. Des.

LOUIS N. DONATO*

A graduate of Cooper Union Art Sch., where he has also taught, his paintings are represented in museum and private collections and he has had 5 one-man shows. Now AD at Will, Folsom & Smith, Inc.

ALBERT DORNE*

New York City born, by 12, having drawn every sculpture and copied many pictures in the Metropolitan Museum, he had completed art training. Got first job sweeping floors in studio in 1921; became free lance artist in 1934 and in 1947 founded the Famous Artists Schools. Is former SOI pres. and honorary mem. of most AD Clubs. Was co-founder of Joint Ethics Committee.

WILLIAM R. DUFFY*

Senior TV-motion picture AD, McCann-Erickson, Inc., he pioneered in early experimental live and film TV shows and commercials as first accredited TV-AD. Taught at Columbia Univ. and is on New York Univ. faculty. Winner four merit awards ADC-NY.

FRANC von DUMREICHER*

Vienna born, studied there and in Paris, Munich, London, Zurich. With McCann-Erickson, Inc. 14 years, 6 years as AD of International Div. during which has traveled through four continents. Speaks 6 langauges, wants to travel even more.

WALLACE W. ELTON*

A graduate of Brown Univ., he has been AD, group head in copy and TV, aviation writer, travel photog. Has lectured widely at 4-A's, New York and Columbia Univ. most Clubs in NSAD. Past pres. NSAD and officer ADC-NY, he was named one of 10 top AD's in the country in 1955. Now v.p. and dir. J. Walter Thompson Co.

SUREN ERMOYAN*

Senior v.p., visual dir., Lennen & Newell, Inc. Former AD at Kudner, Compton, Ruthruff & Ryan Agencies; art ed. *Cosmopolitan, Town & Country, Good Housekeeping* mags. Has lectured widely at univ. and art sch.; mem. SOI. Awards include 24 medals and certificates of merit: ADC NY and Phila., AIGA.

CHARLES FALDI*

After study at Art Students League, Grand Central Art School and in Provincetown, he joined Benton & Bowles, Inc. in 1932 where he is v.p. and dir. of art. Mem. SOI.

STEPHEN FRANKFURT

A graduate of Pratt Inst. where he is now a faculty member, he also studied at New York Univ. and The New School. Worked on staff for UPA and as free-lance designer for CBS, NBC and KNX (Hollywood). Now TV AD at Young & Rubicam, in 1956 he won the ADC-NY Medal, Sylvania Television Award, Advertising Age Award and others for TV.

ALBERTO PAOLO GAVASCI*

New York born, his first job was with a package des.; later was *Vogue* ass't AD. Saw action in World War II, was AD for U. S. Gypsum Co. for 3 years and is AD of *Interior Design* mag. as well as head of his ad. consultant firm, APG Associates, serving a variety of national accounts.

WALTER B. GEOGHEGAN*

Connecticut born, after study at the Art Stud. Lea., he has been successively artist, des., AD and advertising executive at Calkins & Holden, Inc. Twice pres. of ADC—NY, he is mem. SOI and on Advisory Boards of Pratt Inst. and Sch. of Industrial Art.

WILLIAM GOLDEN

Creative dir., advertising and sales prom., CBS Television; born in New York, educated there and Los Angeles: Worked for a lithographer, a photographer, several newspapers and Conde Nast Publ. before joining CBS in 1937. Work has been prominent in ADC-NY and AIGA shows and in *Graphis* and *Print* mags.

JUKE GOODMAN*

Consultant AD. For past 20 years he was AD for leading department stores and agencies, including 12 at Saks Fifth Avenue. Awards number 2 ADC-NY medals and 7 merit certificates for fashion, cosmetics, packages. Mem. SOI.

WALTER R. GROTZ*

AD, Marschalk & Pratt Div. of McCann-Erickson, Inc., he studied at Art Stud. Lea. and New York Univ. Former sec'y. and v.p. ADC-NY.

WALLACE F. HAINLINE*

AD of *House Beautiful* mag., he started with Carson Pirie Scott & Co., Chicago. Then to Meredith Publ. Co., Des Moines as exec. AD handling *Better Homes & Gardens, Successful Farming*, advertising prom. and books. Has restyled many mags; exhibited in shows of ADC-NY and Chicago, AIGA.

A. HALPERT*

Native New Yorker, he studied at Art Stud. Lea. and Nat'l Acad. of Des. before joining art dept. of Frank Seaman Co. Has worked on many large national accounts and conducts own art studio. Life mem. ADC-NY where he has held many offices. Mem. SOI.

HENRY MITCHELL HAVEMEYER*

Mitch has really seen the world at large as well as that of advertising and the graphic arts. From Yale to teaching the tommy gun in the Army, to chr. ADC-NY Education Com., he's seen education. From paste-up boy to exec. AD and ad agency partner to pres. of Hoyt Howard, Inc., consulting AD firm, he's seen business. It took a background like Mitch's to develop the penetrating chart on page 44.

ARTHUR HAWKINS*

Native of Maryland, he graduated from Univ. of Virginia, studied at Art Stud. Lea. His long service to the profession includes: past pres. ADC-NY; charter sec'y-treas. NSAD; founder and pres. Consulting AD Ass'n.; on Advisory Boards ADC-NY, NSAD, Cooper Union Art Sch. Mem. SOI; hon mem. ADC-Seattle and Rochester.

234

EUGENE HEIFFEL*

Charter mem. Consulting AD Ass'n. and a Frank Seaman alumnus, he is art consultant to G. M. Basford Co. and chr. City Coll. Coop. Advertising Training Com. He is a life mem. ADC-NY.

HOYT HOWARD*

The retailer-manufacturer-agency cycle of art direction has taken him 20 years to complete. Although an early flair for lettering enabled him to last out the depression at Macy's, it was an affinity to copywriters that marked his 9 years at Bethlehem Steel and 5 years at Gardner of St. Louis (his home town). Now sec'y treas. Hoyt Howard, Inc., consulting AD firm.

ALLEN F. HURLBURT*

Univ. of Pennsylvania graduate; former AD Bureau of Advertising (1935-40), AD of NBC (1946-50). Now AD *Look* mag. Work has been in ADC-NY shows since 1947, 4 award winners. Mem. exec. com. ADC-NY.

JOHN JAMISON*

AD, J. M. Mathes, Inc. started with N. W. Ayer & Son, Inc., and for more than 20 years has been in the agency art field and active in professional organizations. Among posts held are: pres. ADC-NY, chr. ADC-NY Advisory Bd., hon. chr. Joint Ethics Comm., hon. mem. SOI, mem. Amer. Arbitration Ass'n.

PEIRCE JOHNSON (deceased)

Born Covington, Ky., studied at Cincinnati Art Acad., Herrin Art. Inst., Chicago Art Inst. Began career as newspaper reporter, then became commercial artist. Was AD for J. Walter Thompson 13 years; also conducted own advertising service. Founding mem. ADC-NY (1920), he served as treas., pres. and chr. Advisory Board. Died 1956.

OSCAR KRAUSS*

A native New Yorker who originally began his career as an architect, he later studied advertising design at Pratt Inst. Has been a free-lance des. and consultant AD for past 9 years, was at one time with Lord & Thomas and Buchanan & Co.

GEORGE KRIKORIAN*

235   Connecticut born, after study at Pratt Inst. he worked for a photo studio, two manufacturers, two ad agencies, one newspaper before joining *Look* mag. where he is promotion AD. His work, internationally exhibited, has won honors from ADC-NY, AIGA, Harvard Adv. and Sell. Awards.

PAUL R. LANG*

Brooklyn born, graduate of Pratt Inst., he is v.p. and N. Y. mgr. of Ketterlinus Lithographic Mfg. Co. Was AD and creative sales dir. for Niagara Litho. Co. and Snyder & Black. Has taught advertising design at Pratt and has held numerous offices in ADC-NY and is life mem.

WILSON STUART LEECH*

Ad of Einson-Freeman C., Studied at Nat'l. Acad. of Des., Art Stud. Lea., Maryland Inst. of Art. Operated own commercial art studio for many years before becoming AD for Kindred & MacLean Co. Winner of Elliott, Suydam medals and 20 awards for display advertising and package design.

BERT W. LITTMANN*

A Pratt Inst. graduate, he was with Frank Lindsay Art Service and 6 years promotion AD for Hearst Magazines. Was AD Raymond Spector Co. and H. B. Humphrey Co. Now v.p., Pahmer & Littmann, Inc. Has served in many offices in ADC-NY.

HERBERT LUBALIN

Grad. of Cooper Union, he has been AD of Deutsch & Shea, Reiss Advertising, art ed. of *Menswear* mag. With Sudler & Hennessey Inc. for 10 years and now exec. AD.

TOBIAS MOSS*

Consulting AD and des., advertising mgr. and AD, A. I. Friedman Inc.,; administrative dir. New York Univ. Center for the Graphic Industries and Publishing. Former chief, Graphics Section, Office of War Information; previously associated with *Life* mag., Curtis Publ. Corp., Hillman Periodicals. Mem. SOI, Type Dir. Club, Soc. Typog. Arts, AIGA (chr. publication).

JAN CHRISTIAN MAYER

Born in Belgium, after a printer's apprenticeship in Germany and Switzerland he came to the U. S. in 1927. Former AD of *Charm* mag., he has been AD for *Family Circle* since the mag. started in 1932.

HARRY WAYNE McMAHAN

A recognized authority on television advertising, he has written more than 3,000 commercials and been TV consultant or production head on more than $150,000,000 TV billing. For 16 years he headed his own production company in Hollywood, then was three years on the creative plans board of McCann-Erickson, New York. He is the author of *The Television Commercial* and *Television Production* (Hastings House).

GEORG OLDEN*

Dir. graphic arts, CBS Television, his first job was staff artist of a newspicture mag. at 16. At 19, designed a series of national conservation posters. Graphic des. for Office of Strategic Services in World War II and for UN founding conference. Numerous awards including special ADC-NY medal for overall contributions as TV-AD.

GARRETT P. ORR*

Born on a Michigan farm, attended Univ. of Michigan, graduated from Chicago Art Inst. where he painted signs to earn expenses. Joined Outdoor Advertising, Inc. in 1933, now assoc. AD. Has held numerous offices in ADC-NY. Hobby is painting.

NATHANIEL POUSETTE-DART*

P-D's long and distinguished career of service to the AD profession is attested to throughout this book. Past pres. of ADC-NY, he was also chr. in 1920 of the committee formulating the original Code of Ethics and an early chr. of the Educational Comm. In fact, over the years, he has been active in most of the Club's committees. Minnesota born, he has had an equally noteworthy career in the fine arts as painter, writer, lecturer and teacher. His latest book is *American Painting Today: A Cross-Section of Our Contemporary Art* (Hastings House).

STANLEY RESOR

Graduating from Yale Univ., started in advertising in 1904 with Proctor & Collier, Cincinnati, where he was born. Established J. Walter Thompson office there in 1908. Brought to New York in 1912, became gen. mgr. in 1914 and pres. in 1916, chairman in 1955. Founder and early pres. Amer. Ass'n. Advertising Agencies; helped organize Nat'l Outdoor Advertising Bureau. Dir. many business, banking, charitable organ.

LESTER RONDELL*

Artist and AD, he has exhibited in national museum shows as well as a one-man show in his native New York. Studied at Sch. of Fine and Applied Arts and Art Stud. Lea. Was 8 years illus., des. as free lance and in art studio; agency AD for 20 years. Now group supervisor, Grey Advertising Agency. Past pres. ADC-NY as well as holding other offices. Mem. SOI.

MORRIS L. ROSENBLUM*

Studied and taught at Pratt Inst., formerly AD at Abraham & Strauss and L. Bamberger. Says he: "It took me two years out of art school to acquire title of AD and almost 25 years to get beyond it. I am now Macy's creative advertising mgr."

WILLIAM H. SCHNEIDER*

Came to New York from Rochester at 18 to attend art school but quit because he was too busy doing fashions for Lord & Taylor and Altman's, and theatrical caricatures for the *Times* and *Herald-Tribune*. While he writes here on motion pictures, his experience includes advertising fields as diversified as food and gasoline. Painter and sculptor, he was pres. of SOI for two terms. Now v.p., creative dir. of copy and art, Donahue & Coe, Inc.

PAUL SMITH*

Minnesota born, studied at Univ. of Minnesota, he was pres. ADC-NY for two terms. Has won over 10 medals and numerous other awards from ADC-NY and Chicago. Mem. SOI and formerly head of his own advertising agency, he is now v.p. of Calkins & Holden.

KARSTEN STAPELFELDT*

Born and educated in Germany, he came to U.S.A. in 1926. Former AD for Monroe Dreyer, L. Gumbinner, Robert Orr. Now a free-lance des. and illus.

RICHARD G. STEIN

AIA, partner Katz, Waisman, Blumenkranz, Stein, Weber, Archtitects Associated. Studied at N. Y. U., Cooper Union, Harvard. Worked for Gropius, Breuer, Stone, Raymond. His firm has received numerous awards for commercial buildings, schools, housing, factories, furniture. Teaches at Cooper Union.

ALFRED B. STENZEL*

Massachusetts born, studied at Los Angeles Sch. of Art and Des., Nat'l. Acad of Des. and Art Stud. Lea. and has taught continuity drawing and writing at N.Y.U. AD at Johnstone & Cushing since 1940.

OTTO STORCH*

Now AD of *McCall's* mag., he started out to be a portrait painter. Studied at Pratt Inst., Art Stud. Lea., New Sch., Phoenix Inst. Turned to comm'l art, then AD and des. with Dell Publ., *Time, True, Pageant, Holiday*, RCA Victor, and others. Former art ed. *Better Living mag.*

WILLIAM STROSAHL*

New York born, he is v.p. and a creative director, William Esty Co., and also a practicing AD in both TV and publication advertising. Believes in "advertising for people," not for "art's sake," that a 3-man team produces the best ads. Mem. executive board, Amer. Water Color Soc.

LADISLAV SUTNAR*

AD and des. was dir. of State Sch. of Graphic Arts and exhibition architect in his native Prague before coming to U.S.A. Consulting AD for Sweet's Catalog Service and other companies since 1941. Recent books include: *Catalog Design Progress* (with K. L. Holm), *Design for Point of Sale, Package Design*.

SALVATORE J. TAIBBI*

New York City born, his formal art training began at 11 and paintings exhibited nationally. Graduate of Pratt Inst. Evening Art Sch. and now on faculty, he is a World War II veteran. AD, American Telephone Co. for past 10 years; mem. SOI.

P. K. THOMAJAN

Now an advertising consultant, he has been Hollywood gag man, exploitation representative for Paramount Pictures, public relations dir., N. Y. Sales Executives Club. His articles on advertising and related subjects appear regularly in general and trade publications.

BRADBURY THOMPSON*

AD, des., typog., he was born in Kansas, graduated from Washburn Coll. Now AD *Mademoistlle* mag., he is also des. Westvaco *Inspirations for Printers, Art News* mag. and Annual. Awards include 10 ADC-NY medals and certificates, 1950 Award of NSAD, numerous AIG honors. Mem. AIGA (dir.), NSAD, SOI, Dutch Treat Club.

DANA P. VAUGHAN

Dean of Cooper Union Art. Sch. since 1945 he was formerly dean of Rhode Island Sch. of Design. Past pres. Eastern Arts Ass'n; ed. and author (*Art Professions in the U.S.*, etc.). Chairman, Accreditation Committee, Nat'l. Ass'n. of Schools of Design. Has studied in Europe, the Near and Far East.

ELWOOD WHITNEY*

Began career as apprentice in scenic studio. Free lance design and letering brought him into contact with advertising business. Was v.p. and senior AD at J. Walter Thompson Co. Joined Foote, Cone & Belding as a v.p. in 1943; served as creative chief on many large national accounts. Was elected a director of agency in 1951. Mem. SOI.

GORDON M. WILBUR*

A graduate of Cornell Univ., Coll. of Architecture, he has worked continuously for N. W. Ayer & Sons — as layout designer, product and package designer, and art buyer. Currently associate AD in charge of art buying. Has bought art on most Ayer accounts, with many ADC award winners. Member ADC-NY and Philadelphia.

The wide range of subject matter in this book demanded a variety of approaches. The Editorial Committee decided, therefore, to invite a number of art directors to participate in its design. Each was assigned the task of laying out one complete part or section. The result speaks for itself in the fresh treatments and the changes of pace throughout.

This design group, under the direction of editor-in-chief Nathaniel Pousette-Dart, includes:

ALBERTO P. GAVASCI, *design supervisor*
C. EDWARD CERULLO, *traffic manager*
JULIAN M. ARCHER
WILLIAM P. BROCKMEIER
GREGORY BRUNO
RALPH DADDIO
LOUIS N. DONATO
SUREN ERMOYAN
STEPHEN FRANKFURT
HENRY M. HAVEMEYER
HOYT HOWARD
OSCAR KRAUSS
JACK MCMAHON
GEORGE SAMERJAN, *typography*
LADISLAV SUTNAR
SALVATORE J. TAIBBI

ALBERTO P. GAVASCI designed the jacket, the front matter and two other sections.

Other art directors, artists, designers, photographers, are credited in the book.

For the publisher:

RUSSELL F. NEALE, *publishing director*
ATKINSON DYMOCK, *production design*
ROSE DALTON, *assistant*

Contributors

Photographs/Albert Gommi

Index